Helen Mae Innes grew up on a small farm in New Zealand and studied linguistics and psychology at Victoria University of Wellinton. She has travelled through 30 countries, mostly by train, and has taught English in five countries to adults from more than 100 nations. After teaching for 25 years, she completed a PhD in creative writing and now works copyediting psychology journal articles, editing fiction, teaching academic writing, and writing.

Also by Helen Mae Innes

FICTION

And the Birds Fled to the Bush
Oracles & Miracles & Zombies (with Stevan Eldred-Grigg)

AUTOFICTION

Into the Woods

Warblish, Chirpish, Ticktocklish, & Animalopoeia

Onomatopoeic interpretations for specific species and objects using existing words

Piwaiwaka
Press

First published by Piwaiwaka Press 2024
ISBN 978-1-0670286-1-9
Revised edition 2025
ISBN 978-1-0670286-6-4
163 Rata Street, Naenae
Lower Hutt 5011
New Zealand
All rights reserved.

www.piwaiwakapress.com
Copyright © Helen Mae Innes 2024/2025
Cover Artwork: Sarah Weidig; sarah@imastar.co.nz
Cover Design & Text Layout: Madden Hay

This book is copyright. Except for the purposes of fair review, no part of this book may be stored or transmitted or reproduced in any form or by any means, electronic or mechanical, including recording or storage in any information retrieval system, without permission in writing from the publisher. Helen Mae Innes asserts her right to be known as the author of this work.

The Excel database on which this book is based is available to researchers upon reasonable request. Contact the author via piwaiwakapress@gmail.com

Acknowledgements

Thank you to all the writers, past and present, who have shared their discoveries of warblish with the world, no matter how brief. I especially want to thank Åsa Abelin and Hannah Sarvasy as their articles first sparked my interest in this topic and they kindly communicated with me. Thank you to members of the public who contacted me with warblish and to all the people who translated examples: Michael Weber (Afrikaans); Pavel Pipek (Czech); Virve Vihman (Estonian); Luc Arnault (French); Nikolaus Himmelmann (German); Daisy Coles, Helen Stipkovits, and Balint Koller (Hungarian); Cris Cucerzan (Romanian); Mikaela Nyman (Swedish, Finnish); Viveka Velupillai (Swedish); Nic Wynne (Mandarin); Vladimir Safonov (Russian), Andrey Sabitov (Russian), and Anatoly Chernykh (Russian). Thank you to Sophie Gaffney-Henderson for pointing me towards warblish-laden books and suggesting the term chirpish. Thank you to my PhD supervisors, Damien Wilkins and Miriam Meyerhoff, for, among many other things, allowing me to change my dissertation topic from a perfectly sensible one to this joyful-madcap one. And thank you, as always, to my mother Pauline for proof-reading and being on the constant look out for new examples, and my son David for letting me write my thesis in five-minute intervals between reading stories and playing in the sandpit.

Contents

Acknowledgements	5
Summary	11
Foreword	**13**
1. Introduction	**15**
2. Defining the Phenomenon	**19**
Attributing words to birds	20
Attributed words imitate bird sounds	21
The mechanics of imitation	22
Is meaningful content a defining characteristic?	29
Terminology in the literature	34
3. Revised Terminology	**42**
Warblish	42
Chirpish	43
4. What is the Function of Warblish?	**46**
Is memorability a function?	46
Is humour a function?	51
Does warblish function as a literary form?	58
Understanding warblish in and through prose and poetry	69
What are the mechanics of a literary form?	71
5. Does Warblish Only Exist for Birds?	**73**
Animalopoeia	73
Ticktocklish	75
6. The Shared Features of Different Interpretations	**78**
Imitative + Vocal = Chirpish	79
Imitative + Vocal = Non-Verbal (Whistling, Humming)	79
Vocal + Semantic = Oral Poetry	79
Semantic = Poetry, Anthropomorphism, Description, Metaphor, and Simile	79
Imitative + Semantic = Spectrogram, Musical Notation, and Other Notation	80
Imitative = Musical Instruments	81
Vocal = Nonsense	81
Vocal + Imitative + Semantic = Warblish, Animalopoeia, And Ticktocklish	81
7. Is Warblish Endangered?	**83**
8. Warblish as a Creative Process	**89**

9. Further Research	**91**
Afterword	**94**
Appendix A: Methodology for creating the database	96
Appendix B: How to use the database	103
Appendix C: Warblish Database	**113**
Appendix D: Animalopoeia Database	**263**
Appendix E: Ticktocklish Database	**265**
Works Cited	**266**
Endnotes	**279**

Table of Tables

Table 1: Type I and Type II are Subsets of Onomatopoeia
Table 2: Type II Examples
Table 3: Swedish Type II for the Yellowhammer (Emberiza citrinella)
Table 4: Linguistic Features of Type I and Type II
Table 5: Bird-Related Meaningful Content in Type II Examples
Table 6: Terminology Referring to Created and Existing Words that Imitate Bird Sounds Using the Vocal Apparatus
Table 7: Type II Great Kiskadee (Pitangus sulphuratus) *Names in Central and South America*
Table 8: Terminology for Subsets of Onomatopoeia: Chirpish and Warblish
Table 9: Categories of Non-birding Texts that Contain Warblish
Table 10: Figurative Language Used in Warblish
Table 11: Example of Animalopoeia in Bird Talk *by Bianki*
Table 12: Subsets of Onomatopoeia with Examples

Table of Figures

Figure 1: Relationship of Different Components of Birdsong to One Another
Figure 2: Shared Features of Interpretations of Bird Sounds
Figure 3: Musical notation and alternative notation of Veery song
Figure 4: Alternative notation for Veery song

'The basic criticism of the romantics' love of nature is that they listened to birds and heard only themselves.'

Simon Barnes
Birdwatching with Your Eyes Closed: An Introduction to Birdsong

'I imagine quite a few people have heard waterfalls or rapids break into speech.'

Don McKay
Deactivated West 100

Summary

There is a little-known phenomenon of interpreting the sounds of birds, insects, animals, and inanimate objects as intelligible yet onomatopoeic human words. Common examples include the Yellowhammer's song being rendered as, 'A little bit of bread and no cheese, please,' and the Bush Cricket Katydid saying, 'Katy did, Katy didn't'.

Although such examples are common across in many languages and cultures, in-depth studies are rare. It is not often referred to by any specific term, but North American birders sometimes refer to it as *birdsong mnemonics* and recently an academic coined the term *warblish*. Where it has been discussed, it has been limited to the sounds of birds, often in relation to bird names or onomatopoeia. However, collecting and analysing over 1500 examples spanning 62 languages has allowed me to offer fresh insights into this phenomenon.

In this book, I describe the method used to create the collection; for the first time bring together the sound imitations of birds, insects, animals, and objects; examine what these imitations have in common; and argue for the use of new terminology and classification of these examples.

This book is aimed at researchers, both amateur and academic, but should also be of interest to lovers of poetry, words, birds, and quirky topics.

Foreword

Way back in 2016, I started a PhD in Creative Writing at Victoria University of Wellington in New Zealand and was preparing to write a novel and conduct research into how dialects are represented in texts through respelling. However, as I searched for articles about dialects, I kept stumbling upon articles about bird dialects and how researchers had observed similarities in bird and human dialects. This area should not have concerned me, mainly because it was off topic, but also because I had a secret shame as a New Zealander living in a land that celebrates avian wildlife—I hated birds. Really hated them. Even a picture of a bird or reading about birds made me feel slightly nauseous. However, there were interesting parallels between how birds and humans respond to strangers with different accents, so I read some of the articles. Meanwhile, the sounds of birds, the bush[i], other creatures and objects, and the sounds and silences of people, were appearing in my creative writing.

Then I found an article by Åsa Abelin which covered something completely different—the use of real words in Swedish folklore that acted like onomatopoeia by imitating birdsong. Most examples were in Swedish, but an English example included the Rose Finch saying, 'Pleased to see you'.[1] The article was unusual for an academic article as it was short and listed only four references, three of which had no more examples of what Abelin called *folk rhymes*. However, I was intrigued so veered off on a tangent looking for more examples, but I found next to nothing. It appeared to be a dead end.

The idea of it remained with me as I was reading and writing about other topics and slowly, over time, I found more information, most significantly when my supervisor Miriam Meyerhoff alerted me

---

[i] New Zealand English for forest or woods.

to an upcoming article by Hannah Sarvasy about the same phenomenon which she had named *warblish*.

The list of warblish kept growing and my understanding and interest in it developed over time, and rather than being a sidenote in my main creative component it became the major critical research project in my thesis. I created, at first, a small database of examples which I planned to use to write a small booklet. It was difficult to compile a list of examples, especially across different languages and countries, due to a lack of research and even an agreed term for what this phenomenon is. However, the luxury of having a very flexible PhD and understanding supervisors meant I could chip away at the topic while reading for other components of my thesis. Over time the database slowly grew. I realised that others might be interested in using it, if they, like me, had been intrigued by the idea but frustrated at the apparent lack of information. In my search I identified two more categories that had not been researched before, that of the equivalent type of onomatopoeia for insects and animals, and for objects. I have created new terminology for these as I have found no commentary or analysis of these anywhere.

The present book summarises the research and sources I have discovered and includes my database in order to make it easier for researchers to study this topic in the future. Many of the sources I have used were written by academic researchers but perhaps equally many were written by enthusiastic amateurs. As such, I have tried to make this book as accessible as possible, to as wide an audience as possible, at the risk of teaching some readers how to suck eggs. Forgive me if that's you. And for those who find the topic fascinating but this book a little too technical at times I am currently writing a book aimed at the general public which should be published in 2025.

Please note the common names of birds are presented, as is often the case in birding books, with capital letters. This is to make it clear where a word is part of the name and not just an adjective describing the bird. For example, when William Young refers to the 'loud but elusive noisy pitta,'[2] he structures the sentence so the word 'noisy' is part of the name and not just a description. However, this could also be missed by a reader unfamiliar with the bird's name. Therefore, I have used capitalisation so readers can identify the bird's name easily.

1. Introduction

Every so often (in a birding book, an article, a poem, a novel, or a book of nature writing), a reader might come across a sentence such as this one from a newspaper article in 1893: 'A bird spoke up out of the wood and said, "Sow wheat, Peverly, Peverly, Peverly!—Sow wheat, Peverly, Peverly, Peverly!"'[1]

At first glance such examples may appear to be anthropomorphism. However, other similar entries suggest this is a case of attributing human words to birdsong because they happen to mimic the sounds of such words in some way. In his description of the New Zealand Fantail/Piwaiwaka, Johannes Andersen says, 'It is in the tweeting notes that the words "pretty creature, pretty creature" have been heard.'[2]

Some sources more explicitly identify the connection between birdsong and words. A newspaper article from 1887 says people 'imagine that the bird's song may be rendered in these syllables of human speech.'[3] A comparison of phrases attributed to a specific bird supports this idea. A list for the White-Throated Sparrow (*Zonotrichia albicollis*) shows that the attributed phrases are similar in length, and all contain eleven syllables and three repetitions of the same three-syllable word at the end:

> Dear sweet Canada, Canada, Canada.[4]
> Oh, sweet Canada, Canada, Canada.[5]
> Poor Sam Peabody, Peabody, Peabody.[6]
> Old Sam Peabiddy Peabiddy Peabiddy.[7]
> Sow wheat Peverly, Peverley, Peverly.[8]
> All day whittling, whittling, whittling.[9]
> All day fiddling, fiddling, fiddling.[10]

However, most references offer only fleeting glimpses of the phenomenon in question, often providing just one example, then moving on to other topics. Longer lists of phrases can be found on internet pages,[11] but such sites usually cover just North American birds, have only examples in English, and usually with little to no analysis. Other examples are sometimes shared in birding forums as a response to a question posed by a forum user, but again the phrases are not examined in any depth.[12]

Given this phenomenon is about birds one might expect to find more information in birding books. Sometimes these books do have a brief section which may refer to such examples as *birdsong mnemonics* or just *mnemonics*. These are purported to be a way to remember bird calls or songs by imitating the bird, although they are also often criticised for doing this badly. They can be apologetic, such as Roger Burrows justifying the use of, 'Quick three beers' with 'this interpretation of the male Olive-sided Flycatcher's courtship song may seem silly, but it is surprisingly accurate'.[13] Most birding books however, if they include examples at all, include them under the *voice* section for each bird without further comment.

Usually, a literature review would cover the current state of knowledge on a subject, but what little has been written about this topic has mostly been in isolation, with little to no reference to or commentary about other sources of information. While this can be expected in non-academic sources, the few academic papers dedicated to the topic also had limited references. Asa Abelin, Hannah Sarvasy, Juan Moreno Cabrera, and Adrian Koopman have all written about this phenomenon within the field of linguistics (broadly speaking) and yet have not referenced one another, I believe partly due to the lack of an established term making it difficult to discover each other's work.

Koopman[14] did refer to R. G. Dunning as having the best collection of examples available (and I agree). It is a pity no one else referred to Dunning's brilliant work as he spent 47 years collecting examples and two years writing them up. In his 1947 book he writes:

> Hitherto no work has been published on the cries of birds, this book will open up to all scholars, students and others, a rich unexplored field of expression in Zulu literature and should be of interest and use to them.[15]

It seems every writer who tackles this subject has the same feeling of discovering something new and wanting to share it. In 2016 Hannah Sarvasy states that this phenomenon was 'heretofore unnamed'[16] and says it is 'thoroughly described for the first time in [her] paper,'[17] and she ends her article with a call for other ethno-ornithologists to continue research in this area.

However, Koopman toys with the term verbalisation back in 1990, it being a subset of what he calls ornimatopoeia, and he expands upon this concept in his 2018 papers. R. E. Moreau, like many other authors just calls it onomatopoeia. He identifies this phenomenon as it pertains to bird nomenclature back in 1942 and shows that despite onomatopoeia names making up 44% of birds' names in African languages and 16.5% of English names, only 4% of African bird names and 0.5% of English bird names use the specific type of onomatopoeia we're referring to here.[18]

The terminology has been unclear for a number of reasons: the phenomenon is rare; the concept is not readily acknowledged as existing; a lack of research, especially interconnected research; researchers using the same terms (e.g., onomatopoeia) differently; researchers creating their own terms which are not then adopted by other researchers; and researchers using terminology which I believe is misleading as to the function of this phenomenon. Therefore, before reviewing the literature, I will define here the two types of onomatopoeia I explore and call them by undescriptive names for now so that it is easier to later compare the references to each in a wide range of texts.

> ***Type I*** *uses created/nonce[i] words to mimic a bird's vocal sounds, such as the Ovenbird saying,* 'queecher, queecher, queecher.'
>
> ***Type II*** *uses existing words to mimic a bird's vocal sounds, such as the Ovenbird saying,* 'Teacher, teacher, teacher.'

According to the *Cambridge Dictionary*, onomatopoeia is 'the act of creating or using words that include sounds that are similar to the noises the words refer to'.[19] Type I and Type II are therefore both types

---

[i] A word coined on a specific occasion.

of onomatopoeia. However, as the term onomatopoeia has been used differently by various researchers it could lead to confusion so I will use these unique terms for now (see Table 1) and discuss my preferred terms and own proposed neologisms[i] later.

I was primarily interested in collecting and analysing Type II examples, but I mention Type I where relevant (e.g., some writers contrast and others combine Type I with Type II examples, and some use the same terminology to refer to Type I as another writer uses to refer to Type II)

Table 1: Type I and Type II are Subsets of Onomatopoeia

	Onomatopoeia	
	Type I (using created words)	**Type II** (using existing words)
Ovenbird	queecher, queecher, queecher	teacher, teacher, teacher
California Quail	ki kuu kuu	Chicago

---

[i] A newly formed word which has been recognised.

2. Defining the Phenomenon

A list of Type II examples reveals patterns (see Table 2). What these examples share in common is not language, origin, content, nor seriousness. They all, however, imitate the sound of the bird they are purported to represent, and they all use words that already exist in the lexicon.

Table 2: Type II Examples

Bird	Type II Example	Language/Country
Warbling Vireo	If I sees you, I will seize you, and I'll squeeze you, till you squirt.[1]	English, USA
Wood Pigeon	My toe bleeds, Georgie![2]	English, UK
Eastern Meadowlark	See-you-at-school-today.[3]	English, Canada
Chiming Wedgebill	But did you get drunk?[4]	English, Australia
Indian Cuckoo	বউকথাকও [Baukathā kaō] (Bride, please speak).[5]	Bengali, India and Bangladesh
Common Cuckoo	不如归去, 不如歸去 [Bùrú guī qù] (You should go home)[6]	Chinese, China and Taiwan
Fantailed Cuckoo/Sbaw	*Tap sy ñban – ohoy!* (You are eating stolen food, shame on you!)[7]	Kalam, Papua New Guinea
Reed Bunting	*Ich sing immer noch schlecht* (I still sing badly).[8]	German, Germany
Grey Warbler/Riroriro	*Riro riro, riro riro* (Gone gone, gone gone).[9]	Te reo Māori, New Zealand

Therefore, the most obvious features of Type II examples are that they must do two things:

>   1. *Attribute existing human words to birds.*
>
>   2. *Imitate the sound of the bird's call or song.*

Later, I will explore the other features the examples display, but as the two features above are the only ones most writers have considered, and are the features I consider essential, I will start with those.

Attributing words to birds

Firstly, Type II is often not referred to by any specific term, so its existence is indicated in another way. Often an example is accompanied by use of a verb such as *cry*, *say*, or *call*. This sentence from a book on Iraqi folklore is typical: 'The hen pigeon cries "*Ya karīm*," "O Merciful One".'[10] Sometimes Type II is indicated by a claim the bird is actually speaking human words. A Kattang speaker told researchers in eastern Australia, 'This is a little grey bird ... who "can talk our language".'[11] These types of accounts are sometimes moderated to show if the speaker actually believes the bird spoke the words, such as in Luther Standing Bear's account: 'The larks in our State, at that time, talked the Sioux language—at least, we inferred that they did.'[12]

Some writers add hedging language as well as a brief description. When discussing the White-Throated Sparrow's (*Zonotrichia albicollis*) call, Judson McGehee says, 'To me he seems most often to be crying, in his descending, wistful chromatic, "Oh! Long ago, long ago, long ago-Oh!".'[13] Other examples are accompanied by a more elaborate story to account for the bird's words, such as Robert Cowser's explanation from America:

> [O]ur father would remind us of the whippoorwill was saying, "Chip flew out of White Oak" ... [because] many farmers in the community often went to White Oak Bottom in order to chop wood for use as winter fuel.[14]

Similarly, Bradford Torrey's book *Birds in the Bush* includes a story about the White-Throated Sparrow (*Zonotrichia albicollis*) helping a local farmer:

> A farmer named Peverly was walking about his fields one spring morning, trying to make up his mind whether the time had come to put in his wheat. The question was important, and he was still in a deep quandary, when a bird spoke up out of the wood and said, "Sow wheat, Peverly, Peverly, Peverly!—Sow wheat, Peverly, Peverly, Peverly!" That settled the matter. The wheat was sown, and in the fall a most abundant harvest was gathered; and ever since then this little feathered oracle has been known as the Peverly bird.[15]

Many authors do not use a specific term but do provide a more thorough description to attribute the words to birds, often when documenting cultures other than their own. For example, T. Owen interviewed a Baggari man in Sudan who said, '[N]ot all the birds talk; but some use human words which we can make out.'[16] Likewise, E. S. Stevens translated Iraqi folktales and explains, 'The cries of birds and beasts are often thought to convey a warning, or are translated into human speech by tradition.'[17] R. G. Dunning implies that Zulu phrases attributed to birds are creations of the human listeners: '[B]irds ... have had their cries put into words.'[18] Sonia Tidemann and Tim Whiteside collected Type II examples from Aboriginal Australians and say, '[A] number of bird species are known to be messengers.'[19] Some of these examples are difficult to distinguish from anthropomorphism, so it is the next requirement, imitation, that is essential to determine an example's categorisation as Type II.

Attributed words imitate bird sounds

Many authors allude to the imitative qualities in the attributed words. Henry Callaway describes Zulu imitations like this: 'The natives also affect to hear in the cry of certain birds sounds resembling human speech'.[20] Some authors provide a little more information to account for the imitation, such as Robert Cowser recalling an example from his childhood in a letter to the editor of *Western Folklore*:

> [T]he hoot owl was supposed to communicate the same message night after night: "I cook for my folks. Who cooks for you all?" The vowel sound in *who* and *you* was emphasised by

human imitators to signify its similarity to the call of the hoot owl.[21]

Although the mechanics of Type I and Type II are not frequently commented upon (or, if they are, not in a technical manner), they are important. A few linguists have studied Type I and Type II and have shown the ways in which they mimic the bird vocalisations can vary.

The mechanics of imitation

How exactly are words attributed to bird calls or song? When we say Type II imitates the bird's song or call there are a number of components that can create that impression: pitch, pace, syllable count, and timing.

Birdsong is often divided into notes, syllables (collection of notes), phrases (collections of syllables), songs (collections of phrases), and repertoire (different versions of songs, from one to over 2000 for some thrushes). If we compare birdsong with human language, I believe we can equate notes with phonemes[i], syllables with syllables or words, phrases with phrases, songs with sentences, and repertoire with a person's entire lexicon[ii] (see Figure 1).

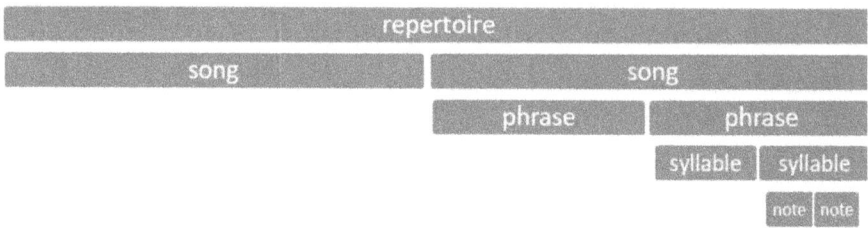

Figure 1: Relationship of Different Components of Birdsong to One Another

---

[i] The smallest unit of sound in a language that can change one word into another, [b] and [p] are different sounds in English which can change the word bat to pat.
[ii] Essentially all the words a person knows.

In Asa Abelin's analysis of English and Swedish Type II examples found in Ingrid Norudde's[22] unpublished document, she compares the phonemes of Type II with the notes in birdsongs. She comes to the following conclusion:

> The sounds (vowels and consonants) of the rhymes for bird song seem to divide birds into birds with high pitched songs, imitated with e.g. [s], [t] and [i] and those with low pitched songs, imitated with e.g. [o], [u], [ʉ], nasals and voiced consonants. Vibrating sounds are imitated as [r].[23]

Her examples of high-pitched songs from the Great Tit (*Parus major*) include, '*Edit!*' (a female name), and 'Whiskey, whiskey, whiskey'.[24] For the Yellowhammer (*Emberiza citrinella*), she gives various Type II examples which she claims, 'are generally on high frequencies, e.g. [i], [s]'.[25] (See Table 3.)

Table 3: Swedish Type II for the Yellowhammer (Emberiza citrinella)

Swedish	English translation
Sitt sitt sitt sitt å skiiit	Sit sit sit sit sit and shit
Se se se se se se shiiit	See see see see see see shit
Nu är sommaren snart slut	Now the summer is over soon
Vi-vi-vi-vi-visingsööö	(Name of an island)
1 2 3 4 5 6 sjuuuu	1 2 3 4 5 6 seven
Fy på dig Nisse lille fyyyy	Shame on you little Nisse, shame on you
Ett två tre fyra fem sex sjuuu, jag är liten jag är guuul	One, two, three, four, five, six, seven, I am little, I am yellow

Abelin also notes that the [r] is used in the human words when the birdsong contains a trill. For examples, the Common Snipe (*Gallinago gallinag*) says, '*Herrarna, herrarna, herrarna*' (The men/boys)[26]. There are other words with the same meaning that could have been chosen but she suggests the [r] has been used because it better imitates the bird's vibrating call.

Abelin also compares the Type II examples for the same bird occurring in both English and Swedish and finds the same number of syllables for both, with correlations between the same vowels sounds used in the phrases. For example, according to Ingrid Norudde the Common Rose Finch/*Rosenfink* (*Carpodacus erythrinus*) says in English, 'Pleased to meet you', 'Glad to see you', and in Swedish says, '*Se video*' (watch a video), '*Köp en video*' (buy a video), '*Skit i de du*' (do not worry).[27] Abelin notes that all these rhymes have four syllables and end with [u] and somewhere contain the sound [i]. So, while there is not a perfect replication of the bird sound, the high/low sounds of birdsong are often reflected with the high and low frequency sounds used in the human words, regardless of language.

Sarvasy compares the sounds and timing of birdsong with both Type I and Type II using spectrograms.[28] Spectrograms have been touted as a modern alternative to written representations used in the past such as musical scores, alternative birdsong notation, and Type I or Type II. This is because, on spectrograms, the sounds are objectively displayed on graphs that digitally plot the frequency of the call (y-axis) over time (x-axis). This is a less subjective technique for presenting sound than Type I or Type II, but Jeremy Mynott notes they scare off readers in the same way musical scores can do and therefore have not often been used in birding books.[29] They can also be difficult to interpret and subject to a lot of variability. Their marking of amplitude at different frequencies does not adequately display the complexity of human language. However, their use by Sarvasy does lend some credibility to the belief that the Type I and II phenomena are imitative. She compares the timing of the Black-Capped Chickadee's (*Poecile atricapillus*) call and its Type I imitation, and conjectures that timing may be 'more critical to a successful onomatopoeic rendition than choices of vowels and consonants'.[30]

Sarvasy then compares the call of the Whip-poor-will (*Antrostomus vociferus*) to its Type II rendition, 'Whip poor Will'. She similarly concludes that the 'tempo, relative timing of component, intonation, and voice quality may be more critical to the acceptability of warblish [Type II] than consonant and vowel qualities'.[31] She also compares the call of the White-Throated Sparrow (*Zonotrichia albicollis*) to two different phrases: 'Poor Sam Peabody, Peabody, Peabody,' and 'Oh sweet Canada, Canada, Canada'. She finds similarities between both phrases and the bird's call in pitch, number of syllables, and timing, and concludes the consonant and vowels chosen are less important than other features for successful imitation.[32]

Juan Moreno Cabrera explores bird names that mimic bird sounds across Central and South America. He believes that the many names for the Great Kiskadee (*Pintangus sulphuratus*), such as *Bem-te-vi* (Well-you-saw) and *Bien-te-veo* (I see you well), derive from an interpretation of their call and the names 'sound more or less like the bird call'.[33] The exact imitation is therefore not necessary for this phenomenon.

According to Moreno Cabrera, the English word 'to chirp' and the Hungarian word of the same meaning '*csipog*' are similar because of their 'use of the vowel [i] in order to convey a high-pitched sound produced by a small bird'. However, 'chirp' [tʃɜːp] does not have a high-pitched vowel but the open mid-central vowel [ɜː]. Moreno Cabrera may have made a mistake and have meant to write 'cheep' [tʃiːp] which does have a close (high-pitched) vowel. If we assume he means 'cheep' then his next comments about Type I are interesting:

> [I]t can be said that neither *chirp* [*cheep*] nor *csipog* are successful imitations of the sounds produced by small birds. They can be seen instead as phonetic interpretations on which some general sound symbolic principles exert some influence.[34]

He points out that Type I and Type II (what he calls onomatopoeia ornithonyms and delocutive ornithonyms, respectively) share four important characteristics:

    a) They can be language/dialect dependent.
    b) They are phonetic interpretations (not imitations) of bird calls.
    c) Such phonetic interpretations are a poor imitation of the actual bird calls, since they are not intended as pure imitations.
    d) The interpretations are based on generally sound-symbolic principles.[35]

The idea that this phenomenon is a 'phonetic interpretation' rather than an imitation, fits with the other features found in Type II. For example, Abelin compares the rising or falling pitch of the birdsong to the Type

II imitations and finds a correlation with the rise or fall of pitch and the meaning of the corresponding words. For example, the Chaffinch/Bofink (*Fringilla coelebs*) has a call which descends in pitch and is rendered in Swedish, '*Trilla nerför trappan – nu är jag här*' (fall down the stairs—now I'm here)[36]. In her example, the matching of the meaning of the word 'fall' with the falling intonation of the song is of more importance than matching the pitch of all the phonemes. Therefore, a recognisable approximation of sounds may be sufficient to convince a listener of imitation.

Moreno Cabrera's idea of a 'sound symbolic principle' could be interpreted as the use of any number of different linguistic features or variables. In Table 4, I have included a range of potential features, such as pitch, stress, and syllable count, alongside examples I have found in various sources. Therefore, a Type II example would not need to contain all features to be considered a successful imitation. I believe Moreno Cabrera is deliberately vague when he says, '[S]ome general sound symbolic principle,'[37] because there are no rigid rules as to how the word or phrase mimics the bird, only that it is perceived to do so.

Therefore, the more subjective auditory measures, which affect how a listener perceives the sounds, may be more important than the acoustic measures, that is the physical properties of sound. Indeed, birders complain that spectrograms are not very successful at indicating the 'colour' of the voice despite their obvious success at recording the acoustic frequency and duration. It may be sufficient that the meaning of the word 'fall' could trick a person into believing the fall in subjective pitch was more than the recorded fall in frequency.

Table 4: Linguistic Features of Type I and Type II

Function	Example
High pitch shown by close vowels	Egypt [ˈiː.dʒɪpt] (Crescent Honeyeater); See see see [siː]; Seat seat seat [siːt] (Cape May Warbler); FEED-me-now, feed-me-now, feed-me-now! [fiːd miː naʊ] (Common Murre); Drink your tea! [drɪŋk jər tiː] (Eastern Towhee);

Function	Example
Alternations in birdsong frequency and phoneme pitch	Chewy-chewy-chewy-chewy-chewy [ˈtʃuː.i] (Common Quaker Babbler); Look-'igh-up, look-'igh-up [lʊk aɪ ʌp] (Golden-Throated Barbet); Var är du? (Where are you?) (Great Tit)
Intonation shown by '?' or '!'	Who are you there? ... Go 'way ... Get out! (White-Eyed Vireo) Fire! Fire! Where? Where? Here! Here! (Indigo Bunting)
Syllable length shown by repetition of letters	Willie, come and have a fight, sca-a-a-a-a-red (Sombre Greenbul); Y-a-a-a-ss (Paradise Riflebird) You-GET-awaaay (White-Eared Monarch Flycatcher)
Loudness shown by uppercase	FEED-me-now, feed-me-now, feed-me-now! (Common Murre); It's-up-to-you, it's-up-to-you, IT'S-UP-TO-YOU (Heuglin's Robin); Think-of-it, think-of-it, THINK-OF-IT (Heuglin's Robin)
Pauses shown by punctuation	Tom-Kelly ... whip-Tom-Kelly! (Red-Eyed Vireo); Cook . . . Cook ... Cook (Greater Green-Billed Malcoha); PLEASE, put-it-HERE. put-it-HERE ... DEAR, put-it. HERE (Brown-Crested Flycatcher)
Syllable count matches	Where are you?; Tomato; Tobacco; McPherson; Dick-Vercoe; ¡Sí señor! (Yes, sir!); Chicago; Rise and run; Wet my lips; Pippy wheat (Quail); One more bottle; 不如歸去;(Bùrú guī qù) (Why not go home) (Indian Cuckoo)
Syllable stress shown by uppercase	VIC-tor, VIC-tor, VIC-tor (Greater Honeyguide) You-GET-awaaay (White-Eared Monarch Flycatcher)
Pace, timing matches	Whip-poor-Will (Eastern Whip-Poor-Will). The sequence of plosives [p] makes a person pause briefly, mimicking the rhythm of the birdsong

Type II are sometimes respelled to show aspects of sound such as the lengthening of a note. The Black-throated Blue Warbler (*Setophaga caerulescens*) from the USA says, 'I'm lazy' but various authors spell it differently, for example: 'I'm laa-zyyyy';[38] 'I am soo lay-zeee';[39] and 'I'm lazeee'.[40] Using the repeating 'y' or 'e' is supposed to show a longer note on the last syllable but it could potentially also lead to confusion as 'lazeee' could be perceived as 'laze' [leɪz] instead of 'lazy' [ˈleɪ.zi] and thus change the syllable count.

The spelling changes some authors use to indicate sounds can get out of hand. Adrian Koopman describes Type I (what he calls onomatopoeia) as 'strings of letters divided by hyphens or spaces that resemble little more than some sort of code language, like *skiz-skizzkiz*'.[41] Koopman notes how problematic these 'words' can be and quotes Jeremy Mynott who describes a particularly striking example as, 'a heroic attempt'.[42] The example Mynott quotes is from *The Collins Bird Guide* which claims the Sedge Warbler (*Acrocephalus schoenobaenus*) says, '*Zrüzrü-trett zrüzrüzrü-trett zrüzrüzrü psit trutrutru-pürrrrrrrrurrrrrr **vi-vi-vi** lülülü **zetre zetre**…*'[43]

Mynott declares that the above example is ultimately a failure. Koopman notes that Type I, '[F]requently includes letter combinations which do not occur in "natural" words in English, like the <tz> and the <dzw> in "*tzzzzzrrr dzweep*".'[44] I would note that Type I can also include *graphemes* that do not occur in English, such as the Hermit Thrush (*Catharus guttatus*) saying, '*chück*' and '*veeüh*'.[45] Not everyone is familiar with an umlaut and so might pronounce *chück* as [tʃʌk] or [tʃyk]. I note that both Mynott and then Koopman fail to copy the long example for the Sedge Warbler exactly from the original which contains German umlauts (ü), which they replaced with the English letter (u). I am against using such graphemes in English-based onomatopoeia since they are not readable by everyone, even if, as in this case, the writer explains how to pronounce such sounds in the preface.[46] The fact the writer feels the need to add to normal orthography highlights how poorly human language approximates bird sounds.

Is meaningful content a defining characteristic?

There is a lack of agreement over whether the content of Type II is essential to its definition. There are many examples of content ranging from farming and seasons to greetings and warnings (see Table 5). Abelin states that Type II, 'seem to both imitate the birds' songs and to describe some content connected to the bird'.[47] She elaborates, saying, 'The choice of words ... is focused on certain areas of common life, e.g. food, seasons, social relations ... the physical appearance of the bird...'.[48] She gives examples such as the Chiffchaff (*Phylloscopus collybita*) saying, '*Salt sill, salt sill, salt sill*' (salt herring, salt herring, salt herring);[49] the Yellowhammer (*Emberiza citrinella*) saying, '*Nu är sommaren snart slut*' (now the summer is over soon);[50] and the Great Tit (*Parus major*) saying, '*Titta hit titta hit, jag är gul och svart och vit*' (Look here look here, I am yellow and black and white).[51]

Sarvasy also gives examples from the field of ethnobiology which discuss seasonal changes, and 'observable avian behaviour'.[52] For example, the Red-Chested Cuckoo (*Cuculus solitarius*) says, '*Gikuyu 'ngwikia ku*' (where do I sow the seed?),[53] and the Black Fantail (*Rhidura atra*) says '*Joley boley*' (Alight in one place, alight in another, call and call again).[54] Sarvasy also notes the occurrence of the following topics in warblish: seasonal changes, farming, birds' behaviour, patterns of avian flight, and traditional stories. She comments on the differences in the content of warblish as revealing 'differences in the ways communities have framed their relationship with birds'.[55] She states birds can figure as 'heralds or transformed mythical humans' such as the example given by Steven Feld of the Chanting Scrubwren (*Crateroscelis murina*) saying, '*Kalu yabɛ*' (A person is coming).[56] However, Sarvasy, unlike Abelin, does not include the content of the utterance in her definition of Type II.

So, despite Abelin's inclusion of 'content that fits the context' in her definition, Sarvasy does not include such a proviso as a defining feature. Looking at Norudde's examples, Abelin seems to have chosen the 'best' examples, the most interesting precisely because they do comment on relevant avian content. The Swedish examples do appear

Table 5: Bird-Related Meaningful Content in Type II Examples

Content	Bird	Type II example
Behaviour	Dimorphic Fantail/Jolbeg	Describes its own movement in Kalam: '*Joley-boley*' (Alight in one place, alight in another, call and call again).
Identity	Eurasian Blue Tit	Says, 'I'm a blue tit'.
Appearance	Goldcrest/ Kungsfågel	Says in Swedish, '*Jag är minst, jag är minst, jag är minst i hela Sverige*' (I'm the smallest, I'm the smallest, I'm the smallest in all of Sweden).
Habitat	Golden-Crowned Sparrow	Says in the gold fields of Reno, 'No gold here'.
Action matches tone	Chaffinch/ Bofink	Says in Swedish, '*Trilla nerför trappan - nu är jag här*' (Fall down the stairs - now I'm here). The falling tone is mimicked in the word *fall* and the action of falling down the stairs.
Emotional prosody	Chaffinch/ Bofink	Calls in Swedish, '*Snälla, snälla*' (Please, please), with begging intonation and begging meaning of the words.
Hunting	Spotted Nutcracker/ Кедровка	Says, 'Идёт идёт охотник идёт' (*Idot idot okhotnik idot*) (Coming, coming, a hunter's coming).
Farming	Yellowhammer	Tells the farmer, '*Spänn för två, spänn för två*' (harness two, harness two), referring to the number of horses needed to carry a load of wood.
Seasonal changes	Noisy Pitta	Says, 'Walk to work' in spring and summer.
Food	European Pied Flycatcher	Says, 'Kiwi kiwi chips kiwi kiwi chips kiwi kiwi'.

Content	Bird	Bird and Type II example
Greeting	Louisiana Waterthrush	Says, 'See you see you see you nice to meet you, chao'.
Warning	Red-chested Cuckoo	Says, 'It will rain'.

to be particularly good at including 'meaningful content', so it is not surprising she tentatively put forward this observation. However, these may not necessarily represent the most typical examples across other languages. I shall explore my observations about what is the most typical content later. Koopman and Moreno Cabrera do not include content as being essential.

Dunning does not explicitly sort Zulu Type II into topics but, using the translations, I was able to sort the examples into broad topics, which in descending order of frequency were: people, food, farming, hunting/trapping, seasons/temperature, locations/travel, the bird's appearance/description, sleep, and greetings.[57] Many of these would appear to feature topics relevant to birdlife.

Abelin states, 'The creation of folk rhymes can be seen as a kind of folk etymology. In folk entomologies an incomprehensible series of sounds is heard, and these sounds are interpreted in terms of already existing words that fit the context'.[58] Although 'by context' implies meaning topics that related to birds, I would contend that it is better understood as words that fit together within the semantic and syntactic rules of the language. If the resulting words or phrases connect in some way to the bird that certainly makes for more interesting examples, but it is not a compulsory component.

Koopman questions if the Heuglin's Robin[59] saying, 'It's up to you' can be considered a 'meaningful utterance'.[60] I assume he says this because he thinks the content is not related to birds nor their surroundings. However, the majority of examples I collected, including this one, are grammatically and semantically correct. Therefore, I think this type of phrase *is* meaningful in that it is a comprehensible utterance. Most of the Type II examples follow the same pattern of being grammatically and semantically sound, while their content is often not about birds. For example, in many examples birds talk about human food and drink. The Rock Pigeon (*Columba livia*) in Hungarian says,

'*Van borunk! Van borunk!*' (We have wine! We have wine!), to which the Duck (Genus: *Anas*) replies, '*Csak csapra! Csak csapra!*' (Only on tap! Only on tap!).[61] This has nothing to do with birds, but by following turn taking, grammar, and vocabulary rules it can be perceived as an intelligible exchange.

In contrast, an example for the Chaffinch (*Fringilla coelebs*) is, '*Chip-chip-chip-chip tell-tell-tell-tell cherry-erry-erry-erry tissy-che-wee-ooo*'.[62] Since 'chip', 'tell' and 'cherry' are existing words it would seem to be Type II, but since it is not grammatically nor semantically meaningful, it reads more like Type I since its main feature is the mimicking of sounds. An old example from Germany is for the Nightingale which sings, 'Is tit, is tit, to wit, to wit – Trizy, Trizy, Trizy, to *bucht*, to *bucht*, to *bucht*'.[63] Trizy is the name for a dog and *bucht* is the word used for a sheepdog when the sheep are to be collected. This does not make a lot of sense, in either English or German, despite being made up of intelligible words. It is accompanied by an explanation of a shepherdess who cursed a shepherd who postponed marriage, but even that does not help comprehension much. So, despite all the components being words, they are not arranged into a semantically intelligible phrase.

There are numerous examples such as this one which appear to straddle both categories, but not as many as you might suspect. I have included some of these in the database, even though I class them as Type I, so they are available for comparing and contrasting with other Type II examples. Sometimes, the information surrounding a possible Type II example was not sufficient to decide if it was imitation or anthropomorphism. Later, if I found a Type I example for the same bird, I could compare linguistic features and see if there were similarities in sound, such as syllable count and stress, to confirm the first example.

Therefore, 'meaningful' is misleading because it implies the birds' message is related to the context of birds, or, in the case of 'messenger birds,' to the meaning of the bird's intention and the human words being the same. Holmer and Holmer explain that the Grey Fantail/Wagtail/Guri Djugi (*Rhipidura albiscapa*) in Australia gives the listener information such as, '*Guri djugi, guri djugi*' (A black fellow is coming).[64] Sarvasy takes examples such as this from traditional cultures that sometimes believe the birds are heralds who may therefore say that the sounds are meaningful even when not comprehensible to most humans. Unless there is explicit questioning of the subjects about their beliefs, I do not think we can always say whether someone actually believes the human words are the birds' intended message or if they are part of a story. Many of the examples I collected contain the same sort of phrasing as Sarvasy's examples, attributing the words to a bird but without, I believe, necessarily believing it to be true. Therefore, deciding if the words are actually believed to be spoken by the birds is difficult, especially as so many examples are from older sources and are accompanied by so little explanation. Consequently, I do not think the differentiation between true belief and fanciful attribution is one that we can or need to make. However, we should note that *meaningful* does not necessarily refer to a topic that is meaningful from a bird's point of view, nor for a human viewing a bird. So, while the Mountain Mouse-Warbler in Papua New Guinea warning other animals of predators with, 'Ñ-o py-ok-ey py-ok-ey' (Son, something is close by)[65] is an engaging example, the Pied Wagtail (*Motacilla alba yarrellii*) in England saying, 'Chiswick flyover,'[66] is just as valid, as it is still an intelligible, if an unlikely and uninspiring, message.

When I questioned Akiko Kawasaki about the differences between Type I and Type II in Japanese (what I termed at the times as 'meaningless onomatopoeia' and 'meaningful onomatopoeia/warblish' respectively), she explained that for Japanese people onomatopoeia *is* meaningful, therefore there is not a strong distinction between the two categories.[67] Indeed, the Japanese language has a very rich lexicon of onomatopoeic words that are difficult to translate into English. Therefore, I concluded that the term *lexical* is preferable to *meaningful* and this means the words can be found in a dictionary or conceivably could be found in a dictionary if one is not yet available for a particular dialect or language. However, as some onomatopoeia can be found in a dictionary so Type II words must have a meaning beyond the simple imitation of sounds. Therefore, an onomatopoeic word such as 'cheep' may be found in a dictionary but has no meaning beyond imitation and therefore is Type I, whereas the word used to imitate a turkey, 'gobble', does have meaning as it can also mean, 'to eat quickly' and therefore is Type II.

Therefore, the phenomena we are exploring is the attribution to birds of existing intelligible words or phrases whose sound characteristics are influenced by bird calls or songs. However, what this phenomenon is called is entirely dependent on who you consult.

Terminology in the literature

Due to the imitative qualities of Type I and Type II suggesting it is a type of onomatopoeia, it has often been called by that term, by a term that incorporates that word, or by a related word such as imitation or mimicry. Nevertheless, I have identified two distinct types of onomatopoeia, Type I and Type II. Many terms used by others can also be applied to these two categories, but the terminology used is not consistent (see Table 6).

Reginald Ernest Moreau organises African[68] and English bird names into eleven groups: motion, colour and pattern, onomatopoeia, food-habits, habitat, shape and size, nesting habits, season and weather, personal attributes, superstition, and personal names.[69] The third group, onomatopoeia, is the largest group for the various African languages he collected, but only third largest for English. This group is further divided into three categories: 'Names, apparently meaningless, that reproduce a noise' (i.e., Type I), 'names that reproduce a noise but by means of interpretable words' (i.e., Type II), and 'Names suggested by a noise made by the bird', a category for descriptive names like Knocker for woodpecker.[70] He gives four examples of Type II, including Klaas's Cuckoo[71]/Seyeikia (*Chrysococcyx klaas*) saying '*Seyeikia*' (Famine will come).[72] He states English names are rare and the only example he gives is the Quail (*Corturnix pectoralis*) saying, 'Wet my lips.'

Steven Feld wrote *Sound and Sentiment* originally in 1982 (with a third edition in 2012) and among other aspects of sound in the culture of the Kaluli people in Papua New Guinea he notes their taxonomic organisation of birds (and other flying animals). The bird names fell under seven categories: *Imilisi Ganalan*/Only Sound (make noises with their bodies and 'don't speak words'; *Holan*/Whistle (have human tongue); *Yɛlan*/Weep; *Ene Wi Salan*/Say their Name; *Mada Ganafodan*/Make Noise; *Gisalo Molan*/Sing Gisalo; and *Bosavi to Salan*/Speak *Bosavi* Language (have human voice).[73] There are only seven birds that fit in the last category, i.e., Type II, who can speak

Table 6: Terminology Referring to Created and Existing Words that Imitate Bird Sounds Using the Vocal Apparatus

	Onomatopoeia	
	using created words (Type I)	**using existing words (Type II)**
Cooke (1884)	Imitation, Mimicry	
Andersen (1921)	Vocalization	
R. E. Moreau (1942)	Meaningless onomatopoeia	Onomatopoeia made with interpretable words
Dunning (1946)		Bird Cries
Bulpin (1966)		Interpretation
Feld (1982; 2013)	*Ene Wi Salan!* (Say their names)	*Bosavi to Salan!* (Speak Bosavi language)
Wainwright (1986)	Praise name* [i]	Unsophisticated Praise Poem* [ii]
Koopman (1990)	Ornimatopoeia,* Onomatopoeia*	
	Verbalisation	
Bush (1999)	Memory phrase	
Young (2003)	Word-based mnemonic, mnemonic phrase, birdsong mnemonic [iii]	
Gorst (2010)	Interspecies mimicry	
	Vox confuse	A combination of *vox confusa* and *vox articulata* [iv]
Abelin (2011)		Folk rhyme, expression
Moreno Cabrera (2016)	Onomatopoeic Ornithonym*, 'Syllabic sound symbolic onomatopoeia'	Delocutive Ornithonym,* 'Lexical sound symbolic onomatopoeia' [v] 'Phrasal sound symbolic onomatopoeia' [vi]
Sarvasy (2016)	Onomatopoeia	Warblish
Zingesser (2017)	*Vox discrete*	
Koopman (2018a)	Verbalisation [vii]	
	Partial-verbalisation	Full-verbalisation
Koopman (2018b)		Vocalisation [viii]
Kawasaki (2018)	Onomatopoeia	聞きなし (*Kikinashi*)

* Refers to only bird names
i. Not all praise names are Type I.
ii. Not all praise poems are Type II.
iii. These terms also cover descriptions and metaphors.
iv. These terms are not usually nor solely used for bird imitations. For a discussion of these terms, along with *vox discrete/articulata, inarticulate, litterata* and *illitterata,* see Zingesser 2017.
v. Refers to using only a single existing word.
vi. Refers to using an 'existing phrase.'
vii. 'Verbalisation' also encompasses descriptions, metaphors, similes, and bird names.
viii. 'Vocalisation' is used here the way he uses 'verbalisation' in his 2018a paper. It is only a passing comment, and I wonder if he has just made a slip.

---

phrases. Two birds, the New Guinea Friarbird and the Brown Oriole (considered by locals to be one bird, the *Bɔlo*), are part of the myth that is said to have created this category:

> Once parents sent their two children off to fetch water. The children did not return. More and more the parents called out for them to come home and bring water. The children remained out of sight, but the parents heard them calling 'we'll bring some.' Finally the parents went in search of the children. They found them dead, killed by enemy people; *bɔlo* had taken their voices.[74]

The *Bɔlo* also calls the words, '*Dowo, nɔwo*' (Father, mother), and '*Hɛ gɔ fɔn*' (Where are my feathers).[75] Interestingly, locals believe that while other birds make 'bird sound words' the birds in this category 'speak real Bosavi words.' All birds can understand these words, whether they are said by people or the birds of this taxa.

Koopman names his paper *Ornimatopoeia* (a neologism created by fusing ornithology with onomatopoeia) and explores 'song-references in English, Afrikaans, and Zulu bird names'.[76] He does not explicitly define ornimatopoeia but divides song-referenced bird names into three categories, *Descriptive*, *Metaphoric*, and *Onomatopoeic*. The Onomatopoeic category includes both Type I names, such as the Hadedah Ibis[77] (*Bostrychia hagedash*)[78] and Type II, such as the Go-away bird (Genus: *Corythaixoides*).[79] After the main section he has an additional short section headed *Verbalisation*, which includes Type II songs and some Type II names which are derived from Type II song, such as verbalisation in three languages for the Fiery-Necked Nightjar (*Caprimulgus pectoralis*): In English it is also known as the Litanybird because it says, 'Good Lord deliver us'; In Afrikaans it is known as *Die Wewenaarvoël* (The Widower) because it says, '*Jaag weg die wewenaar …*' (Chase away the widower …); In Zulu the bird sings, '*Zavolo, Zavolo, sengal' abantanakho*' (Zavolo, Zavolo, milk for your children) because, as in folklore in the Americas, it is believed the bird sucks cattle teats in the night.[80]

Later Koopman builds upon what he explores in his 1990 paper and looks beyond bird names. He abandons the term ornimatopoeia and incorporates what he observed earlier into a fully encompassing theory of how people verbalise bird sounds. In his aptly named paper, *From Vocalisation to Verbalisation, Strategies for Turning Bird Calls into Language*, Koopman's reveals five verbal strategies for rendering birdsong:

1. Descriptive: using adjectives and adjectival phrases.
2. Metaphor and simile.
3. Partial-verbalisation: using 'semi-words' and 'semi-phrases' that are 'lexically meaningless'.
4. Full-verbalisation: using phrases that are 'lexically intelligible'.
5. Bird names: using any of the above strategies to create bird names.[81]

It is his third and fourth categories that are of interest here, although the fifth category can use any of the other four strategies to create bird names, so it is also relevant.[82]

Koopman names Type I *partial-verbalisation* as it uses 'apparent words' such as the Great Reed Warbler (*Acrocephalus arundinaceus*) saying, 'tuckle-tuckle-tuckle'.[83] He names Type II *full-verbalisation* as these use 'recognisable words' such as the Ring-Necked Dove (*Streptopelia capicola*) saying, 'how's father, how's father'.[84] He compares the two types of verbalisation with examples for the Black-Collared Barbet (*Lybius torquatus*): It says, '*two-puddly*' (Type I) or 'clean-collar clean-collar' (Type II). Although 'two' *is* a word, 'puddly' is not and the phrase as a whole is not semantically meaningful. I would note that the 'apparent' words of 'two-puddly' appear to be a different beast to the strings of consonants also attested to be partial-verbalisations, such as *'tzzzzzrr dzweep,'* but Koopman groups them together due to their being 'meaningless'.

Juan Moreno Cabrera, like Koopman in his 1990 paper, only explored bird names. As a result of his research in Central and South America he creates two categories: onomatopoeic ornithonyms and delocutive ornithonyms. An example of an onomatopoeic ornithonym (Type I) is 'cuckoo', as the name of the bird is the imitation of its call.[85] He describes delocutive ornithonyms (Type II) as 'a meaningful interpretation of [a bird's] characteristic call'.[86] He gives the example of the various names for the Great Kiskadee (*Pitangus sulphuratus*) in various dialects (see Table 7), including Bicho-feo (Bug ugly) and Quit-a-fé (It takes faith).

Despite using the term onomatopoeic, Moreno Cabrera states that describing his Type I and Type II examples as imitative is misleading, and they are each better understood as a 'meaningful interpretation of its call. This call can be *interpreted* or *understood* as similar to a particular phrase or expression of a natural language'.[87]

He goes on to note that the only difference between onomatopoeic ornithonyms (Type I) and delocutive ornithonyms (Type II) are that the former, 'interpret[s] bird sounds from a phonetic point of view,' and the latter, 'interpret[s] them from a morpho-syntactic point of view'.[88] Therefore, only semantically meaningful words and phrases count as Type II.

Sarvasy splits the imitation of bird sounds into categories along similar lines but does not limit her explorations to bird names. She states that, in the field of ethnobiology, Type II has been 'largely overlooked by researchers' and that at an ethnobiological conference 'it lacked even a name'.[89] However, she then rejects the term 'mnemonics' (for reasons I'll discuss shortly) thereby admitting it does have a name, albeit not an academic one, nor one that she thinks is accurate. Her paper, *Warblish: Verbal Mimicry of Birdsong* analyses three types of imitation: non-verbal vocal mimicry (whistling, hissing etc.), onomatopoeia (Type I) and warblish (Type II). Her focus on imitative techniques means she also focuses on the imitative qualities of Type II examples, including comparing examples with bird sounds using spectrograms, as previously mentioned.

Table 7: Type II Names for the Great Kiskadee (Pitangus sulphuratus) *in Central and South America*

Country	Spanish/Portuguese bird name	Literal English translation
Brazil	*Bem-te-vi*	Well you saw
Argentina, Bolivia	*Ben-te-ve-o*	Well you see
Mexico, Peru	*Bien-te-ve-o*	Well you see
Argentina	*Quit-a-fé*	It takes faith
Argentina	*Gente-ve-o*	People I see
Argentina	*Bicho-feo*	Bug ugly
Columbia	*Bicho-fu-é*	Bug was
Honduras, Venezuela	*Cristo-fu-é*	Christ was

However, in Sarvasy's definition, 'The phenomenon of vocal imitation of avian vocalizations by humans, using existing non-onomatopoeic word(s)' she states warblish uses 'non-onomatopoeic word(s)'.[90] I find this confusing since warblish *does* imitate sounds and therefore is a form of onomatopoeia. I interpret her definition as meaning warblish uses not *merely* nonce onomatopoeic words, like the California Quail saying, 'Ki kuu kuu' but rather uses imitative words like 'Chicago.' However, I think she unnecessarily confuses the issue with her category labels, of onomatopoeia (Type I) versus *warblish* (Type II). The fact that she and Moreno Cabrera specifically contrast Type I and Type II, using the term onomatopoeia for one and not the other, implies that Type II are not *also* onomatopoeic.

Koopman originally makes a similar error when he includes both Type I and Type II under the term onomatopoeia,[91] but he remedies this in his later paper when he chooses new terms to show their similarities (both are types of verbalisation) but also their differences (one is partial-verbalisation and the other is full-verbalisation).[92]

On first reading, Emma Gorst appears to use the terms *vox confusa* (meaningless speech like that of an animal) and *vox articulata* (meaningful speech, like that of a human) in a similar way to partial-verbalisation and full-verbalisation in her article *Interspecies Mimicry—the Practice of Mimicking the Song and Speech of a Different Animal*.[93] She looks at the humour of listening to geese and sparrows trying to communicate together in Chaucer's *The Manciple's Tale*, and the exclusion of a crow for mimicking a nightingale, a cuckoo, a swan, and a person in his poem *Parlement of Fowles*. She raises the interesting point that both humans and birds can imitate one another: 'Interspecies mimicry opens up the possibility that certain birds stand apart from the class Aves, just as we might like humans to stand apart from the class Mammalia.'[94] However, she, like Moreno Cabrera, notes that the difficulties in humans creating sounds for birds results in poor imitations on our part, and that there are differences in onomatopoeia across languages due to any given language's limited range of phonemes.

Gorst notes that in *Parlement of Fowles*:

> [T]he English *caw* and the Latin *crocio* sound a little like the Middle English pronunciation of the word 'care' (*ka*) — so when Middle English speakers mimicked the crow's 'Caw!' they could have heard what Chaucer calls the 'crow's vois of care'.[95]

Therefore, in Middle English, 'Caw' would be considered a Type II example because it sounds like the word 'care'. (However, this could be disputed since the word care in Middle English was likely to have been pronounced with an [r].) Similarly:

> [W]hen the crows says 'Cokkow!' ... it engages in a doubly interspecies mimicry: it imitates the English words *cuckoo* and *cuckold* while mimicking the sound of the cuckoo bird. The crow's rude word 'swyve'[96] is also a double mimicry: its rudeness mimics the tenor of Phebus's wife's adultery, embodying the word that 'cosyn be to the working'..., and fusing polite songs counterfeited from Phebus with the crow's own crude words. Unlike the goose's 'kek kek' in the *Parlement of the Fowles*, the crow's 'Cokkow!' fuses *vox articulata* (meaningful speech) with *vox confusa* (meaningless speech,

including the mimicry usually considered characteristic of birds).[97]

Therefore, although she and others treat *vox confusa* as the equivalent of Type I, she does not treat *vox articulata* as the equivalent of Type II. Instead, she claims the rarer Type II is a combination of both *vox confusa* and *vox articulata*, since *vox articulata* does not have the imitative qualities necessary to make it Type II on its own.

Kawasaki appears to have similar categories that she calls onomatopoeia (Type I) and 聞きなし (*Kikinashi*; Type II).[98] However, I may have missed any subtle distinctions as I am not fluent in Japanese but as her examples are from American sources in English, I believe she was translating the concept from English to Japanese.

Therefore, numerous terms have been proposed over the years, with varying definitions, so where to from here?

3. Revised Terminology

Sarvasy states:

> North America English-speaking birdwatchers often call warblish "mnemonics" (e.g., Feith 2002). But in only a minority of cultures around the world does it seem that warblish is just an aid for learning to recognize calls.[1]

I agree that the term mnemonics is a poor name, but mainly because it is too vague. The works of William Young,[2] John Feith,[3] and many websites include descriptions, metaphors, and Type I and Type II under the term *mnemonics*. The term seems to have been mostly used on websites, and to a lesser extent in some birding books, but not so much by those interested in examining exactly what it is.

As Table 6 shows, a number of researchers name or refer to Type II by terms other than mnemonics. Those who have explored the concept most fully have usually attempted a systematic distinction between Type I and Type II.[4]

Warblish

I prefer Koopman's emphasis in his later paper on the various strategies for verbalising birdsong and the equal weight given to Type I and Type II in his terminology partial-verbalisation and full-verbalisation.[5] I also admire his avoidance of the term onomatopoeia. However, as I wanted to approach the public to elicit examples and aimed to write a book, I preferred to use terms that are catchy, concise, memorable, and less academic sounding. Sarvasy's Type II term, warblish, is a neologism and so avoids the problems that the words onomatopoeia and mnemonic had run into being defined differently by various people and being used in areas other than birdsong. Hopefully, if adopted, the term warblish will enable future researchers to build on previous research rather than contributing yet another term as has happened in the past. Her article and the new term attracted some attention from non-academic sources, I believe, in part, because of the unique and interesting sounding name.

Therefore, I adopted the term warblish early on and found it captured people's attention. I have made a slight adjustment to the wording of her definition, but not, I believe, any difference to its intending meaning. I incorporate Moreno Cabrera's idea of interpretation rather than imitation of birdsong, thus placing less emphasis on the accuracy of the mimicry of sounds. I use the word onomatopoeic, whereas Sarvasy used non-onomatopoeic, as I want to highlight that it is a subset of onomatopoeia.

> *Warblish*: onomatopoeic interpretations of a specific bird vocalisations using existing word(s), e.g. the California Quail says, 'Chicago,' or 'Where are you?'

Chirpish

If we continue to use the term onomatopoeia for Type I examples this is still problematic because it implies warblish is not also a type of onomatopoeia. However, I believe Moreno Cabrera's argument that it is the definition of onomatopoeia that should be changed is flawed. The term is used in so many disciplines and is so widely used outside of academia that redefining it is problematic, and his call for, '[A] new definition of onomatopoeia as a language dependent interpretation of non-linguistic sounds instead of the traditional notion involving animal sound imitation'[6] completely ignores all the onomatopoeia for inanimate actions. (I will also at the end of this book consider a category for inanimate objects that is relevant). Therefore, I have created a new term for the onomatopoeia used for bird calls and songs, and that is inspired by Sarvasy's term warblish: I will use the term *chirpish* for onomatopoeic nonce words.

The focus of this book is warblish. However, I think chirpish needs its own term not just to differentiate a similar phenomenon from warblish. The chirpish found in birding books appears to often be quite different to the onomatopoeia found elsewhere. While I will not explore the idea in any depth, there are a few issues I want to cover first.

Sarvasy refers to onomatopoeic imitation as using 'nonsense words that may combine into set expressions evoking bird calls according to the grammars of their own languages'.[7] However, Koopman notes that partial-verbalisations often do not look like the language they are used in.[8] Later in her paper Sarvasy also notes that 'although onomatopoeic birdsong imitations largely fit phonological systems' they may also use consonant clusters normally only used in expressives and birdsong imitations, such as word initial <kr> and <br> combinations in Nungon.[9]

I think Type I needs its own term. Firstly, to differentiate it from warblish. Secondly, to highlight the fact it's also a *subset* of onomatopoeia. There also appears to be something interesting going on with Type I as most examples, like the *tzzzzzrrr dzweep* examples, do not seem to be of the same family as bang, pop, or hiccup, i.e., the types of words thought to be indicative of onomatopoeia.

A better term for describing of Type I may be nonce words. Sarvasy uses the words nonce and nonsense interchangeably. However, nonce words are invented to suit 'a particular occasion or situation,'[10] or 'a word coined on a specific occasion,'[11] as opposed to just being silly. Most Type I words and phrases for birdsong are created to mimic specific bird sounds rather than for specific sound *qualities*. For example, the onomatopoeic word bang means 'a sudden very loud noise'.[12] This can be used for the sound of a gun firing, a car crashing, or a door slamming. It can refer to a range of actions. Birdsong onomatopoeia found in birding guides, however, is specific to a specific bird, and therefore rather than a 'particular occasion or situation', I would argue for a specific species.

Therefore, I have termed this particular type of onomatopoeia, Type I, as *chirpish* (see Table 8).

> *Chirpish***:** onomatopoeic interpretation of a specific bird vocalisation using a nonce word(s), e.g. the California Quail says, 'Ki kuu kuu'. (Type I)

Table 8: Terminology for Subsets of Onomatopoeia: Chirpish and Warblish

	Onomatopoeia	
	Type I **Chirpish** (using created words)	Type II **Warblish** (using existing words)
Ovenbird	queecher, queecher, queecher	teacher, teacher, teacher
California Quail	ki kuu kuu	Chicago

4. What is the Function of Warblish?

Sarvasy's rejection of the name mnemonics on the basis that not all cultures use it as a memory device is perhaps confusing its name with its function. While Sarvasy argues that other cultures do not use warblish as a mnemonic, I would question whether English-speaking and Western cultures always do either. In order to decide if mnemonics is a legitimate name, we need to look at how warblish functions.

Is memorability a function?

Sarvasy implies that an instance of warblish might be only used as a mnemonic in English but in other cultures it has other purposes, such as conveying actual messages from birds or being part of a traditional story. She does not provide any evidence to ascertain who does and who does not believe the words attributed to the birds are the birds' intentions. Many of the examples I found in English (such as the 'Sow wheat Peverly' example) were told in a way that could suggest belief in birds talking. Her references include a notable number of examples from indigenous cultures but only two sources with English examples and all but one example were from one CD by John Feith,[1] who uses chirpish and warblish, along with descriptions and metaphor, to help birders identify bird calls and songs.[2] Feith, as well as other sources (books, apps, websites, CDs, etc.) aimed at birdwatchers, often refer to these as mnemonics precisely, I think, because for a birdwatcher they *can* serve as mnemonics. A birdwatcher's primary interest is to identify birds so chirpish and warblish are merely another tool (albeit a poor tool according to many birders) to use in their quest for identification. It is understandable that the onomatopoeic qualities of chirpish and warblish have led many to conclude that they are mnemonics.

However, many birding books, while they use chirpish and warblish, rarely explicitly explain or comment on them or explore the concepts in any detail. The research I have found on this subject is mostly from linguistics, not ornithology. When birding books do comment, they point out the shortcomings. The entry in the *RSPB Guide to Birdsong* for a short text entitled *Word-based Mnemonics* is typical:

> [F]or some birds, you can aid your memory by using English phrases that do not attempt to accurately transcribe the sounds but provide a memorable approximation. So, while the Yellowhammer doesn't actually sing 'little bit of bread and no cheese' (or the polite version with a 'please' at the end), the sound has enough of the same pattern, duration and timbre to remind us of it.[3]

More often, naming or referring to such examples is almost taboo. Crowe's book *Which New Zealand Bird?* has a list of bird calls and songs which includes descriptions, simile, chirpish and warblish, but makes no distinction between the different imitative techniques, nor are any or all of them named.[4] These imitative techniques all appear in Koopman's[5] categories, which is not surprising because he based his analysis on birding books from southern Africa. They are all commonly used, although warblish more rarely so, in the birding world.

Most birding books that include warblish do not have a separate section for it. Examples are just found under the voice section, and they are simply presented as a feature of birding books without any further comment. However, when there is a comment, it is evident that many birding books (and birders) do not like warblish because of defensive remarks such as 'We do not share the opinion that written voice transcriptions are so subjective that they have little value at all.'[6] However, that author does not clarify what their value actually is.

The use of the term mnemonics and the assumption that these are mere memory aides is understandable when we remember that conspicuous examples of warblish are often found listed under the vocalisation section of birding books, where people are interested in the sounds made by birds and how to identify them; however, it is also where their lack of accuracy is most noticeable and bothersome. Perhaps it is because birdwatchers are so attentive to sounds that they correctly identify the lack of precision in the imitations. Nevertheless, the classification of these phrases as purely mnemonic is not, as far as I can find, supported by any evidence from the wider study of other mnemonics, notwithstanding William Young's claim that it is 'an effective learning technique is to translate the vocalizations of a species into familiar words or phrases'.[7]

If chirpish and warblish are mnemonics we would expect both of them to be memorable, but the '*Zrüzrü-trett zrüzrüzrü-trett zrüzrüzrü psit trutrutru-pürrrrrrrrurrrrrr **vi-vi-vi** lülülü **zetre zetre**…*' example is definitely not memorable. Most chirpish examples with strange spellings are not at all memorable, and they are more common than warblish examples. Therefore, this suggests this phenomenon has a different function.

If warblish is merely a memory device to help identify birds, then we would not expect a large number of phrases for the same call, as remembering all the different phrases would be cumbersome. However, some birds have a great many warblish phrases attributed to them. There are vastly different versions for the Song Thrush in Swedish. Just some (translations of) examples are: 'Take a cookie, take a cookie, spit in the cup and dunk it, dunk it'; 'Pedal on you, you have a long way home, pedal on you, you have a long way home'; 'Are you fishing, Ola? Are you fishing, Ola? Pull it up, pull it up, pull it up!'; 'If you need to shit then take a shit, if you need to shit then take a shit'.[8] The sheer number of examples could suggest they are operating as something other than an *aide memoire.*

The most useful mnemonics might be expected to be the dominant ones in circulation. For example, we might consider the analogy of pangrams designed for testing a keyboard's functionality or a person's typing skills. The most common is: 'The quick brown fox jumps over the lazy dog'. Another is, 'Jaded zombies acted quaintly but kept driving their oxen forward.' There are many such pangrams, but all but one are longer than the 'fox' version. That one is, 'The five boxing wizards jump quickly'. Many of the alternatives are far more exciting but the traditional pangram, one that is very economical in numbers of letters used is the most well-known. It also uses easily spelled familiar words, making it perhaps the best choice. Therefore, if warblish is a mnemonic, we would expect that the warblish best approximating the sound of the bird would be the most well-known.

Word mnemonics are often used for lists that need to be

remembered in a particular order, such as the order of sharps on a musical scale: Father Charles Goes Down And Ends Battle (F♯, C♯, G♯, D♯, A♯, E♯ and B♯); or for the scientific classification applied in taxonomy: Kings Play Chess On Funny Glass Stairs (Kingdom, Phylum, Class, Order, Family, Genus, Species); or finally, the colours of a rainbow: Richard Of York Gave Battle In Vain (Red, Orange, Yellow, Green, Blue, Indigo, Violet). Warblish has the same necessity for elements to be in a particular order, so the sound imitation is obvious. However, warblish has a lot of variation even within the same phrase. For example, the Yellowhammer (*Emberiza citrinella*) is reported as saying:

> A little bit of bread and no cheese, please.[9]
> A little bit of bread and no cheese.[10]
> Give me bread and some more cheese.[11]
> Bread and butter but no cheese.[12]

It is conceivable that these differences could be accounted for by regional, seasonal, and individual differences in the birdsong. However, some phrases are vastly different from others, such as those for the Song Sparrow (*Melospiza melodia*):

> Sweet, sweet, sweet, towee.[13]
> Pres-pres-pres-pres-by-ter-ri-an.[14]
> Welcome to Campton, tra-la-la-la-la-la lay.[15]
> Welcome to Campton's flow'ring meadows gay.[16]
> God be with you till me meet a--- (a famous song lyric cut off).[17]
> Wail, wail, fickle wife is she, flown away and left me![18]
> Sad, sad, what a tale of sorrow, she may return tomorrow.[19]
> True, true, very true you see, she's come again to live with me.[20]
> Maids, maids, maids, put on your tea kettle-ettle-ettle.[21]
> Maids maids maids pick up the tea kettle kettle kettle.[22]

Aside from lists of warblish on the internet and in the odd magazine article there was another source of examples that stood out, that of illustrated books or posters. I found four children's picture books: Bianki's *Птичьи Разговоры* [Ptich'i razgovory] (*Bird Talk*);[23] Allen's *Waddle Giggle Gargle*;[24] Jonas' *Bird Talk*;[25] and Donaldson's *Go-away Bird*;[26] and Mosco has made two colourful posters using warblish as part of her series on nature called *Bird and Moon Comics*.[27]

Rosemary Moscos's posters seem designed to appeal to both adults and children. Each poster shows twelve birds and their warblish is within speech bubbles, but they also illustrate the bird in a way that relates to the content, such as the Red-breasted Nuthatch (*Sitta canadensis*) walking through ink and saying, 'Ink. Ink. Ink'[28].

Julia Donaldson's *Go-away Bird* is also beautifully illustrated but only contains one example of warblish with the Go-away bird's name[29]. It plays with other bird names, inventing new ones that also describe the birds featured on the pages.

Bianki, Allen, and Jonas, however, dedicated their entire books to warblish. Vitaly Bianki's Птичьи Разговоры [Ptich'i razgovory] (*Bird Talk*) was originally published in in Russian in 1939 in the Soviet Union. It sets the story in a farmyard where all the poultry and farm animals speak meaningfully and onomatopoeically using warblish and Type II for animals (i.e., animalopoeia; see chapter 5).[30]

Allen's book *Waddle Giggle Gargle* is a story based around one phrase attributed to magpies. New Zealand poet Denis Glover's famous poem *The Magpies* famously rendered the bird's call in chirpish in the second to last line of each verse: 'And quardle oodle ardle wardle doodle/The magpies said'.[31] In contrast, Allen's phrase is, 'Waddle giggle gargle paddle poodle.'[32] Normally, I would say that a string of unconnected words appears to act more like chirpish than warblish. However, in this case Allen appears to be alluding to one of the most famous lines in New Zealand poetry. She is also incorporating alliteration, and the falling intonation suggested by the change in vowel sounds mimics the Magpie's song, and the choice of words has a silliness that is not accidental. Therefore, this little ditty is more sophisticated than a random choice of words that happen to sound like the bird and I decided to list it as warblish.

Ann Jonas' book *Bird Talk* only contains warblish. It dedicates itself to North American warblish but has a few chirpish examples such as the Chickadee saying, 'chicka dee dee dee'.[33] Each double-page spread shows a scene full of birds 'talking' about the same topics. All the birds talking about food appear on the same spread regardless of whether they would normally be found in the same habitat. The pictures show speech bubbles for each bird with their phrase. There's no other text but there is an identification glossary at the back which marries the phrases up with the names of the birds.

Jonas takes the commonly shared phrases in North America and illustrates them beautifully. However, Bush, a reviewer, points out that the 'joke' might be lost on the younger readers.[34] Admittedly, the type of illustration makes it look like a picture book which would suggest a younger readership than would perhaps know the mnemonics or be able to identify the birds. However, I know local children would have no problem identifying a Morepork or understanding that its call sounds like 'more pork,' so I do not think the criticism is entirely justified.

If the purpose of warblish is not to act as mnemonics though, the bright cheerful illustrations in the above authors' work could be indicating another purpose. Bush's use of the word 'joke' inadvertently suggests questioning if humour is an aim of warblish.

Is humour a function?

References to the humour of warblish is, like so much around this topic, often brief and sometimes dismissive. It seems humour is not something to be taken seriously.

In his thesis *The Use of Bird Sound Imitations and Recordings Among Estonian Birders,* Sugata Bhattacharya, surprisingly, only dedicates one paragraph to warblish and includes only two examples. He states that the warblish 'remembered by the Estonians, was not just a source of humour, but a mnemonic device to distinguish the call of the Ural Owl from that of other owls heard during the trip'.[35] The warblish is, '*Uhu, kas tüdrukud kodu*'.[36] I have had it translated as either, 'Uhu, are the girls at home?' or 'Uhu, are the girls going home?'

Thomas Bulpin makes a similar comment about the Zulu people: 'The calls of the birds seemed to have a particular fascination to these primitive tribespeople and many of their interpretations are beautiful and amusing.'[37] An example he gives is the Hamerkop (*Scopus umbretta*) saying, '*Thekwane, Thekwana, nganqimuhle kodwa ngoniwa yilokhu nalokhu nalokhu*' (Thekwane, Thekwane, I would have been a handsome chap but I am spoilt by this and that and that).[38]

Sarvasy considers 'facetiously irrelevant and incongruous warblish' such as the Northern Waterthrush saying, 'nice old ladies do not chew' to be 'more typical of industrialised societies and those with a history of colonization'.[39] However, later she does concede that her example is humorous by saying, 'Humor and off-color warblish are not limited to these societies, however,'[40] and gives an example of the New Guinea Friarbird/Bɔlɔ (*Philemon novaeguineae*) insulting men about their genitalia in the Kaluli language.

A. J. Moreau collected bird names in Zulu, Xhosa, and Afrikaans including chirpish and warblish names. He notes that 'In general, … the names very often give evidence of good observation and show an appropriateness that is at times witty.'[41]

As Moreno Cabrera points out, warblish is poor at mimicking the bird sounds and should be thought of as interpretation instead of imitation. I think the idea of interpretation allows more room for humorous content and for understanding examples as not being irrelevant, but humorous. Take the following examples, which have been interpreted as imparting information: the Eurasian Blue Tit (*Cyanistes caeruleus*) announces, 'I'm a blue tit';[42] the Goldcrest (*Regulus regulus*) says, '*Jag är minst, jag är minst, jag är minst i hela Sverige*' (I'm the smallest, I'm the smallest, I'm the smallest in all of Sweden);[43] the Great Tit (*Parus major*) says, '*Titta hit titta hit, jag är gul och svart och vit*' (Look here look here, I am yellow and black and white).[44] It can be argued that these phrases are informative for beginner birders who are trying to identify birds and match what they see with what they hear. However, it has to be acknowledged that they are the exception to the rule, in that they refer to something related to the bird when most warblish does not. When we hear a Blue Tit introducing himself, I propose that we do not think, 'that's useful information' or 'that's a clever mnemonic that has helped me identify the bird,' but rather, it makes us smile.

Sarvasy states, 'North American and Australian English warblish are rife with flippant warblish, such as several referring to "beer" in the United States.'[45] I would contend that much of warblish is light-hearted and witty and the Acadian Flycatcher (*Empidonax virescens*) asking for 'pizza,'[46] or the Alder Flycatcher announcing, 'free beer!'[47] are perfect examples of this. We know birds do not really eat pizza or drink beer, they prefer nectar or insects or seeds, so perhaps these are not 'flippant' as Sarvasy alleges, but examples of humour, which can be found in traditional/indigenous populations as well as modern urban populations. According to Feld, the New Guinea Friarbird (*Oriolus szalayi*) says, '*Ninɛli monowo id alu nagalakɛ-o hɔɔ!*' (I just ate and my asshole really hurts, ha!).[48]

For a long time, I assumed the words chosen for warblish were just the ones which most suited the rhyme pattern due to the linguistic demands of such a restrictive form. However, that would not explain why there is so much swearing and silliness. If we look at all the examples of birds talking about food and drink the vast majority of them are about substances that birds don't actually consume, such as beer, whiskey, wine, tea, coffee, pizza, potato chip, Doritos, *salt sill* (salt herring), egg, *smörgas* (sandwich), crackers and cheese, bread and cheese, tomato, nut, cooked apple, and bean porridge. The only two fruits mentioned by birds, the pandanus palm by the Wasio[49] in Papua New Guinea and the bayberry by the Indian Cuckoo (*Cuculus micropterus*) in Nepal[50], are not fruits eaten by those birds in natural settings. Of all the examples of birds talking about food only a couple seem to refer directly to bird food: the Red-Eyed Vireo (*Vireo olivaceus*), who says to a mate, 'Fat worms ... plenty to eat ... gobble 'em up ... they're so sweet ... come dear ... don't delay ... fly this way'; and the Warbling Vireo (*Vireo gilvus*) says to a caterpillar (in the cleaner version), 'If I sees you I will seize you, and I'll squeeze you till you squirt!'[51] What these two last examples share with the list of human foods mentioned is that they are silly: silly because of the way the Red-eyed Vireo talks directly to its partner, and the Warbling Vireo to its food, or silly because of the absurd food choices. The former foods are all silly because they are absurd food choices for birds and the later are silly because the Warbling Vireo talks about its food in cute friendly language and not the violent language more fitting for a predator. It uses the wrong register for this violent act. The Warbling Vireo uses alliteration and a regular rhyme pattern and anthropomorphises its food source, all which add to the humour, not least the image of squeezing a caterpillar till it bursts. The only warblish example about food that sounds believable and not humorous is 'wheat': The Australian Golden Whistler (*Pachycephala pectoralis*) says, 'wheat-wheat-wheat-WHITTLE!';[52] the Black-Backed Forktail (*Enicurus immaculatus*) says, 'wheat, wheat';[53] and the Common Snipe (*Gallinago gallinago*) says it four times.[54] These examples are not shared as often and with such obvious delight by people as the other food and rhymes examples. The only phrases I found about wheat were rarer, with only one source for each: 'Sow wheat, Peverly, Peverly, Peverly' for the White-throated Sparrow;[55] and for the Indian Cuckoo there is: '快快割麥' [*kuài kuài gē mài*] (Go to cut wheat); and '阿公阿婆, 割麦插禾' [*āgōng ā pó, gē mài chā hé*] (Grandpa, Grandma, cut wheat, transplant rice).[56] The fact they are all not only about wheat but about farming I think is significant and I shall refer to the topic of farming later. The other food examples may be newer; the inclusion of pizza, Doritos, and potato chips certainly are. The predominance of ridiculous foodstuffs is best explained not by the fit of the words to the bird sounds but because of their ludicrousness adding to the humour.

The humour does not appear to be evenly spread across different verbal interpretations, which is using Koopman's categories of *description*, *metaphor and simile*, *partial verbalisation* (chirpish), *full-verbalisation* (warblish), and *bird names*.[57] On searching through A. J. Moreau's lists of African bird names and their translations it strikes me that the descriptive names are often true descriptions based on observation, such as the Sparrow (*Shorwe wanda*) translating as, 'bird of the backyard'.[58] In English there are numerous descriptive names, such as Hedge Sparrow, Willow Warbler, Honeyguide, Fantail, Broad-winged Hawk, Black-masked White-eye, Grey-sided Laughing Thrush, and so on. However, the warblish names are often silly, funny, and not at all informative. For example, South American bird names such as the Great Kiskadee (*Pitangus sulphuratus*) saying and therefore being named, *Bicho-Feo* (Bug Ugly).

Insults can be also humorous, and birds talking is funny, so it is no coincidence that there are books of birds insulting people. These do not usually contain much warblish, but the combination of expletives or insults and birds is interesting and may give insight on the use of humour in warblish. In the *Guide to Troubled Birds,* the birds make sarcastic observations, and are accompanied by noticeably short, weird, funny stories and beautiful artwork. In a rare example of warblish in the book an Owl says, 'Whom.'[59]

Aaron Reynolds has authored a similar book, *Effin' Birds*, which is wonderfully illustrated and contains obscene comments allegedly from the birds, although obviously anthropomorphism. The reason I mention these works is they illustrate that the mere idea of birds talking is funny, let alone birds swearing. I believe a lot of warblish also contains insults, expletives, and taboo topics because these too can be amusing. However, such offensive language has not always been recorded by researchers and writers. Daniel Tammet interviews a Nahuatl speaker in Mexico whose mother warned him as a child not to listen to things with 'dirty mouths' such as strong gusts of wind, wells, and various birds. Although Tammet gives examples in Nathuatl for other topics, he does not list the exact words for 'dirty' topics. I contacted him and he said he did not receive those examples so the censorship may have been with his contributor or the mother.

Many other authors are hesitant about spelling out what the birds are saying. Sarvasy tells us:

> Twentieth-century ornithologist Arthur Allen is credited with the English warblish for the Eastern warbling vireo (*Vireo gilvus*) song; this warblish is known in two variants with more or less veiled reference to male (human) genitalia.[60]

After I approached Sarvasy she provided me with the original, 'First you seize it, then you squeeze it, then you please it, 'til it squirts.'[61] Sarvasy, writing within the confines of an academic journal, also censors other examples. When writing about Feld's discussion of the Bɔlɔ (considered by locals to be both the Brown Oriole (*Oriolus szalayi*) and New Guinea Friarbird (*Philemon buceroides novaeguineae*)) she says, 'men heckled with these insults about their genitalia "shout back, with both laughter and scorn" (Feld, 1982, p. 78).' However, Feld does not use euphemisms, stating the birds are calling about erections and say, '*Ku genelɔ!*' (red cock!) or '*Ku halaid!*' (hard cock!) or '*Hɔ, hɔ, Gigio ku genelɔ!*' in which a man, in this case Gigio, is singled out as being the one who has the 'red cock'.[62] Feld elaborates:

> *Bɔlɔ*'s special skill is the ability to heckle all men with this call. On the trails Kaluli men blush when they hear *bɔlɔ*'s insults and shout back, with both laughter and scorn, *wɛfio, kɔm!* 'shut up, retard!' or *towɔ dabɛno mobiakɛ!* 'we're unwilling to listen to your talk.'[63]

This type of language is not unusual. The Giant Nuthatch (*Sitta magma*) has a harsh, corvine voice and says, 'Get it up! Get it up!'[64] There are examples of chirpish which are spelt in an inoffensive manner making them homophones of rude words. The Crimson Chat (*Epthianura tricolor*) says, 'Dik-it, dik-it,'[65] but it could just as easily be spelt Dick-it, dick-it.

When translating bird names Reginald Ernest Moreau comments:

> [I]t seems to me pedantic to translate names as "the cunning one" or "the crested one": the African has named his birds light-heartedly and colloquially, and the spirit is much better conveyed by such renderings as "the impostor fellow" (the bird is a great natural mimic) and "the crested chap", or best of all, illiterately, as "him with the crest".[66]

Just as some researchers have modestly left out rude examples, it is conceivable that some translators have not been as careful as Moreau to conserve the humorous element, either because it is rude or considered too frivolous. Others may respell warblish to make it more palatable. I suspect some chirpish examples appear to be deliberated spelled, so they do not look like warblish. For example, according to Schmalz the Acadian Flycatcher (*Empidonax virescens*) says, 'peet-suh',[67] but this could be respelled 'pizza' with no changes to the pronunciation. So, just as I found myself keen to respell chirpish to make it become warblish, others may have been doing the opposite.

In Australia, the Red-capped Robin says, '*Gunibuu*' (Mum the balls).[68] It is a reference to a young bird asking mum for the kangaroo testicles that are cooking,[69] but it is unclear whether the original or just the translation can be interpreted as lewd. It is hard to tell with so little information around some translations. Some phrases may not appear to be rude because of cross-cultural differences or the meaning being lost in translation. The Ornate Melidectes/Golyad (*Melidectes torquatus*)[70] in Papua New Guinea says, '*Gol nak, gol yad*' (your exposed brightly coloured skin, my exposed brightly coloured skin).[71] The phrase may not necessarily sound offensive in translation, but it is hard to know if it is impolite and if so, how impolite without further information. Similarly, one of Reginald Ernest Moreau's four examples of warblish is identified as an insult: The Crested Francolin (*Francolinus sephaena*) says in Kikami, '*Ngilikilajako*' (warthog your tail!).[72] Without the note from Moreau, the insulting nature of this phrase might be lost on a reader.

In Papua New Guinea both the Belford's Melidectes/Alawna and the Reichenow's Melidectes/Nol say, '*Ss kyan kyan*' (urine, you pass, you pass),[73] but it is unclear if the bird is using polite language, or the translator is being coy. Since it is a very noisy bird, I could imagine it sounding more uncouth, saying, 'You're pissing! or, 'You're taking a slash!' When Kalam tribespeople hear the bird call, they say the rain will soon come. Interestingly, the bird is the second to call in the morning, before sunrise, and this is significant since people usually 'pass water' when they wake up. I found numerous references to bodily functions such as the White-Crowned Sparrow (*Zonotrichia leucophrys*) saying, 'I gotta go wee-wee now.'[74]

The Chestnut-Backed Scimitar-Babbler (*Pomatorhinus montanus*) is not so harsh, saying, 'Poop' two or three times,[75] while the Chestnut-Winged Babbler (*Cyanoderma erythropterum*) says it four times.[76] However, in Sweden the Yellowhammer/Gulsparv (*Emberiza citrinella*) says, '*Se se se se se se shiiit*' (See see see see see see shit) or '*Siit sitt sitt sitt sitt å skiiit*' (Sit sit sit sit sit and shit).[77] The White-Plumed Honeyeater (*Lichenostomus penicillatus*) in Australia says, 'Shit-a-brick!';[78] the Great Tit (*Parus major*) in Sweden who says, '*Kyss en skit!*' (Kiss a shit!);[79] and the Common Rose Finch (*Carpodacus erythrinus*), also speaking Swedish, who says, '*Se video, Köp en video, Skit i de du*' (Watch video, buy a video, you shit you).[80]

The Common Starling (*Sturnus vulgaris*) just says, 'Dick!'[81] and although this could be a name for Richard, it could also be an insult. There's no mistaking what the Ring Dove/Ringduvan (*Columba palumbus*) in Sweden means with, '*Du är tokig, du är dum*' (you are crazy, you are stupid).[82] The Cetti's Warbler (*Cettia cetti*) is not ambiguous either, saying, 'Me? Cetti? If you don't like it, fuck off.'[83]

I believe the joy of warblish lies not in its attempt to exactly imitate birdsong, but in its playful approximation of birdsong. Warblish representations of birdsong share common characteristics with the sounds of birds, just as a caricaturing cartoon shares characteristics with its subject; there is enough similarity for the observer to recognise the intended target. An exact likeness would cease to be a caricature or warblish, and therefore the humour would be lost. The content of the words does not necessarily need to be humorous as the very act of 'translating' or 'interpreting' the bird sounds as words is itself ridiculous and therefore comical, but entertaining content certainly helps.

Not everyone finds toilet humour or insults humorous, but there is a case to be made for talking birds being inherently funny, especially when they mention incongruous topics. The humour of warblish reminded me somewhat of limericks, and I began to wonder if warblish is a literary form.

Does warblish function as a literary form?

Categorising warblish under mnemonics or imitations, I believe, leads us down the wrong track. Warblish passages might be memorable the way a mnemonic is, or even help in bird song identification, as they do, of course, have a resemblance to the bird sounds they mimic. However, consider this: birdsong could serve as a template to be used in a creative exercise. It could be a form of verse, with rules as to length and cadence, rules that change according to which species of bird is singing. It's like a creative-writing exercise of the 'write a funny poem in iambic pentameter about something in your fridge' variety. So, like another type of nonsense poem, the limerick, there are limits on where the word stresses are, the syllable count, and a fondness for transgression, for rudeness and silliness. Nonsense literature subverts language conventions and creates humour from the nonsensical content. The idea of birds talking can be thought of as nonsensical and therefore having the bird saying anything at all is nonsense and therefore humorous, but adding specific content words, especially rude or humorous ones, or even nonsense chirpish, adds to the effect.

A clue suggesting this function may lie in observing which sources yield comments (as opposed to just examples) of warblish (see Table 9). The sources that are more likely to give a description are ones where language itself, not birds, is held in high esteem. The majority of texts with commentary on warblish examples have something to do with literature, oral or written. Despite the fact that a number of authors, usually linguists, have written academic articles which analyse, define,

Table 9: Categories of Non-birding Texts that Contain Warblish

Text type	Author	Genre or Topic: number of warblish examples
Oral poetry or folklore collections with little commentary	Kuhn (1859) Callaway (1868) Cooke (1884) Torrey (1893) Ottó (1901) Standing Bear (1928) Stevens (1931) R. E. Moreau (1942) Dunning (1946) Owen (1947) Bulpin (1966) Cowser (1969) Breedlove (2006) Norudde (2009) Koopman (2018b)	German legends & fairy tales: 1 Zulu nursery tales, & traditions: 4 Chippewa Indian bird names: 1 US birding, poetry, & literature: 1 Hungarian book on birds: 16 Sioux autobiography: 2 Iraqi folktales: 11 birds & animals East African bird names: 34 Zulu proverbs, idioms, warblish: 4 Sudanese warblish: 12 Natal and Zulu natural history: 15 Letter to folklore journal: 2 US chirpish & warblish: 10 Swedish warblish/folk rhymes: 120 Zulu bird names: 3

Oral poetry or folklore analysis
 	
(can include examples given in previous category)
	Holmer & Hol. (1969)
	Wainwright (1986)
	Koopman (1990)
	Hunn (1991)
	Tidemann &
	    Whiteside (2010)
	Abelin (2011)
	Moreno Cabrera
	    (2016)
	Sarvasy (2016)
	Kawasaki (2018)
	Koopman (2018a)
		Australian indigenous stories: 3
		Xhosa oral poetry, bird names: 12
		Zulu, Engl, Afr. bird names: 6
		Sahaptin bird classification: 1
		Australian indigenous bird
		    stories: 1*
		Swedish folk rhymes: 53
		Spanish language bird
		    names: 7
		Indigenous chirpish & warblish: 23
		American folk mnemonics: 9
		Engl., Afrikaans, Zulu bird calls: 16

Literature	Chaucer (1478/1977) Bianki (1939) Frame (1957) Jonas (1999) Budhwar (2019)	Poem: 1 Kid's book: 45 birds, 12 animals Novel: 2 Children's book: 30 Poem: 1

Text type	Author	Genre or Topic: number of warblish examples
Literary criticism	McGehee (1958) Gorst (2010)	Nature essays: 1 Analysis of Chaucer: 2
Dictionary		Romanian Dictionary: 1

* I believe Tidemann and Whiteside (2010) have paraphrased the example from Holmer and Holmer (1969) incorrectly; therefore, readers should consult the original.

and categorise warblish examples, they use as their source material the poetry, folklore, myths, tales, or bird names from various cultures. They usually analyse the material from a linguistic point of view, comparing the sounds of the imitations with the sounds of the birds they are imitating as previously mentioned. This analysis is interesting and useful for comparing how well the imitations work but overlooks a key element—the purpose of this phenomenon is not necessarily to imitate birds nor to act as mnemonic. It could be argued that imitation functions to display the aesthetic or ludic aspects.

Koopman, in exploring the separate ways in which birdcalls are 'verbalised', lists various techniques and he names the categories accordingly: 'descriptive' (adjectives and adjective phrases), 'metaphor and simile', and 'partial-verbalisation' (i.e., chirpish). All these are also types of figurative language.[84] When we consider other types of figurative or poetic language, such as personification, assonance, and alliteration, these also appear to be components of warblish (see Table 10). Many examples display more than one type of figurative or poetic language. For example, another version of the Warbling Vireo's (*Vireo gilvus*) song is, 'When I see you I will squeeze you, and I'll squeeze you till you squirt',[85] which uses alliteration and a cacophony of [s]; assonance and rhyme of [i:] in *sees*, *seize*, and *squeeze*; personification; parallelism of 'I + verb + you'; and of course, onomatopoeia.

Given that most sources of discussion about warblish are from texts related to language, specifically poetry or folklore, rather than avian life, can the phenomenon be understood from the point of view of literature? While my project's aim has been to find examples, there are some indications from research that it could be thought of as a literary form and I think it important to quickly consider this possibility.

Table 10: Figurative Language Used in Warblish

Figurative Language	Example	Bird
Alliteration	If I sees you, I will seize you, and I'll squeeze you till you squirt[86]	Warbling Vireo
Assonance/ rhyme	One, two, three, I'm lazy[87]	Black-throated Green Warbler
Assonance/ rhyme	Will you live with me? Way up high in a tree, I'll come right down and ... Seeee![88]	Wood Thrush
Sarcasm	Don't you have work to do?[89]	Chicken
Anaphora	*Asifuni bantu! / Sidiniwe ngabantu! / Asifuni ndwendwe! / Asifuni ndaba!* (Xhosa: We do not want people! / We are tired of people! / We do not want visitors! / We do not want any news!)[90]	Chicken
Anaphora	I wish, I wish, I wish, to see Miss Beecher[91]	Chestnut-sided Warbler
Tautology	*'Herarna, herarna, herarna'* (Swedish: boys, boys, boys)[92]	Common Snipe/Enkelbeckasin
Parallelism: tone and content	*'Trilla nerför trappan – nu är jag här'* (Swedish: Fall down the stairs - now I'm here)[93]	Chaffinch/Bofink
Personification	Here I am! Don't you see me? Well, why don't you?[94]	Red-eyed Vireo

    A. T. Wainwright's paper only had four warblish examples in one short paragraph and was so different from the other sources I read that I did not consider it carefully at first. In it he explores 'bird poetry' in Xhosa culture. He describes a type of oral poetry (*ukubonga*) called praise poetry (*izibonga*). Praise poetry is, 'usually recited very fast, at the top of one's voice and in an emotionally charged manner' and the specialist poet 'dresses in a regalia befitting his status'.[95] The praise poems are typically for one's cattle, friends, dogs, children, spouse, or for birds. Wainwright divides the process of writing this type of poetry into three stages which are: 1. Creating a praise name, 2. Creating an unsophisticated praisepoem based on the name, and 3. Creating a sophisticated praise poem.

Wainwright outlines the first step is to give the subject a praise name, which illuminates some feature or characteristic that the praiser wants to emphasise.[96] The praise name can be based on appearance, feeding habits, or, not surprisingly for birds, call, or song. Hence, a praise name can, but need not necessarily, be chirpish or warblish. This has parallels with Koopman's[97] and Moreno Cabrera's research on ornithonyms. In the second phase, literary devices such as imagery, metaphor, parallelism of form and meaning, and repetition, can be incorporated to make an 'unsophisticated praise poem'. It seems more than coincidental that so much figurative language occurs in the same places that warblish does. Wainwright notes that some of the phrases:

> do not even remotely approximate to the sound of the bird's cry. However, certain birds do have praises rendered more "accurately" the sound approximating as closely as possible to the original but with a very significant loss in meaning for the human audience.[98]

Therefore, there appears to be a direct trade-off between meaning and imitation. This could explain why so many names are descriptive whilst warblish is often made of existing words and yet not necessarily very meaningful content. The difficulty in marrying chirpish and warblish because of phonological restraints results in incongruous words being used. Wainwright goes on to say:

> It is common knowledge that bird calls are very repetitive; thus when these calls are rendered as "praises", they too are consequently uninspiring poetically: yet for all that they do serve to illustrate an intermediary stage in the development from simple praise names to fully developed *izibongo* [praise poetry].[99]

He proceeds to describe the more 'creative' third stage, which is a fully developed poem. It is however, the second stage, the unsophisticated poem, which offers up warblish examples which I have collected for this study. The implications of Wainwright's categorisation of the entire process as poetry would suggest that both chirpish and warblish are better understood as literary forms rather than either mnemonics or mere onomatopoeia.

R. G. Dunning spent forty-seven years collecting examples for his book, *Two hundred and sixty-four Zulu proverbs, idioms, etc. and the cries of thirty seven birds: fully translated*, and two years writing it up. His book, like Wainwright's, stands out for not focussing on the imitative aspects but the literary aspects of warblish. He lists proverbs and idioms and then has a section of warblish examples which he heads 'Bird Calls'.[100] In it, he lists the Zulu name, the English name, and then the bird call in its entirety in Zulu then English. He mentions if the line is said by the hen or the cock and gives more information at the end of each entry, if necessary. What is interesting about his list is he includes all repetitions of words or phrases where others who later quote him shorten the examples. Yet, it is the repetitions which I think give the examples credence as bird imitation as they sound more like the birds than single unrepeated phrases do. For example, the Pigeon/Ijuba (Ringdove or Turtledove) says of the mabele corn:

> *Amdokwe, avuthiwe* (It is reddening, it is ripened),
> *Amdokwe, avuthiwe* (It is reddening, it is ripened),
> *Amdokwe, avuthiwe* (It is reddening, it is ripened).[101]

Along with assonance, the repetition suggests a poetic slant to these phrases. Repetition would not be necessary in a mnemonic. While the repetition in 'Sow wheat, Peverly, Peverly, Peverly' could easily be explained by the number of syllables in the birdsong, it can also be explained as being a literary device. Dunning's line breaks are also similar to Wainwright's in that they mimic poetic conventions. Given that their examples were originally oral poetry it is interesting that Wainwright says, 'The arrangement of these praises into lines to illustrate linguistic and literary devices, and the comments on poetic features such as parallelism, imagery and the use of ideophones, is also my own work'.[102] If warblish occurs at a step in the process towards full poetry, Wainwright's concern to comment on all these features makes sense.

Henry Callaway's book, *Nursery tales, traditions, and histories of the Zulus, in their own words, with a translation into English and notes* published in 1896 lists four warblish examples. Three of the examples appear to be conventionalised and one is a personal interpretation by one of the author's students. The example of the Southern Ground Hornbill/Insingizi (*Bucorvus leadbeateri*) is especially interesting. The female cries, *'Ngi y' emuka, ngi y' emuka, ngi ya kwabetu'* (I am going away, I am going away to my people), and the male replies, *'Hamba, hamba, kad' u tsho'* (Go, go, you have said so before).[103] It includes personification, repetition, and humour.

However, if we compare the example given in Callaway's book to that of Dunning's, the difference is striking. In Dunning's rendition the Southern Ground Hornbill/Insingizi (*Bucorvus leadbeateri*)[104] 'couple' has the following (translated) conversation:

Hen:	Where, where is (the) meat?
	Where, where is (the) meat?
Cock:	There's none, it's up in the trees above.
	There's none, it's up in the trees above.
Hen:	Where, where are the worms?
	Where, where are the worms?
Cock:	There are none, there are no worms.
	There are none, there are no worms.
Hen:	Are there none, are there none over there?
	Are there none, are there none over there?
Cock	Oh! Get away with you! Where will I get them from?
	Oh! Get away with you! Where will I get them from?
Hen:	Look for them, look for them over there,
	Look for them, look for them over there.
Cock:	There are none, there are none over there,
	There are none, there are none over there.
Hen	I am going, I am going, I am going home to my people (parents),
	I am going, I am going, I am going home to my people (parents).
Cock:	Go, go, you have long since said so,
	Go, go, you have long since said so.[105]

Dunning's example is much longer and much more detailed than Callaway's. Each line is repeated twice and within each line there is often repetition of words or phrases. It is hard for anyone to justify this being a mnemonic as its length makes it not very memorable. Overall, Dunning provides more examples than most sources with 34 in total, and they are all comparably long and often full of repetitions.

In comparison, many of the examples I have found in other sources are short, lacking repetition or explanation. They are treated like interesting asides, put in footnotes,[106] endnotes,[107] or information boxes.[108] Many are limited to only one paragraph in a book or a short section.[109] R. E. Moreau treats warblish as one phenomenon among many others and only has one paragraph; Thomas Victor Bulpin dedicates only two pages in his book; Nils Holmer and Vanya Holmer have two paragraphs in their book. Even Koopman had only one page on warblish examples in his article in 1990 (although admittedly he expands the number of examples in his 2018a paper). Most telling was the fact Koopman shortens Dunning's example for the Insingizi couple. Possibly he does so because of a lack of space in his journal article in 1990 and because warblish is not the focus of the article. However, he does not look at any of Dunning's long examples in his latter paper either, which is dedicated, at least in part, to warblish. He just comments that Dunning, Bulpin, and Lugg[110] devote several pages to warblish.

Arthur Bent devotes a whole book to Nuthatches, and he states for the Caroline Wren:

> Among the 28 references to the song of this bird that I have consulted, I find an almost endless variety of interpretations, expressed in human words or in expressive syllables. I shall select only a few of the best of each which, to my mind, most clearly recall the song. Among the human words, those that please me best are "tea-kéttle, tea-kéttle, tea-kéttle"; others are "sweet heart, sweet heart," "sweet William, sweet William," "come to me, come to me," "Richelieu, Richelieu, Richelieu," "Jew-Pet-er, Jew-Pet-er," "tree- double-tree, double-tree, double-tree," "sugar to eat, sugar to eat, sugar to eat, sugar," "which jailer, which jailer," etc.[111]

So, although Bent found an 'almost endless' number of warblish examples he was prompted only to listing nine examples. This may have happened numerous times with other writers because the examples were not considered interesting or worthy of recording for their purposes, or perhaps they were so well known they didn't need to be written down. While this is understandable that not everyone is interested in this topic, it does mean that there are quite possibly many more examples that have been heard but not recorded by researchers. After giving just one warblish for the Brown Thrasher (*Toxostoma rufum*), Bent says, 'Many other wordings have been attributed to this versatile bird, but there is not room to quote them all here.'[112] As we have seen Koopman[113] uses Dunning as a source, and yet he too only provides a truncated version of the original bird 'conversation' by reducing it to a couple of lines. Andersen was interested in creating musical notation for various birds found in New Zealand, but he also includes chirpish and warblish examples which he terms 'vocalizations'. For example, the Grey Warbler/Riroriro says, 'Dear dear dear dear tee tee dear dear'.[114] Andersen however insists that these are of less importance than the musical scores he produces.

So, while there is an argument to be made that even interested writers have trouble finding a wealth of examples, it can also be observed that many writers chose to ignore, shorten, or leave out multiple examples. This is important because, as we can see with Dunning's example, the length, the line breaks, the repetition may be significant. The truncation or elimination of lines hides the poetic nature that at least some warblish seems to have.

Given Dunning's interest in proverbs and idioms it is not surprising that he notes the care he has taken when translating them to include notes on the literal, metaphoric, and implied meanings of the bird cries. Indeed, for one example the notes are approximately seven times longer than the example, and many other examples have extensive notes.

The long example for the Southern Ground Hornbill/Insingizi from Dunning was originally in Zulu, and many of his other examples are equally long. There are some slightly longer ones in Swedish too, such as:

> *Det var en gång en flicka som tjänte hos en fruuuu, Då sa frun att jag stulit hennes silkesnystan och hennes saaax Men hade*

jag stulit hennes silkesnystan och hennes sax, hade jag stoppat nystanet under hakan och saxen i min stjärt och sjunkit ned i havets djuuuup. (There once was a girl who served with a lady, and the lady said that I had stolen her ball of silk and scissors, but if I had stolen her ball of silk I would have put the ball under my chin and the scissors in my tail (bum) and sank down to the ocean depths).[115]

The longest one I have found in English was for a Brown Thrasher which mimics a telephone call:

> Hello, hello, yes, yes, yes. Who is this? Who is this? Who is this? Well, well, well, I should say, I should say, How's that? How's that? I do not know, I do not know, What did you say? What did you say? Certainly, Certainly, Well, well, well, Not that I know of, Not that I know of, Tomorrow? Tomorrow? I guess so, I guess so, All right, All right, Goodbye, Goodbye.[116]

Understanding warblish in and through prose and poetry

The repetition in the above example is clearly an imitation of the bird since Thrushes are known to repeat the same short phrase twice, sometimes three times, and then go onto a long phrase, as is commented upon by Robert Browning's poem 'Home Thoughts from Abroad':

> That's the wise thrush; he sings each song twice over,
> Lest you should think he never could recapture
> The first fine careless rapture![117]

Alfred Lord Tennyson's poem 'The Thostle' is also inspired by the Thrush and mimics the repeating phrases sung by the bird:

> "Summer is coming, summer is coming,
> I know it, I know it, I know it.
> Light again, leaf again, life again, love again,"
> Yes, my wild little Poet.
> Sing the new year in under the blue.
> Last year you sang it as gladly.

> "New, new, new, new!" Is it then so new
> That you should carol so madly?
> "Love again, song again, nest again, young again,"
> Never a prophet so crazy!
> And hardly a daisy as yet, little friend,
> See, there is hardly a daisy.
> "Here again, here, here, here, happy year!"
> O warble unchidden, unbidden!
> Summer is coming, is coming, my dear,
> And all the winters are hidden.[118]

Tennyson includes warblish within speech marks in amongst lines with narration. The abundance of repetition within the warblish phrases contrasts with less repetition and the grammatical sentences in the narration. Tennyson's and Browning's poems are 'better' than the one collected by Bent but they have similarities. The song of the bird has inspired a poem that also, to a certain extent, mimics aspects of the birdsong. Bent's example could be an 'unsophisticated poem', that is, stage two in Wainwright's three stage process. It is an imitation, with repetition and humour. There is some alteration of number of repetitions of each phrase and some truncation to provide more variation. Meanwhile, Tennyson and Browning, have gone beyond simple imitation and have thus created 'sophisticated poems', that is, their renditions are stage three in Wainwright's process.

This creative process can be seen in another writer's work. Poet Kartika Budhwar shows a modern example in, 'To the Redwing Blackbird':

> The ornithologist puts grapes
> in his garden for orioles, colorless
> sugar water for hummingbirds. But no
> sunflower seeds for you. *I don't want it
> here*, he says, *I don't like the sound
> it makes: Gonhorrheaaa, Gonhorrhhea.*[119]

She uses respelling here to help indicate that the final words are types of onomatopoeia, as unusual spelling could be thought of as part of the convention for this type of imitation. For this example of warblish she also includes humour in her word choice.

Henry Van Dyke finishes each stanza of his poem *The Song Sparrow* with, 'What bird it is, that every year, / Sings "Sweet—sweet—sweet—very merry cheer."'[120]

John Burroughs includes the Vesper Sparrow (*Pooecetes gramineus*) saying, 'Peace, good-will,' in each stanza of his poem 'The Vesper Sparrow'.[121] In New Zealand we have Eileen Duggan's Bell Bird/Koromako saying, 'So slow, so strong! So slow, so strong!' and 'So sweet, so long! So sweet, so long!'[122] It is not entirely clear from the text if this is warblish but after listening to the bird I have decided to include it. In all these examples warblish is not identified as something separate from the poem or prose and therefore can be even harder to identify, so Bill Manhire's (2020) poem 'The Dotterel' looks like warblish, with italicised repeated phrases throughout, such as:

> Little whistle
> little dartaway
> I can hardly hear you
> What's that you say?
>
> *follow me, follow me*[123]

However, upon inquiry the poet said it is not an example of warblish: 'They're my translation, as it were, of what I think its "little whistle" means when a large dangerous human being comes along.'[124]

Janet Frame also includes two examples of warblish in her first novel about a family struggling with poverty, insanity, disability, and death. They are included as just one poetic device in a novel full of figurative language. The first example is for birds that 'mock the intuitive who-dunnit, who-dunnit of the summer thrush'.[125] In 1891, Oscar Wilde had the House Sparrow (*Passer domesticus*) in his short story 'The Happy Prince' saying, 'What a distinguished stranger!'[126] Although it is not obviously warblish, after listening to sparrows I am inclined to include it.

What are the mechanics of a literary form?

Warblish is, as Wainwright has noted, an unsophisticated poem, but it is not as unsophisticated as it first appears. Warblish has many constraints on it making its creation all the more difficult. A particular type of poem may have constraints on its rhythm, rhythm, the number of syllables in a line and whether those syllables are long or short, accented or unaccented. It may also have constraints on the number of lines. In the case of a limerick, it has five lines, and the ends of lines A, B, and E must rhyme, while C and D must rhyme with each other. There are also expectations on the content, in that it will often be humorous, even raunchy.[127]

The haiku also has strict constraints, having seventeen morae[i] (or *on* in Japanese) distributed over three lines in the pattern 5, 7, 5 morae. It also has other constraints on words, the qualities of sounds (hard or soft sounds, and word stress) within words, and also on the content. A traditional haiku will often contain a *keriji* (a 'cutting word' often shown by punctuation in English, somewhat similar to a volta or turn[ii]) at the end of one of the lines which, depending on where it is placed, will change where the dramatic shift is felt. It will also contain a *kigo* (a figure of speech like metonymy[iii]). The content of haiku is often about some aspect of nature such as the seasons or animals. This focus on content as well as the careful consideration on choosing sounds in haiku[128], although for other reasons, has some parallels with warblish.

Even in prose there can be restrictions. Much flash fiction has constraints, usually on word count. It is best illustrated by the much cited six-word poem by Ernest Hemmingway: 'Baby Shoes. For sale. Never worn'.[129] Like warblish, it needs to adhere to semantic rules in order to work.

Warblish, too, has constraints. It is limited by the number of

---

[i] Note, it's morae, not syllables, that are important: A mora is the shortest length of time a short syllable takes, so a long vowel (which may change the meaning from a short vowel) is counted as two morae in Japanese but one syllable in English.
[ii] A volta in poetry is a turning point or dramatic shift in argument, thought, tone, or theme, often accompanied by words like but, yet, or however.
[iii] Metonymy is referring to something with a word that describes one of its qualities or features, such as referring to the whole government with crown.

syllables of the bird's song or call. The phonemes can mimic the pattern of the sound frequency of the bird's notes. The intonation can be imitated by framing the elements that make it up as a question or statement, or the meaning of the words can influence the tone. As we have seen, phrases can also mirror the sounds of birds. The falling intonation of the Chaffinch (*Fringilla coelebs*) sounds like begging and has therefore been rendered as, '*Snalla, snalla*' (please, please).[130]

The metre for the Warbling Vireo's 'If I SEE you, I will SEIZE you, and I'll SQUEEZE you, till you SQUIRT!'[131] is the third paeon,[i] ending with an anapaest.[ii] Some writers use uppercase to show the syllable stress in warblish, as is seen in the example above. The third paeon is considered to be rare in English. *The Princeton Encyclopedia of Poetry and Poetics* says it 'is found only in ancient metrical theory'[132]. However, there are examples in modern English, such as this line from Gilbert and Sullivan's *Mikado*: '[And the LA-dy, [from the PROV-in] [-ces, who DRES-ses] [like a GUY], // [And who DOES-n't] [think she WALTZ-es], [but would RATH-er] [like to TRY]'[133]. Given the (alleged) rarity of the third paeon in English it is impressive perhaps that Allen created the Warbling Vireo's original line.

In Simon Singh's book about mathematical jokes in the TV show *The Simpsons*, he says that one of the show's writers:

> [D]rew some parallels between puzzles and jokes and suggested they have a great deal in common. Both have carefully constructed set-ups, both rely on a surprise twist, and both effectively have punchlines. Indeed, the best puzzles and jokes make you think and smile at the moment of realisation.[134]

Warblish acts in the same way. The set-up is the identification of the bird and the constraints the birdsong imposes on language. The punchline is hearing the similar word or phrase, especially if it is rude, surprising or has relevant content to the bird. There's a surprise at hearing a bird 'speak'. However, it is the thinking and smiling at the moment of realisation which I think is most applicable here. It is unusual and unexpected to hear someone using human words and at the same time sounding like a bird singing. We have the same moment of

---

[i] I.e., it contains a four-syllable poetic foot and the stress is on the third syllable.
[ii] I.e., it finishes on a strong syllable.

realisation hearing such a thing as when we understand a joke that relies on a pun. The Golden-Crowned Sparrow's (*Zonotrichia atricapilla*) words, 'I'm so tired'[135] is clearly anthropomorphism while also mimicking the tone with the meaning of the words. There is admiration for the cleverness of the poet who created the tiny oral poems. The personification of feelings helps to build a connection through empathy between listener and the bird. There is surprise and laughter at the silliness, naughtiness, or cleverness of the poem.

Therefore, I believe warblish is better thought of as a literary form rather than a mnemonic. Warblish does not seem have the respectability of other forms of poetry, which may be why it has been ignored, lost, forgotten, and ridiculed. It may not have this status because, like limericks, it is silly, and sometimes rude. Like many other forms of oral poetry, it is not recorded nor revered. It is subversive. Anthropomorphism and personification are not currently fashionable and usually only found in children's books or old-fashioned poetry or prose (like in many of the older birding books I consulted). This, combined with its 'unsophisticated' nature, results in warblish not being considered high art, but I believe should still be thought of as an important cultural artifact.

5. Does Warblish Only Exist for Birds?

If warblish is only used to remember birdsong we would not expect to find any examples for animals or objects. While identifying birds may be difficult due to the number of distinct species in an area and the fact they are often heard and not seen it is understandable that people may think we need mnemonics to learn their songs and calls. However, the sounds of farm animals are easily traced back to their source and they are usually restricted to one species of each type, so there would be no need for such examples, nor for sounds of objects represented by existing words to exist. And yet, I found such examples.

Animalopoeia

> *Animalopoeia:* onomatopoeic interpretations of a specific animal or insect vocalisation using existing word(s), e.g. a frog says, 'Rip it, rip it', and the Bush Cricket says, 'Katy did, Katy didn't'.

When looking for examples of warblish I occasionally have found examples from other creatures. There are two conventionalised examples from insects in David Gunson's *The Big Book of New Zealand Wild*life: the Katydid (family: *Tettigoniidae*; a type of cricket) saying, 'Katy did, Katy didn't' in America, while the New Zealand insect of the same name says, 'Zip zip'.[1] It is similar to the Go-away Bird and others whose names are also taken from its spoken phrase. While insect sounds are often more likened to birds than to other animals it seems sensible to list them separately from birds given the significant discrepancy between the number of examples found for birds versus insects.

There are more examples of animalopoeia from animals than

insects, but the majority of them (57 examples) are from the Russian children's book *Птичьи Разговоры* (*Bird Talk*) by Vitaly Bianki.[2] I assume they are his creations, although I imagine it is possible he was inspired or influenced by existing examples. Bianki organises the phrases of farm birds and animals, then later wild birds and frogs, into storylines. A short excerpt, about a bull threatening the other farm animals, shows how the phrases are strung together (see Table 11).

Table 11: Examples of Animalopoeia in Bird Talk *by Bianki*

Russian	Romanisation	English
- Убью-у! – кричит	Ub'yu-u! – krichit	'I'll kill you!' he yells.
Голуби с крыши спрашивают:	Golubi s kryshi sprashivayut:	Pigeons ask from the roof,
- Кого-с? Кого-с?	Kogo-s? Kogo-s?	Whom? Whom?'
А овцы с перепугу все сразу:	A ovtsy s perepugu vse srazu:	All the sheep become frightened, and say,
- Меня-я! Меня-я!	Menya-ya! Menya-ya!	'Me! Me! Me! Me!'
Воробьи с плетня:	Vorob'i s pletnya:	The Sparrows call from the wattle fence,
- Чем? Чем? Чем?	Chem? Chem? Chem?	'With what? With what? With what?'
Боров из лужи:	Borov iz luzhi:	The pig in the puddle says,
- Рюхой! Рюхой!	Ryukhoy! Ryukhoy!)	'With blocks of wood! With blocks of wood!'[3]

Russian appears ideally suited for creating warblish as so much semantic and grammatical information can be contained in a single word, where English often needs a couple of words or more to express the same meaning.

E. S. Stevens's noticeably short story in Arabic from Iraq has four examples of animalopoeia and one of warblish:

> Children are told that the beasts hold an auction sale of the house. The cow moos, '*Ab'ia ad dār, dār, dār!*' 'I sell the house!' The cat bids, '*Khams mīa—au, khams mīa—au!*', 'Five hundred!' The dog outbids her, '*B'alf!*' 'A thousand!' The cock

says, '*Ma abi'a ū-ū*', 'I won't sell it!', but the sheep bleats, '*Mb'a-'a-'a-, mb'a-'a-'a-!*', 'Sold!'[4]

The phrases in both stories are short, include repetitions of words, and are clearly onomatopoeic. The animal and bird phrases are treated and behave the same as each other within the text and resemble the warblish examples I found elsewhere, suggesting that both animal and bird imitations belong to the same subset of onomatopoeia. This would suggest one term would be sufficient to encompass the imitative phrases using existing words from any living creature. However, I chose to label the imitations of birds and animals separately for a number of reasons. Firstly, birds make up the vast majority of examples found. Secondly, all the research I have found commenting on this type of onomatopoeia deals solely with birds. Thirdly, Sarvasy has created an excellent term for describing the imitations of birds. Fourthly, I want to have some continuity in the research and build upon previous studies, and I therefore have chosen to use the term warblish for birds, so Type II imitations for animals needed a different term and I have fused animal and onomatopoeia to create animalopoeia.

Ticktocklish

> *Ticktocklish*: onomatopoeic interpretation of sounds made by an inanimate object using existing word(s), e.g. the Limited Express train says, 'Go-it go-it go-it de-light-ed-ly de-light-ed-ly the Lim-it-ed'.

I also, very occasionally, found examples of Type II for inanimate objects. These included the old-style ambulance sirens in South Africa sounding like they were whining, *'Ry daar, ry daar'* (Drive there, drive there) in Afrikaans.[5]

Daniel Tammet's Nahuatl-speaking informant also spoke of inanimate objects talking. The only example given in his language was for the clock, which I note sounds similar to the English onomatopoeia, 'tick tock':

> And occasionally to Mexicano ears, things can speak. 'My mother, she would say to me, "You hear the clock? Listen to

what the clock is telling you." Always, work this and work that. That is what it was saying. Work. You have to work. *Tequiti* — it means "to work".[6]

In Romanian, a train says, *'Te duc, te a-duc'* (I'll take you (there); I'll bring you (back).[7] In New Zealand, novelist Janet Frame also mimics a train, this time the specific passenger express train called the South Island Limited, which says, 'Go-it go-it go-it de-light-ed-ly de-light-ed-ly the Lim-it-ed'.[8]

The children's book *The Little Engine That Could* by Watty Piper was published in 1930. The very first lines of the book start with onomatopoeia: 'Chug, chug chug. Puff, puff, puff. Ding-dong, ding-dong. The little train rumbled over the tracks.'[9] This sets the scene for the coming ticktocklish. Later an old rusty tired engine refuses to take a train full of toys over the mountain and says, 'I can not. I can not. I can not.'[10] Then a little blue engine wonders if she can make it up the mountain and says, 'I think I can. I think I can. I think I can.'[11] As she gets faster she says, 'I think I can—I think I can—I think I can—I think I can—I think I can—I think I can—I think I can—I think I can—I think I can.'[12] The punctuation is important for these aid in the imitation. The last line of the book is when the little blue engine makes it over the peak and comes down the other side saying, 'I thought I could. I thought I could. I thought I could. I thought I could. I thought I could. I thought I could.'[13] The slowing down of the train is indicated by the slowing sound represented by lines breaks and indentation:

> And the Little Blue Engine smiled
> and seemed to say as she puffed steadily
> down the mountain. "I thought I could.
> I thought I could. I thought I could. I
> thought I could.
>   I thought I could.
>   I thought I could.

Again, these examples behave just like the warblish and animalopoeia examples do, suggesting they all belong to a group of onomatopoeia that uses existing words to mimic specific sounds, differentiating them from onomatopoeic words that are created for that purpose.

Therefore, the term onomatopoeia should be used for the larger category used to describe the creation or use of any words to mimic sounds. Warblish, animalopoeia, and ticktocklish are all subcategories, and they are all using words to mimic *specific* birds, animals, or objects (see Table 12).

I propose a new term for the onomatopoeia usually found in birding books. This type of onomatopoeia is used for specific birds, and I want to differentiate this from the general term that covers objects, animals, insects, birds, and the like. I propose using the term chipish for Type I onomatopoeia referring to birds.

Table 12: Subsets of Onomatopoeia with Examples

Onomatopoeia			
Type I (using created words)	Type II (using existing words)		
Animate	Animate		Inanimate
Chirpish	**Warblish**	**Animalopoeia**	**Ticktocklish**
ki kuu kuu (Quail)	Chicago (Quail)	Rip it (Frog)	I think I can (Train)

6. The Shared Features of Different Interpretations

Given the evidence so far of overlap between poetry and warblish, I decided to compare warblish to other ways of interpreting bird sounds and see what they did and did not have in common. Figure 2 illustrates the features that warblish has with other art forms or interpretations that refer to birds. ticktocklish and animalopoeia have been added to show their kinship with warblish despite their having no connection to birds.

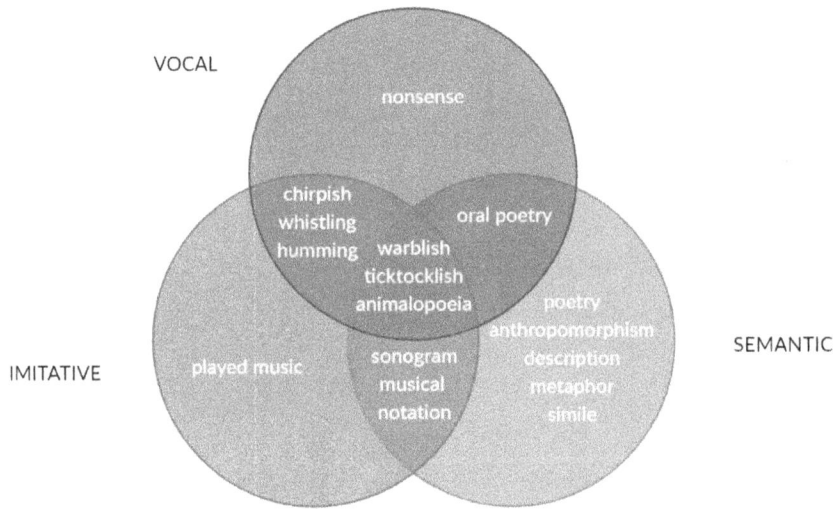

Figure 2: Shared Features of Interpretations of Bird Sounds

Key: **Vocal** = Any interpretation of birds made with the vocal apparatus.
Imitative = Any mimetic interpretation that seeks to imitate or represent the sounds of birds.
Semantic = Any interpretation of birds that is semantically meaningful

Imitative + Vocal = Chirpish

In Mozart's opera *Die Zauberflöte* (The Magic Flute) Papageno and Papagena stammer *'pa pa pa pa'* in a duet, before saying each other's names and singing in full sentences. The sounds they make are very loose imitations. They do not mimic particular sounds recognisable as a particular bird call or song, but have the suggestion of imitation in their timing, turn taking, and the unintelligibility (the *vox confuse*)[1] of bird 'language'.

Imitative + Vocal = Non-Verbal (Whistling, Humming)

Sarvasy and Koopman[2] look at non-verbal methods that imitate bird sounds. Whistling can create more realistic renditions than chirpish or warblish. The call of the extinct Huia was imitated by Kingi Ihaka whistling for the New Zealand Broadcasting Corporation in 1967 and is the only record of the bird's alleged sound.[3] I note that hunters or birders would never use onomatopoeia, neither chirpish nor warblish, to call a bird—they would whistle, gurgle, hum, chortle, etc., (as there are a number of other vocal methods for imitating birds, the most well-known of which are the various calls used by wild turkey hunters) as these are the most realistic imitations of birdsong.

Vocal + Semantic = Oral Poetry

Wainwright's analysis of Xhosa oral poetry, especially praise poetry, fits this category. He also notes that European court poetry appears to be the closest 'equivalent to African praise poetry' but is 'all but extinct'.[4]

Semantic = Poetry, Anthropomorphism, Description, Metaphor and Simile

Although the latter three components of this category could be grouped together under 'descriptive features' I have listed them separately partly because Koopman[5] has them as distinct categories for verbalising bird sounds, but also because they deserve naming as related but different approaches. Anthropomorphism is often found not only in children's books, but also in nature writing and even birding books, and it is difficult sometimes to tell apart from warblish.

Imitative + Semantic = Spectrogram, Musical Notation, and Other Notation

While these show the sounds of birds, they do not provide a vocal sound themselves, so I apply the term *imitative* here very loosely, meaning to represent the sounds in some form. Writers such as Schuyler Mathews, Aretas Saunders, and Johannes Andersen have tried, in vain, to write down the birdsongs using musical notation. While they can serve as approximations, they do highlight how birdsong can change according to season, time of day, individual birds, and so on. The musical scores created can be difficult to read the more exacting they are, and not everyone can read music. Likewise, not everyone can read spectrograms, and both can be intimidating. However, the problems these two pose does lend credibility to using warblish, since warblish uses existing words that everyone can read. S. Mathews (see Figure 3) and Saunders (see Figure 4) have created a notation for people who cannot read music. Mathews' notation consists of very decorative curling lines above the musical stave while Saunders uses straighter lines, sometimes with little squiggles at the ends.

Figure 3: Musical notation and alternative notation of Veery song by S. Mathews (1921)

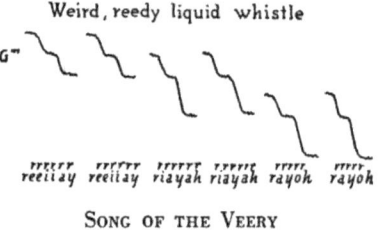

Figure 4: Alternative notation for Veery song by Saunders (1951)

Imitative = Musical Instruments

Cupped hands, leaves, whistles, boxes, and other objects can make sounds to imitate birds. The oldest musical instruments are flutes made from bird bones which we assume were to imitate birds. The very oldest are about 35,000 years old and found in Germany. The oldest non-flute musical instruments (harps and lyres) are from 2600 BC in Sumeria. Simon Barnes comments:

> Surely it would have been easier to make a plucked instrument from a length of gut. Or melodic percussion instrument, like a xylophone, from chunks of wood. But that didn't fit our first ideas of music. We wanted to sound like birds.[6]

Vocal = Nonsense

It was difficult to find an example for this category, but I did find one. Wolfgang Müller is an *avant-garde* musician who created *Séance Vocibus Avium,* an audio project which recreates the sounds of extinct birds. Various musicians use voice descriptions, which sometimes are extremely limited, to recreate the sounds of birds. Most of the tracks sound plausible and are presented as a conventional birding CD would be with narrated track numbers and bird names before the calls. However, the last track for the Great Auk (*Pinguinus impennis*) sounds like joyful nonsense. It is better placed in this category than any onomatopoeic category as its main aim does not seem to be imitation but entertainment. It is exaggerated, ridiculous, and very funny. It is difficult to say if any of the other tracks are imitations given that they are not based on audio recordings, and they are guessing at the extinct birds' calls and not listening and mimicking them. These are more like creative reconstructions if anything.[7]

Vocal + Imitative + Semantic = Warblish, Animalopoeia, And Ticktocklish

These three types of onomatopoeia vocally mimic a sound using existing words. Warblish mimics bird sounds; animalopoeia mimics animal sounds (including insects, frogs, and mammals); and ticktocklish mimics the sounds of inanimate objects, such as clocks and trains.

7. Is Warblish Endangered?

My experience of searching for warblish was one of finding old forgotten books, often difficult to get hold of, with examples that although supposedly common at the time of writing had become rarer now. The more I looked the more evidence I seemed to find that not only are birds and ecosystems endangered or extinct, so too is the language used to describe them. Even within supposed robust languages like English the vocabulary used to describe nature is disappearing. When *The Oxford Junior Dictionary* removed 'bluebell' and 'beech' in favour of 'broadband' and 'blog' Robert MacFarlane responded by writing *Landmarks*. In this book he catalogues little used or almost lost terms for elements in nature, such as 'the variant English terms for icicle: aquabob (Kent), clinkerbell and daggler (Hampshire), cancervell (Exmoor), ickle (Yorkshire), tankle (Durham) and shuckle (Cumbria)'.[1]

What is striking about Norudde's collection is that many respondents comment on how old their examples are, often by saying when their parents or grandparents, who had told them the warblish, had been born, and/or their relative's dialect or hometown. It suggests that the older generations knew more examples and that this is knowledge that is handed down orally through families. However, as I do not know the methodology or any background to the document nor when it was collected, I do not know if this information was specifically asked for, nor when the information was collected.[2]

My husband's father Mikhail used to hunt for food in the tundra and taiga[i] of the far north-east of the Soviet Union. Mikhail used to share many examples of warblish with my husband when he was younger, but Vladimir could only remember one example to share with

---

[i] Biome characterized by coniferous forests

me, and Mikhail is no longer alive to ask for other examples. I have repeatedly heard comparable stories from people whose grandparents had told them warblish. Often, the older generations had lived in rural areas, and had been farmers, forestry workers, gardeners or otherwise close to nature. Only rarely were the grandparents available to be consulted. Some of my informants who asked their grandparents at my instigation have proven able to give me warblish that they themselves had never heard.

Older texts I have consulted often have examples about farming, such as the Red-chested Cuckoo (iNkanku):

> Who announced the approach of spring with "Phezukomkhono" ("On your shoulder"), thus telling the tribespeople to put their hoes on their shoulders and be off to the fields. With the approach of autumn the same bird changed its cry to "Khawula, khawula" ("End the work, end the work").[3]

Sarvasy[4] notes that in S. G. Goodrich's 1849 book, the Bobolink (*Dolichonyn oryzivorus*) said, 'Bobby Lincoln-Lincoln time to plant corn, if you plant any this year, this year, this year'.[5] However, more modern sources just include something like 'Bob-o-Lincoln', often accompanied by chirpish, with the farming references having been removed. The 'Sow Wheat Peverly' phrase has been replaced by most sources with 'Poor Sam Peabody'.

There are also a number of phrases for the Brown Thrasher (*Toxostoma rufum*) related to farming:

> Plant a seed, plant a seed, bury it.[6]
> Drop it, drop it, cover it up, cover it up, pull it up, pull it up.[7]
> Drop it, drop it - cover it up, cover it up - pull it up, pull it up, pull it up.[8]
> Shuck it, shuck it; sow it, sow it; Plough it, plough it; plough it; hoe it, hoe it.[9]

Of the last example, Schuyler Mathews says it is found in 'various books', although I have seen it nowhere else. He presents a much longer version under a musical score (see Figure 5). It is not clear if other writers have shortened this longer version, or if only snippets are remembered, or if Mathews has joined other shorter versions together to create this comprehensive version:

Hurry up, hurry up, plough it, plough it, harrow it, harrow it, hoe it hoe it. Scatter it, scatter it, seed it, seed it, seed it, cover it over, rake it, rake it, tut-tut tut-tut, push it in, push it in, weed it, weed it, pull 'em up, pull 'em up, leave it alone![10]

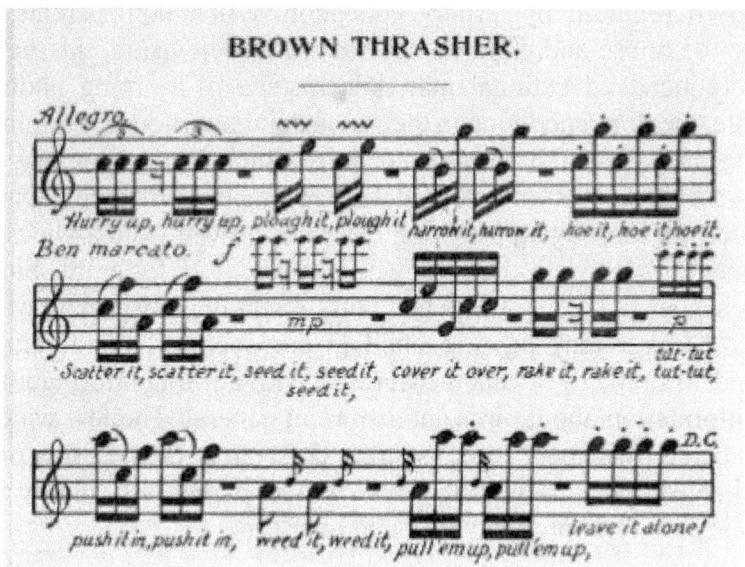

Figure 5: The Song of the Brown Thrasher[11]

The warblish with farming information appears frequently to be dropped in favour of other versions, or is not often quoted, whereas 'pizza' and 'beer' examples are more readily shared these days. I wonder if 'plough', 'harrow', or 'hoe' are even in *The Oxford Junior Dictionary* anymore. I have heard that children in Europe cannot answer the question, 'what sound does a cuckoo make?'

As a society we may also have forgotten many of the warblish phrases that normally would have been handed down through the generations. Feld notes that between writing the first edition (1982) and third edition (2012) of *Sound and Sentiment*, 'many of the beliefs, practices, knowledges, rituals, and experiences described are either considerably muted or are no longer believed, practiced, known, performed, or experienced'.[12] He implicates 'evangelical missionization and government neglect' which have 'collided with transnational intrusions to produce varieties of cultural dissonance'.[13]

However, there could also be ongoing loss of cultural information in the Western world, even now. These days Western families seldom live in intergenerational households, or even in the same cities or countries as older generations of families. Populations have become urbanised, education has become nationally standardised, and apprenticeships have been replaced by tertiary education. Often both parents work outside the house and children have access to television, internet, and mass-produced educational materials instead of learning about, for example, the flora and fauna in their own neighbourhoods. Farming has become mechanised, as have other jobs which in the past may have nurtured a keen observation of nature. People buy their food rather than grow or hunt their own. Watching birds has moved from a widespread necessity for survival to becoming a leisure activity for a few. Some of these changes have only happened fairly recently. I suspect all of these factors together may have resulted in our society having forgotten, changed, or found irrelevant the warblish with farming information, and with information about birds and nature in general. The few which are remembered from more recent sources do seem to be the sillier ones.

Indeed, R. E. Dunning says of one particular Zulu warblish example that it has probably changed over time:

> The cries of the birds have been handed down for generations and generations, that before the advent of civilisation on the present scale, the natives stayed more at home in at their kraals, and that history, traditions, and all other facts, were handed down from father to son regularly, daily and in the evening, in a reliable and exact manner.

However, if English warblish is more 'facetious' than indigenous warblish due to colonisation, as Sarvasy claims, then we should expect to find a difference between the English warblish in England where there has been a long history of relationship with the native birds and the English warblish found in the 'new world'. I found no such differentiation. Indeed, the example from Gorst shows birds being rude in the same way as the New Guinea Friarbird does with them both mentioning something potentially offensive: genitalia or copulation. Many birds swear in many different languages, which I will cover later. I found many examples from European countries including Romania,

Hungary, Sweden, Germany, France, and Russia which were in their native languages, and they did not appear to be markedly different in tone or subject matter than the warblish of colonising cultures, nor indigenous colonised cultures.

What could account for some of the differences however was the society in which the warblish was created. The 'Sow wheat Peverly' version of the Peabody bird's call was interesting because it was about farming, but most other variations were not. This could be explained by a changing pattern in occupations of a population. The 'colonised' populations were often less urbanised, less industrialised than the 'colonising' populations. The more 'meaningful' warblish of indigenous populations can be explained by people being involved with hunting or farming, with working outdoors and having occupations where being observant of bird behaviour was important for survival.

Even warblish embedded with cultural knowledge can be lost as its content becomes outdated or its history is not taught. For example, Schuyler Mathews interprets the Yellow-throated Vireo's song as listing battles in the Boer War: 'Mafeking, Modder River, Buluwago, Malappo, Boer War!'[14] However, someone unfamiliar with this information may interpret it as chirpish, or irrelevant, or boring. Similarly, I thought the Red-Winged Blackbird's (*Agelaius phoeniceus*) song was chirpish, and thus nonsense: 'O-ka-lee, kong-quer-ree, You-choo tea, Oolong tea! Gl-oogl-eee, Conk-a-ree, Quang-se tea, Shoo-chong tea!'[15] However, because I recognised the name of one type of tea, I asked a Taiwanese friend, and she said they were *all* types of tea.[16]

Vocabulary can also become dated. The African Grey Hornbill[17] (*Lophoceros nasutus*) complains, 'Ṣeif wa kharif ma dugtu ferik' (All summer and rains I've never had a ripe dura-head)' and the Red-Billed Hornbill[18] (*Tockus erythrorhynchus*) replies, 'T'akul um baṭn, t'akul um baṭn' (All you'll get is gripes).[19] Anyone unfamiliar with the less well-known and more dated meaning of gripes (to have a sharp pain in the bowels) might not get the joke. Although I am pointing to a translation being dated and not necessarily the original, it is possible that, when warblish contains vocabulary children are unfamiliar with, it is not remembered and therefore not handed down. The warblish Sarvasy objected to: 'Nice old ladies don't chew' may not be flippant but actually might encode social norms about polite behaviour in times past.

I thought it interesting how many of my sources were old. Eight were more than 100 years old. Seventeen were between 50 and 100 years old. The oldest is by Charles Darwin, published in 1839. I have also found earlier editions of the same book including warblish and later ones excluding it; or older examples of nature writing being more fruitful than modern equivalents. This could be for several reasons. The older books were often written by English speakers who were exploring unfamiliar places, whether having been stationed for work in colonised countries or exploring other territories. They therefore might have been encountering more rural people in pre-industrialised societies. Also, due to the fashions of the era, the writers may have been more romantic than scientific in their outlook and therefore more accommodating in recording the warblish examples they heard. Many of them were amateur naturalists, which also may have contributed to their 'less scientific' approaches.[20]

I discovered by chance late in my research that first edition birding guides sometimes had warblish examples whereas the later editions had these examples removed. Therefore, I disregarded many books based on the later editions having had no warblish. I did not find Koopman's articles until late in my research, and note he consults all seven editions of one book and multiple editions of others. This confirms my suspicion that I may have missed examples because of this. If I had had more time and been more systematic in my record keeping (keeping a record of all books consulted that did *not* have any examples) I could have gone back and consulted other editions. I would recommend future researchers look at all editions of books before discounting them. A deliberate strategy of finding the oldest editions may yield more results.

Many earlier editions were discarded when the 'better' up-to-date versions were acquired by my university library. Many older books were thrown out during the Christmas break into large skips. My local rare book specialist searched in his databases containing 150 million books and could only find one copy available, which I couldn't afford. So, searching for warblish has also given me a new appreciation for old forgotten books.

8. Warblish as a Creative Process

We have undoubtedly lost some warblish and some we have retained may be obsolete. However, that is not necessarily a problem as literary forms are capable of renewal. We can write new ones, we can adapt old ones, just as we do with other forms of literature. Warblish is especially open to this since it is such a democratic artform. Being a type of oral poetry people do not need any materials to create it. Anyone who lives where there are birds can create it. It is a way children and adults alike can improve their observation skills and actively listen to sounds in a new way. They may find, like I did, that they have a newfound appreciation for birds and their calls and songs.

I think the variation in warblish attributed to some birds could be explained by the fact that some people enjoy *making* these phrases. It is a creative and intellectually challenging exercise, as is creating a phrase that fits to the tune of a birdsong. So, while warblish and these other types of mnemonics may *look* like mnemonics people can often create them for a different reason.

The importance of recording and collecting warblish to prevent it being lost should not eclipse the importance of creating new versions. I did not limit my collection to only conventionalised, well-known examples, since all examples, even those that have not been widely adopted, can be beautiful. Just as bird songs evolve and adapt to modern life so can and should warblish. Birds can 'talk' about pizza instead of sowing wheat because, rightly or wrongly, pizza is part of our modern diet.

When collecting idioms and warblish R. G. Dunning says that he 'confined' himself 'strictly to only those given to [the birds] by the Natives and have not invented any [himself]'.[1] This implies that he could, and may have wanted to, include his own inventions. I certainly found not only myself, but friends and family inventing our own. For example, the California Quail usually says, 'Chicago' or 'Where are you?' but I heard, 'Call Margo', 'Otago' (a New Zealand placename), 'Embargo', 'Watch Fargo' (a 1990's film), and my friend heard, 'Tomato'.[2] My ten-year-old son created his own animalopoeia, writing this joke: 'What do frogs do with their homework? Rip it! Rip it!'[3] and his friend wrote this joke: 'What do cats say when they fall over? Me—ow!'[4]

If the idea of warblish, animalopoeia, and ticktocklish becomes more well-known there is an opportunity for creating new examples. This provides a wonderful technique for making children and adults pay greater attention to the sounds of nature. It provides an opportunity to respond to nature in a creative way. I think warblish has a role to play in raising awareness of conservation because as Richard Louv notes in his book *Last Child in the Woods: Saving Our Children from Nature-Deficit Disorder*:

> People protect what they value, and they value what they know and appreciate. If children don't cherish the natural environment, there is a good chance that they won't grow up to be good stewards of the earth that sustains us.[5]

We will not save that which we do not love. I have used warblish in my own family and in a school, to help people pay attention to birds; to notice birds and appreciate their voices. Warblish has helped me pay heed to birds, the same creatures I previously loathed, and by paying careful attention to birds I have learned to like them and love their songs. Warblish was the thing that led me to watch birds more closely and maybe one day I too will love birds.

9. Further Research

In my opinion, the best source of warblish are Dunning's Zulu examples and the best explanation is Wainwright's coverage of Xhosa poetry. I also found six other sources which contained Zulu or Xhosa warblish. This is no accident as Zulu and Xhosa are languages rich in ideophones[i]. So are Japanese and Korean. Therefore, we would expect Japanese and Korean to also be rich in warblish. I believe we have not found them yet because while there are many authors from southern Africa writing in English and Afrikaans about Zulu and Xhosa culture there has not been comparable writing in English dealing with such aspects of culture in Japan and Korea. Therefore, there is scope for researchers fluent in those languages to explore this concept. Given the Japanese love for haiku and for nature writing I would be surprised if there are not many examples of warblish in that language.

Koopman states that:

> Identification of an appropriate theoretical framework or frameworks for this study has not been easy, Semiotic theory, with its emphasis on signs and sign process, including meaningful communication, appears on the surface an appropriate framework, but is too broad for this specific study on how bird vocalisations are transformed into human language. The sub-branch zoo-semiotic focuses entirely on intra-animal communication. It would be suitable were this article to on the ways birds communicate with each other, but that is not the case. In addition, semiotic theory does not cover the converting

---

[i] Also called sound-symbolic words or iconic words, ideophones are generally not found in English. They are a type of vocabulary that cover "perceptions of the external world as well as inner sensations and feelings" (Dingemanse, 2019, p. 15). Onomatopoeia can be considered a subset of ideophones as they only mimic perceptions of sound, whereas ideophones include other sensory experiences.

of one type of meaningful communication into another.[1]

Koopman went on to discuss the shortcomings of translation theories for tackling warblish. I agree with all of Koopman's points above and similarly found there was no appropriate theory on which to base my observations and thus I created my own models. Koopman did go on to propose his own 'articulatory conversion theory' to cover the vocalisation of birdsong but not the verbalisation, i.e., the ways in which birdsong is turned into language such as warblish. He very briefly proposes a theory based on a combination of discourse analysis and conversion theory, but I found these to be unhelpful.

The other researchers I consulted did not try to fit their finding into theoretical frameworks and so future researchers could try to incorporate other theories that may shed more light on such types of onomatopoeia as are covered in this report. An avenue that I have not explored is the idea of language play. Guy Cook starts his book *Language Play, Language Learning* with a children's hopscotch rhyme which he describes as, 'a hotchpotch of language' and 'a collage of disjointed and elliptical phrases,'[2] and adds, 'Its carefully controlled rhythm and bizarre fleeting images are a considerable source of delight,'[3] which are phrases apt to describe many warblish examples. The area of language play is therefore one which should be explored, and which may provide theoretical frameworks that are fitting.

As translation is a specialised area, and translation of warblish has added the complications of needing to satisfy both meaning and form requirements of mimicking phrases, this an area which can be tackled by future researchers. There are approximately 62 languages in the database but no doubt there will be more languages that could yield results. Of particular interest to me was te reo Māori. Since New Zealand is a country with so many birds and so few mammals, birds have played an important part in Māori mythology, culture, language, and as a food and feather source in everyday life. I expected that there would be many warblish examples in Māori, however, I realised early on that explaining warblish to English speakers was difficult enough, mainly due to it being a novel concept, and I often was given chirpish rather than warblish examples in reply. I recognised that this happened in Māori too, but I was less confident in pointing out the mismatch between what I was looking for and what my interlocutors were giving me. I imagine that anyone collecting Māori examples would need to be fluent in te reo Māori so they could tease out the chirpish from the warblish given to them and discuss the concept in depth with contributors.

If I am correct that urbanisation and the accompanying indoor lifestyles of people results in warblish dying off, research needs to be done soon to prevent examples becoming extinct. Feld notes that between writing the first and third edition of his book (thirty years) new mines had opened up and men had moved away from their tribes for work.[4] Many of the customs he had originally recorded were no longer practised. He did not explicitly mention warblish in this observation, but it is certainly conceivable that this too was in the process of being forgotten.

Books are also in danger. Many of the books I consulted were old, not digitised, and available from very few places. My own university frequently threw many old books away during the holiday periods, including some books I then had to interloan from overseas libraries. Nowadays, many of the books I consulted would not be considered politically correct, having been written by civil servants in colonial governments, or using language and observations of indigenous populations that are dated. Therefore, they may not be valued as sources of information. In New Zealand, the authors Elsdon Best and Johannes Andersen are now seen as problematic, but they are also the authors who recorded folktales including warblish, so at the very least their works provide a basis for the beginning of a conversation about these stories and beliefs. Andersen is less well known, and I had to buy my own copy in order to access his work.

Earlier I stated that it is plausible that the word 'fall' might trick a person into believing the fall in subjective pitch was more than the recorded fall in frequency. This could be studied in psychology.

Of course, warblish should be studied as a type of literature. If warblish, animalopoeia, and ticktocklish are poetry, and they encode cultural knowledge and they are not being handed down, this is a problem. We need to preserve this knowledge. Especially, I feel, because these examples of playing with words are joyful and humorous, virtues that should make this artform more valuable, not less.

Afterword

While writing my PhD thesis I was surrounded by birds: Articles about birds, recordings of birdsong, pictures of native birds. People bought me coffee mugs with birds on them, tea-towels, bags, and books. So many books!

All these images and sounds worked like exposure therapy, subjecting me to my fears, my phobias. I stopped noticing any discomfort. As I focused on the poetry, I forgot about the likelihood of claws getting caught in my hair or inadvertently eating bird-poo sandwiches (again!) or getting bitten by a Cockatoo. Then I noticed the beautiful sheen on a Tui's back, the song a Grey Warbler sings in the spring, the intelligence of a Kea solving a puzzle, the cheekiness of a Weka stealing a spoon.

Warblish is such a freeing literary form. Anyone can create their own warblish, ticktocklish, or animalopoeia. It can be practised inside with recordings or in the field. We don't need any equipment, not even pen and paper, not even literacy. For me, thinking up warblish is a bit like spotting images in the clouds mixed with completing a cryptic crossword: it's both a creative, peaceful pastime and and an intellectual puzzle.

Friends and acquaintances have told me that after learning about warblish they listen to birds differently, more attentively. This has certainly been true for me. The combination of being in and interacting with nature and engaging in perhaps the toughest of flash fiction challenges is wonderful. I'm not totally at ease with birds just yet, but warblish has given me a gift of listening to and watching birds in a whole new way. Warblish has been a blessing that I hope you too can enjoy and share with others.

Appendices

Appendix A: Methodology For Creating the Database

I describe how I found sources of warblish here in the hope it will aide future researchers in this area. There is some repetition from the text in the body of this book as this section aims to give as much information as possible to future researchers. Lay readers can skip ahead.

Data collection

I have used approximately 170 sources for the database. However, given its nature warblish was not easy to spot in many sources, so I have read vastly more than this, approximately 1000 texts. I have been lucky in that by doing a creative-writing PhD I could justify reading a wide range of texts in my search as it would inform the fiction and autofiction writing projects. Sometimes I would read an entire book and find one or two examples. Often, I would find no examples. However, a researcher solely dedicated to finding warblish could still expect to find examples by limiting themselves to books about birds for conventionalised examples

I found many more examples of warblish than I expected to find but it was a long time coming. I spent approximately four years part-time collecting examples while also writing other pieces and working. Finding warblish was my side hustle. I tried to read texts that would also benefit my other writing while hopefully containing warblish. If I had dedicated myself to reading birding books I may have found a greater number of examples, but reading old, eccentric books allowed me to find interesting and unusual examples and ones that appear to be rare or in danger of extinction. It also allowed me to find a greater number of examples in languages other than English.

In the following sections I outline first how previous researchers collected their data and then some details about specific sources I have mined for data. I summarise the criteria for a token to be included in my database and then move on to explain the structure of the databases.

Previous researchers' methodology

I did not search in some fields which might contain warblish. For example, Sarvasy uses ethnobiology texts, and I assume that since she named warblish and she researches in this field, that she would have found the most obvious examples there (such as Feld), so my time would be better spent looking elsewhere. So, there may be scope here for others to look further in this field.

Also, Sarvasy says she collected examples from literature and music but did not include them in her published article, 'choosing to focus on folk traditions rather than literary innovations'[1] My goal was to include all examples I could find, regardless of which discipline they come from. However, I have found academic music texts too technical to read easily so have not explored this field in any depth and will leave that field to someone with more musical expertise.

As an ethnobiologist Sarvasy is interested in how conventionalised knowledge can be in a community. However, I have decided to include examples, if they are plausible, even if only one person has used the word, including literary examples not necessarily used in daily life by others. I also decided to include examples that have not been published in hard copy, such as examples from websites, online forums, and from people I have interviewed.

Abelin obtained warblish from an unpublished document by Norudde which was available at one time on a Swedish ornithology society website. The examples were mostly sourced from the public, though I do not know the methodology used. I had noted early on from talking to people that this type of folk knowledge was of the sort that was often not written down but could be elicited when talking to people. Therefore, to try and elicit these types of examples I made two websites,[2] flyers, posters, talked to anyone I met, and posted on social media, and online forums.

I have discovered from talking to people about my topic that their elderly relatives often know or knew more warblish than they do, which is the case with Norudde's examples also. Therefore, I started reading older books about nature.

Koopman's speciality is onomastics, so I read some books about bird names aimed at the general public. If a bird had a name which suggested it might originate from the bird's call or song I listened to recordings and looked in other sources to find more evidence. This is another field that could be more thoroughly scoured for examples.

Where the secondary texts refer to any original sources, I checked these to see if they had more examples not included in the secondary texts.

My methodology evolved over time. When a new warblish phrase was found, the specific wording indicating the existence of the phrase was examined to find new search terms. The problem of warblish not having a distinct name was a major one. For example, one particularly mind-numbing afternoon I searched for "bird talk" on Google and trawled through 10,000 irrelevant website suggestions before finding a children's picture book about warblish by Ann Jonas.

Early in my research I often did not include examples that combined chirpish and warblish, unless the warblish was dominant. Nor did I include 'boring' examples as I was looking for the type that Abelin had described, that is, interesting content related to birds. As many researchers had focused on mnemonic properties of chirpish and warblish I read less literature and poetry, and more non-fiction that I would if I did it again. I found Dunning's and Wainwright's work only a few months before I finished. They did not fit the narrative of the other papers, and I did not know how to or if to incorporate them, as I was still focused on the mnemonic aspects of warblish. I eventually concluded, aligned with Wainwright, that warblish is a literary form, and began to understand that Dunning's was an extraordinary collection that should not be discounted because its examples were so different from all others.

Text sources

Fiction, poetry, and creative non-fiction: I read most of these books in their entirety, even if they had no warblish. I read a lot of fiction, especially novels with respelled dialogue or narration, for my main project. Most of these do not have any warblish but there are some surprises, such as Janet Frame's *Owls do Cry*. I also read nature writing, memoirs by nature lovers, and poetry about nature, and in particular about birds.

Bird guides: For most bird guides I scanned for the headings on birdsong (keywords: vocalisation, calls, song, voice, birdsong, etc.) looking for examples of warblish under entries such as California Quail and Yellowhammer as these are the most commonly cited examples. If I found any warblish, I skim read the entries for each bird in the guide. Books that did have warblish would usually have it for these birds as well as their examples are very well known and used in birding circles. For British books I'd look up the Yellowhammer, for American books the California Quail or Peabody Bird, for African countries the Go-away Bird, and for other countries I'd look up the Dove first. Warblish was sometimes indicated by speech marks or italics so once this was identified I could more quickly scan the book for these punctuation cues.

Academic texts (eBooks and digital journal articles) and webpages: I used databases, library catalogues and search engines to search for keywords anywhere in text. Examples of search terms and Boolean strings include: warblish, vocalisation OR vocalization, verbalisation OR verbalization, ornimatopoeia, "birdsong mnemonics", "bird says", "birdsong interpreted as", "bird talk", birdsong, bird AND song, "bird call", bird AND rendered, "bird says", etc.

Non-fiction books: I read books about birding, ornithology, sound, music, folklore, ethnology, and searched contents pages for topics such as those pertaining to folk stories/knowledge, ethnobiology, representing birdsong. I searched index pages for keywords such as, birdsong, bird calls, vocalisation/vocalization, mnemonics. As with birding books I looked up Yellowhammer, Peabody Bird, or Dove first. Old books written by civil servants etc. in British colonies seemed to have interesting but few examples

Reference lists: I checked the original references of any warblish found in the above sources to see if they contained more examples.

Criteria for inclusion

Originally, I used Sarvasy's definition of warblish: 'The phenomenon of vocal imitation of avian vocalizations by humans, using existing non-onomatopoeic word(s)'. Like Sarvasy and Moreno Cabrera, I differentiated between imitation based on real words (warblish) and nonsense words (chirpish). Words that merely mimicked the sound of the bird and did not have any independent meaning, i.e., chirpish, were not usually included. Words needed either to be found in a dictionary or conceivably to be found in a dictionary if one was available for that language or dialect. So, words from languages or dialects that are not written, including slang, were permissible. Respelled words that reflected pronunciations not considered standard but in use were included as well as obsolete vocabulary.

Koopman[3] and others refer to the birds that say their own names. However, I have excluded bird names as words on the basis that these do not mean anything other than identifying a bird. The only birds included in the database with a name the same as their call are those whose names also operate independently as words, such as the Go-away Bird, who says, 'Go away,' and the Riroriro who says, 'Riro riro' (gone gone in Māori).

The purpose of this database was originally to enhance my own creative writing by documenting human creativity related to nature, especially birdsong, along with sounds and silence in various aspects (a wide range of topics related to sound and silence such as: being ignored, dealing with miscommunicating, speaking in foreign languages, body language, dialects, accents, tinnitus, mistranslation, etc.) of which warblish was just one of many themes.

The database includes examples from any written or verbal source regardless of whether it is the personal opinion of one person, or an example widely accepted and recorded in multiple published books. Examples were accepted if they appeared to be warblish. If an example did not appear to mimic the sounds made by a bird and was merely anthropomorphising bird's thoughts into speech it was not included. Where it was unclear if warblish or anthropomorphising was being discussed I listened to various example of songs and calls online to establish if it was plausible that the example was warblish. When deciding this I took note that 'the same call can vary considerably depending on a bird's mood and urgency and the conditions at the time'.[4] Dialectal differences in bird sounds means that absolute correlation of, for example, syllable count, was not necessary for examples to be included as the warblish creator might hear a different call or song from myself. Borderline examples were included and given the benefit of the doubt if dialect, season, or sex of the birds might account for differences. The notes section sometimes includes reasons for inclusion or details on any doubts.

Limitations of the database

Punctuation: It was only after I had collected well over one thousand examples of warblish that I considered the actual database itself might be of interest to others, and not just the tiny book (at that time) I was writing about warblish which would not include all examples collected. Up until then I was standardising all the punctuation to conform to the book I was writing as punctuation can vary widely in warblish examples. For example, underlining, use of bold script, hyphens, repetition of letters to distort the spelling, are all commonly but differently used according to each author's preference. For the purposes of my book, I wanted standardised punctuation and spelling. Therefore, the punctuation and spellings used in the sources were changed in many of the examples when recorded in the database. As I was not initially expecting anyone else to look at the database, I did not concern myself with recording exactly how the original sources presented the information, in terms of punctuation. Many authors devised their own methods of showing various aspects of sound, like syllable breaks, hyphens, apostrophes, spaces, superscript, subscript, etc. As these differed widely and I was not going to replicate them in my writing I ignored them. This of course constitutes a limitation as a consequence. The database does not necessarily include the type of information or depth that a linguist or ornithologist or folklorist might want. I do not track the changes in the binomial names over time nor provide detailed information about the types of calls or songs the birds might be producing. Therefore, a researcher wanting to quote the spelling of warblish attributed to a bird should consult the original sources. Sometimes I included information such as 'call' or 'song' in the notes if it was available.

    Pronunciation: I do not provide International Phonetic Alphabet (IPA) representations of warblish as I did not find it relevant for my purposes. Abelin, Sarvasy, and Moreno Cabrera did provide some analysis of the frequency of the human phonemes versus the high and low frequencies of the bird calls, and Sarvasy did compare spectrograms of the bird sounds and the corresponding warblish which indicates some aspects of the IPA could be useful. However, most of my examples were taken from written texts where there was no indication of IPA in the original sources and usually no indication of which dialect of a language was used. As I collected examples from numerous countries, in different languages and many different dialects, I felt that it would be misleading to assign IPA to written examples that at best would only offer a very rough interpretation of the phonemes intended by the warblish creator or recorder. For example, I might assume they meant [ɔ] but actually they meant [ɒ]. Most sources did not give enough details for any meaningful guess at which dialect was being used. Even Abelin (who worked almost exclusively with Swedish warblish) and Moreno Cabrera (who worked almost exclusively with Spanish warblish and chirpish) did not include IPA for their examples, I presume because there is a lot of variation within those languages. Norrude's unpublished document, cited by Abelin, does mention numerous dialects but does not use IPA. I collected examples from many different languages that I am not familiar with so any assigned IPA could be unreliable. Also, my conclusion that warblish is actually a literary form which plays with sounds rather than an accurate imitation means the accuracy of matching warblish phonemes with bird sound frequencies as Sarvasy and Abelin did, is not my primary concern.

Binomial nomenclature: Koopman states 'because scientific names change on such a regular basis, they will not be used in this article unless for a specific stated reason'.[5] While I understand his sentiments, I do provide scientific names with the understanding that they are a snapshot in time which I have used to simply sort data and to add some clarity to which birds were being referred to. Koopman discusses bird in one geographical region (southern Africa) whereas I collected examples from all over the world where the same common names can be used for many distinct species of birds or different common names can refer to the same bird. Often the name used by locals is different from the common name that might be used in birding books, whether it be in a simplified form or in a different language, so I needed terms that would be transparent to those not familiar with the local bird names from disparate locations.

One of my main interests was in comparing warblish for the same bird from different languages and dialects, and even the same or similar species across different countries and continents. I needed some way to group the same birds together from many diverse sources, and sometimes warblish in different languages where the same bird will necessarily have different common names. Also, I did not have enough knowledge of bird species to know which were related by looking at their common names. My solution was to include the binomial name for each example using the information in the source, or more commonly surmising the binomial name using other means. While the practice of changing or adding such information to a database may not be acceptable when creating a database for academic uses, I did not initially envisage use by others, and it served my purposes for sorting information. I started adding the source's binomial names as well as the current name and later typing the added information in red to make it clearer what information I was adding. As I am not an ornithologist and not even an interested birdwatcher, my knowledge of even common names when I began was extremely limited so I cannot guarantee the names I have added are correct, but I have consulted multiple sources when assigning names. Where I am most unsure, I have signalled this with a question mark.

Appendix B: How to use the database

The expanded Excel spreadsheet with ten columns is available upon request from the publisher: piwaiwakapress@gmail.com. As a spreadsheet the data is sortable. However, the simplified database printed in this book has most of the same information combined into four columns: 1. Common Name, other name (language) *Binomial name*; 2. Location; 3. Warblish (language), translation, (explanation); 4. Source. The notes below refer to the original ten columns and my rationale for each column as that information is still relevant for the four columns in this book.

Definition of categories used in database

I entered the data I collected into an Excel spreadsheet, the Warblish Database, and eventually organised it according to ten categories. I used 10 columns so the whole database could be sorted alphabetically by column of choice by using the 'sort' function. Data is sorted alphabetically by 'Most descriptive common English name' as a default.

Column A: Most descriptive common English name: The most descriptive commonly used English name was used in column one to list the bird. I used descriptive common names since the shortened common name was often used in sources but referred to the most common species in that area. Therefore, for example, locals might refer to the only owl in their location as Owl, although it might be a Tawny Owl or Barn Owl. Occasionally, the name used in the original text was different to the one now commonly used. The name in the first column was the most commonly used even if it differed from the one in the source text in order for sorting by name to find similar examples. This means that birds known by different names in different regions, languages, or even different sources, are grouped together (when sorted by default settings) so their warblish can be compared.

The common names are presented with capital letters as is often the case in birding books. The reason for this is to make it clear where a word is part of the name and not just an adjective describing the bird (e.g. Western Meadowlark).

Column B: Name used in source: Where the name in the source differed from the that assigned in column A, the source name is included to help future researchers locate examples when referring to original sources. Sometimes when adding new entries for the same bird from a different source extra information in the second source helped in confirming what I had in other entries. New additions carried extra information, perhaps the binomial name, about the bird which allowed me to double check the common name I had assigned to the bird (especially when translating or using older sources). I did not fill in all cells for this column as column A was used for sorting data.

Column C: Alternative/old/non-English name

Other commonly used names, older names, and non-English names are given in the third column. If the name is in another language the language is included in brackets.

Column D: Location

The location is the one mentioned or surmised from the source text where possible. If it was unclear, then I researched the geographical location of the bird. Some texts mention single countries, whereas the bird may be found over a whole continent. Some books, usually birding guides, list multiple locations where the bird is found, although the warblish may not be known beyond a small area. The location is therefore given as a very general guide only as mentions of the same bird could be listed under North America, another under America, another under Canada, and they might all be found over the same geographical area. Where a small area was mentioned, the location was given as the country or continent to make searching easier (rather than state, or descriptions like 'eastern Australia'). The rationale for this is that this is not an ornithological study, and the location information is given for basic sorting and information only. Some warblish is found in multiple English-speaking countries and has been imported along with the exotic bird species, e.g. the California Quail and its warblish 'Chicago' have been introduced to New Zealand. The location listed is where the bird is mentioned in the source material, e.g. New Zealand, and not where the warblish may have originated from. Location labels should therefore be used with caution.

Column E: Binomial name/Linnean name/scientific name:

These are often given in birding guides and academic articles, though not always, but usually not given in other types of texts. Where the binomial name was not given other sources were consulted to assign a binomial name. Often in non-scientific texts a general name (such as 'Lark') was given which technically refers to a family of birds and not a specific species, even though the warblish may have been intended to refer to a specific locally found bird, a species, or subspecies. Locals can often use the more generic name to refer to one species, not a family, such as calling a Gray Lark or a Greater Hoopoe-lark by the name Lark. Therefore, I researched the location of the warblish, and which species were usually found in that area. If there were more than one species in that area, I listened to recordings and evaluated if the sounds from one species were significantly different to another and matched the warblish. Where it sounded obviously more likely to be one species than another, I have annotated the entry accordingly. Where there was convincing evidence for one species and not another, I have used the name of the most likely species and put any misgivings in the notes. Where it was difficult to determine the species referred to, I have given the genus or even family of birds and indicated this in brackets, e.g. *Aphelocoma* (genus).

Sometimes the warblish itself assisted in this disambiguation process. For example, a text might use a general name such as 'Lark' but because the warblish came from a Siouxan tribe, I was able to triangulate this with geographical information about the distribution of the language and geographical information about the distribution of more specific species of bird (e.g. Eastern Meadowlark and Western Meadowlark). This sometimes allowed me to infer if one species was more likely intended. In this example, it was not clear, so the genus Sturnella (Meadowlarks) was chosen rather than a specific species.

The most significant problem I encountered with binomial names was with old names. Due to reclassification decisions, sometimes based on recent DNA evidence, some birds that have previous been classified as one species are now recorded as two separate species, or even vice versa. Where a species has been split into two species after the source text was written, I have researched both new species and decided if the warblish clearly belonged to one new species and not the other, for example, if they had distinctively different calls/songs and only one matched the warblish. If it was not clear which of the new species the warblish belonged to, or if it could conceivably belong to both, I wrote both names, along with the original binomial name.

Usually, the assigned name therefore is listed first, the source name is listed second. Sometimes synonyms are listed, the most commonly used listed first.

Column F: Warblish language: The language used for the warblish in the text is the one given. Sometimes more information, such as family or dialect, is given in brackets. For less well-known languages, such as Kaytetye, the family it belongs to is given in brackets (e.g., an Arandic language). For dialects of well-documented languages, where there are examples in that language, the dialect is given in brackets, such as 'Swedish (dialect from Vindeln, Västerbotten)'. The language was not always explicitly stated therefore I used online translators and dictionaries to identify the language and then consulted native or near-native speakers to confirm which language was used. In most cases the language was not stated in the source and has been surmised.

Column G: Warblish: As my original purposes for creating this database was to collect examples to use in a book, I wanted to standardise the spelling and punctuation for all examples so that these factors were not distracting to the reader as the use of these features has differed greatly from writer to writer. In the beginning, I therefore simplified the punctuation (removing capitalisation to show syllable stress, hyphens between whole words, ellipsis etc.) and standardised the spelling (many authors use diverse ways to show emphasis, vowels length often by repeating a vowel an unspecified number of times, such as the Black Guillemot saying, 'swweeeeeer'). Later, I changed to listing the respelled version in the 'translation' column.

The novel ways of punctuating and spelling warblish used by many authors did not follow set patterns. By standardising the spelling and punctuation I was able to search for different birds saying the same word. This was important for my book as I grouped phrases by content, such as warblish related to food and drink. Respelling and punctuating words allows searches to be done for the same word, whereas without repunctuation and the use of standard spelling this could not be achieved.

However, where warblish examples were in a language other than English the original warblish is written in this column as it appears in the source. Changes to punctuation and spelling have not occurred in other languages although there appear to be examples of doubling vowels, for example, to show longer notes. I do not have the expertise in these other languages to make any such changes and did not ask any of the translators to make such changes, so researchers should be aware of this when searching for keywords in the database.

Column H: Translation: Translations are provided by the source texts, or by native or near-native speakers, or as a last resort via dictionary or Google translate. Where warblish has been translated by someone other than the author of the source text the translation is written with the name of the translator in brackets. If only the gist of the warblish was provided in the text rather than the direct translation, then the words are enclosed in brackets.

Column I: Source: In this column the surname, date, and page number for the source is included (where possible). The intext reference refers to a reference list (in APA7 referencing style) on tab 2. Examples gained through personal communication are not included in the full reference list. Sources without page numbers, such as websites, give source info only.

If more than one source gave the same warblish example they were listed as separate rows/entries. This was partly because many of the websites went offline over time and some sources were difficult to obtain (many of the books were classified as rare and not available via library interloan) so there are multiple sources given, where applicable, to allow other researchers to find at least one of the sources listed. However, if the same entry occurred both on a website and in a published book then I might only list the example from the published text.

Column J: Notes: I included any information that I thought was pertinent here, but I was not consistent in how detailed the information was. Sometimes I included whether the warblish was a call or a song. I wrote here if I had doubts as to whether an example was warblish or not. Sometimes these notes were removed once I had other sources confirming that they were warblish.

I sometimes include chirpish in the database which helps me to ascertain whether other examples were likely to be warblish or not. Some warblish examples seemed unlikely for assorted reasons, but their similarity to onomatopoeic phrases provided some basis towards including them in the database.

Number of examples, sources, languages represented

I collected approximately 1600 examples of warblish for birds. I also found other similar types of examples: eighteen examples of animalopoeia for animals and insects, and four examples of ticktocklish for objects. This represented approximately 800 different birds, five animals, two insects, and three objects.

Examples were collected from approximately 160 sources, mostly written texts but also collected from friends and strangers. I had seven replies via my websites, some of these using the anonymous option for submitting an example of warblish. Examples from individuals were not included in the database if I already had found the same in print elsewhere. I also recorded 32 examples from conversations with friends or strangers, although I received many more via word-of-mouth but as most were repetitions of examples found in print sources, I did not include them.

The database contains approximately 1405 examples from English, which comprises 70% of the total, but noteworthy contenders for most common came from Swedish (149) and Russian (49).

The languages and number of examples for each are: Afrikaans (6), Arandic (1), Belarusian (2), Bengali (2), Brazilian Portuguese (1), Burmese (1), Chadian Arabic (11), Chinese (9), Croatian (1), Czech (1), Danish (1), Dinka/Thuɔŋjäŋ (1), Dutch (1), English (1163), Estonian (2), Fiji Baat (1), Finnish (8), French (8), German (5), Gikuyu (2), Guanano (1), Hebrew (1), Hungarian (19), Irish/Gaeilge (1), Kalam (30), Kaluli (23), Kattang (7), Kaytetye (1), Kikami (1), Somali/Kisomali (1), Kapon (2), Latin (1), Malayalam (1), Māori (23), Meru (2), Nepali (2), Norwegian (1), Ojibwe and/or Chippewa (1), Portuguese (2), Romanian (2), Russian (48), Sahaptin (2), Samoan (1), Secwepemc (1), Serbian (1), Sioux (2), Spanish (4), Swahili (6), Swedish (149), Swiss German (1), Vietnamese (1), Xhosa (11), Yuwaalaraay and/or Gamilaraay (1), Zulu (27)

There were examples from approximately 62 languages. Not all language tags were confirmed as often there was no indication of what language was used, or the phrase was so short it could have been from more than one language. Sometimes the phrases were single words, or short phrases so positive identification of exactly which language was not possible. My hope is bilingual researchers will be able to confirm or update my findings.

Sources

The sources that provided the most numerous tokens did not necessarily form any pattern. Most birding books do not contain warblish, but the ones that do included either just a couple of conventionalised examples or a substantial number of examples. Australian ornithologist Graham Pizzey provided over 100 examples; King and Dickinson had 144; *Higgins' Handbook of Australian, New Zealand and Antarctic Birds* provided 44; Burrows' *Birds of Atlantic Canada* had 88 examples.

Original research into warblish by Norudde (used by Abelin) contained about 149 examples, and Feith's CD liner notes[6] (used by Sarvasy) had 77. Poetry and fiction sources typically only had one or two examples. Sources dedicated to only warblish had more, for instance, Jonas' children's book had 40 examples, and Bianki's book had 57 (but this also included examples for creatures other than birds).

The majority of warblish examples (70%) were found in English. It should not be inferred that this was because English has more examples, but because that is my native language and therefore English texts were more easily accessed and searched. The examples from other languages were usually found in research or other texts written in English. Some examples, like those in Russian were accessible because my husband is Russian, and he and friends were able to recommend sources and help with translating them. I was also sent texts in other languages in response to my flyers, website, or personal communications which were kindly translated by the senders.

The attempt to elicit examples from the general public was not highly successful in terms of quantity or quality. Most responses contained examples that were well-known, and I had already found in books. When talking to people I had interesting responses: people were often very enthusiastic about the topic and wanted to give me an example but were crest-fallen when they could not help, or they just could not understand the concept and told me what a monumental waste of time it was and that it did not help conservation efforts at all. It is a very polarising topic. Anecdotally, I noticed that people who were interested in literature, poetry, music, and the arts who also liked nature were sympathetic, but bird watchers, scientists, conservationists (if not also part of the first group) often did not like the topic at all.

This would also tally with the books which had interesting examples, they were often generalist books covering many topics, rather than specialist birding books, such as Bulpin's *Natal and the Zulu Country*, a book combining natural history, history, travel writing and bush stories, and Owen's *Sudan Notes and Records*.

Appendix C: Warblish Database

English Name, Other Name (language) *Binominal name*	Location	Warblish (Language); Translation (Explanation)	Source Author YEAR: page #
Acadian Chickadee, *Penthestes hudsonicus*	N. America	Tsickaday-day-day Respell: sick-a-day-day-day or sick-today-day-day	Saunders 1951:111
Acadian Flycatcher, *Empidonax virescens*	N. America	Pizza	Feith 2003a
		Peet-suh Respell: pizza	Schmalz n.d.
Acorn Woodpecker *Melanerpes formicivorus*	N. America	Wake up! Wake up!	Mosco 2017b
African Emerald Cuckoo, Intananji (Xhosa), Intatshongo (Xhosa), Ubantwanyana (Zulu), *Chrysococcyx cupreus*	Africa	Hello Ju-dy	Paine 2020
	South Africa	*Ziph'iintombi* (Xhosa) Where are the girls?	Wainwright 1983:299
		Bantwanyana! Ning' endi! (Zulu) Little children, don't get married	Wainwright 1983:299
		Bantwanyana ningendi (Zulu?) Children, don't get married	Bulpin 1966:26

English Name, Other Name (language) *Binominal name*	Location	Warblish (Language); Translation (Explanation)	Source Author YEAR: page #
… African Emerald Cuckoo … *continued* …	South Africa	Cock: *bantwanyana ningendi, bantwanyana ningendi, bantwanyana ningendi.* (Zulu) Cock: Children, don't get married (and multiply); Children, don't get married; Children, don't get married.	Dunning 1946:
African Grey Hornbill? Lesser Grey Hornbill, Abu Mangur (Chadian Arabic), *Lophoceros nasutus?*	Africa, Sudan	Call: *Şeif wa kharif ma dugtu ferik* (Chadian Arabic?) Call: All summer and rains I've never had a ripe dura-head (Response by Red-billed Hornbill: *t'akul um baṭn, t'akul um baṭn*: All you'll get is gripes)	Owen 1947:194
African Olive Pigeon Wood Pigeon Black Pigeon Ivukuth (Zulu), Ijuɓa Elimnyama Lehlathi (Zulu) *Columba arquatrix*	South Africa	Cock: *Dududu uliqili! Uthi izimvu zethu zinotwayi! Usuthu! Ngagwaz'indoda!* ×3 (Zulu) Cock: Dududu you're a (deceitful) crafty fellow! You say our sheep have the scab! Usuthu! I killed a man ×3	Dunning 1946:43
		Cock: *Gigigi uliqili! Uthi izimvu zethu zinotwayi! Usuthu Ngagwaz'indoda!* ×3 (Zulu) Cock: Gigigi you're a crafty fellow, You say our sheep have the scab, Usuthu! I liked a man. ×3	Dunnning 1946:44
African Paradise Flycatcher, *Terpsiphone viridis*	South Africa	Willie Willie Willie wee wooo	Barnes & Behrens 2017:175

English Name, Other Name (language) *Binominal name*	Location	Warblish (Language); Translation (Explanation)	Source Author YEAR: page #
African Wood Owl?, Mabengwana (Zulu), *Strix* (old)/*Syrium Woodfordi?*	South Africa	Cock: *Woza, woza, Nobathekeli.* (or *Mabengwana*) ×3; Hen: Wee! *Ngeke ungithole* ×3 (Zulu) Cock: (in deep bass voice) Come here, come here, Nobathekeli, (or Mabengwana). ×3 Hen: (in shrill voice an octive higher) Wee! (That's all very fine!) You'll not get me (coming). (I'm certainly not coming, so there!) ×3	Dunning 1946:39–40
Albert's Lyrebird, *Menura alberti*	Australia	Whisk-whisk	Higgins et al. 2001:138 citing Keast 1944
Alder Flycatcher, (Previously considered a subspecies of the Willow Flycatcher, *Empidonax traillii*), *Empidonax alnorum*	N. America	Free beer	Burrows 2002:201; Feith 2003a
		Great deal	Saunders 1951:88
		Wie viel (German) How much	Saunders 1951:88 citing Allen
American Crow, *Corvus brachyrhynchos*	N. America	Car	Feith 2003a
		Crow	Feith 2003a
American Goldfinch, *Carduelis tristis*	N. America	Potato chips	Feith 2003a
		Potato chip	Young 2003:2; Ovenbird43
		Po-ta-to-chip	Yuhas 2024:28
		Baby	Feith 2003a
		Dear-me, see-me	Yuhas 2024:28

English Name, Other Name (language) *Binominal name*	Location	Warblish (Language); Translation (Explanation)	Source Author YEAR: page #
American Redstart, Redstart Warbler, *Setophaga ruticilla*	N. America	Seeseeseeit	Feith 2003a
		See see see see-it	Feith 2005
		Chewy-chewy-chewy, chew-chew-chew	Jonas 1999:8
American Robin, *Turdus migratorius*	N. America	Tut, tut, tut	Jonas 1999:10
		Cheerily cheer-up cheerio (Call is a rapid) tut-tut-tut	Burrows 2002:242
		Cheerily, cheer up	Feith 2003a
		Cheerily-cheer-up! Cheerily-cheer-up!	Jonas 1999:12
		Cheerily, cheer-up, cheer-up, cheer-up, cheerily, cheer-up!	Kawasaki 2018:7
		Cheer up, cheerily, cheerily	Schmalz n.d.; Young 2003:2 citing Walton
		Cheerily, cheerily, cheerily, cheer up, cheer up, cheer up	S. Mathews 1921:66
American Woodcock, *Scolopax minor*	N. America	Paint	Feith 2003a
American Yellow Warbler, *Setophaga petechia*, (formerly *Dendroica petechia*)	N. America	Sweet sweet sweet, I'm so sweet	Yellow Warbler, Wikipedia
		Sweet sweet sweet a little more sweet	Young 2003:2
Aphelocoma Jay, *Aphelocoma* (genus)	N. America	Cheek, cheek, cheek	Bent 1945:90 citing Grinell & Storer 1924

English Name, Other Name (language) *Binominal name*	Location	Warblish (Language); Translation (Explanation)	Source Author YEAR: page #
Ashy Bulbul, *Hypsipetes flavala (cinereus)*	Asia	Keep, keep it going;/Kick me, when-do-we- go	King & Dickinson 1975:268 cite Smythies
Asian Fairy-Bluebird, *Irena puella*	Asia	Be quick, be quick, be quick	Smythies 1953:79; 2001:367
Asian Koel, *Eudynamys scolopaceus*	Asia, Burma	You're ill, you're ill	Smythies 1953:327; 2001:251
Australian Boobook, *Ninox boobook*	Australia	Boo-boo-boo-boo-boo Book book	Pizzey 1958:67 Wheatbelt 2018:89
Australian Golden Whistler, *Pachycephala pectoralis*	Australia	Wheat-wheat-wheat-WHITTLE!	Pizzey 1980:251
Australian Painted Snipe, *Rostratula asutralis*	Australia	Cook-cook-cook…	Birdlife Australia 2020
Australian Ringneck, Twenty-Eight Parrot, *Barnardius zonarius*	Australia	Twen-ty *Vingt-huit* (French) 28 Twentee-eight Respell: twenty-eight	Wheatbelt 2018:111 Tracey et al. 2007:110 Tracey et al. 2007:111
Australian Wood Duck, *Chenonetta jubata*	Australia	Now? Di-di-di-did (stuttering)	Wheatbelt 2018:43
Baltimore Oriole, *Icterus gaibula*	N. America	Over here here here, come right here, dear I can wash, sir, I can spin sir, I can sew, and mend, and babies tend. (song in the opera of Martha) Here; here; come right here; dear	Feith 2003a S. Mathews 1921:64–69 Roth 2012:78; South Bay Birders n.d.

English Name, Other Name (language) *Binominal name*	Location	Warblish (Language); Translation (Explanation)	Source Author YEAR: page #
Banded Bay Cuckoo, *Cacomantis sonneratii*	Asia	Smoke-yer-pep-per Respell: smoke-your-pepper	Kennedy et al. 2000:164
Banded Dotterel, *Charadrius bicinctus*	NZ	Wit wit wit	Williams 1976:32
	N. America	Wit wit	Feith 2003a
Barn Swallow, Ladusvala (Swedish), Scissorelf (Swedish dialect), *Hirundo rustica*	Sweden	*Mamma har sagt att inga stygga barn får röra meeeej* (Swedish) Mom said no naughty kids are allowed to touch me	Norudde 2009
		Tjyfliip, tjyfliip (Swedish) (a derogatory name for a small boy)	
		Jungfru mari se att i a stuli ge silversked men e då in nnt saaant (Swedish) Virgin Mary said that I had stolen a silver spoon but it isn't true	
		I fjol när ja for, va boa full me korn, i år när jag kom va det oppitt och utskitt på en breee (Swedish) Last year when I left the barn was full of barley, this year when I returned it was all eaten and shat out on a board (the long drop)	
		I ladan i hö ligger pigor och drängar och klappas och kyssas och kyssas och klappas och jag, jag seree (Swedish) .... continued ...	

English Name, Other Name (language) Binominal name	Location	Warblish (Language); Translation (Explanation)	Source Author YEAR: page #
...Barn Swallow ...continued...	...	... continued ... In the haybarn the maids and farm-workers are stroking and kissing and kissing and stroking and I, I SEE IT.	...
	Sweden	Jungfru Maria ha vite me' för att i ha stöle saxa, men se vitt som i ha silkesmössa se je' int he jig, se je' int' he jig (Norwegian); Jungfru Maria har straffat mig för att jag har stulit saxen, men så sant som jag har silkesmössa så är det inte jag, så är det inte jag (Swedish) Virgin Mary has punished me for stealing the scissors, but as true as I have a silk hat, it is not me, it is not me (translator: Mikaela Nyman)	Norudde 2009
	Finland	Jungfru Maria ha skylt ma för och ha stöle silverskia sii. Tvi vale, tvi vale, it vare jee (Finnish) The virgin Mary accused me of having stolen her silver spoon. How despicable, how despicable	
		Det var en gång en flicka som tjänte hos en fruuuu, Då sa frun att jag stulit hennes silkesnystan och hennes saaax Men hade jag stulit hennes silkesnystan och hennes sax, hade jag stoppat nystanet under hakan och saxen i min stjärt och sjunkit ned i havets djuuuup (Finnish) ... continued	

English Name, Other Name (language) *Binominal name*	Location	Warblish (Language); Translation (Explanation)	Source Author YEAR: page #
...Barn Swallow ...*continued*...	...	...*continued* ...There once was a girl who served with a lady, and the lady said that I had stolen her ball of silk and scissors, but if I had stolen her ball of silk I would have put the ball under my chin and the scissors in my tail (bum) and sank down to the ocean depths	...
Barred Owl, Hoot Owl, *Strix varia*	N. America	Who cooks for you? Who cooks for you all? Who cooks, who cooks, who cooks for you all? Who cooks for you? I cook for my folks. Who cooks for you all? Madame, who cooks for you?	Burrows 2002:181; Feith 2003a Dormon 1969:58 Sarvasy 2016:774 Cowser 1969:43 Young 2003:2
Bat Hawk, *Macheiramphus alcinus*	Africa, Asia	Quick quick	Smythies 1960:143
Bay-Breasted Warbler, *Setophaga castanea*	N. America	Teasy, teasy, tease Cheesy cheesy cheesy	Feith 2003a Feith 2005
Belford's Melidectes, Alnjawnm (Kalam), *Melidectes belfordi*	PNG	Ss *kyan kyan* (Kalam) Urine you-pass you-pass	Majnep & Bulmer 1977:62

English Name, Other Name (language) *Binominal name*	Location	Warblish (Language); Translation (Explanation)	Source Author YEAR: page #
Bellbird, Korimako (Māori), Makomako (Māori), *Anthornis melanura*	NZ	Pek pek pek Respell: peck peck peck	Chambers 2007:113
		So slow, so strong! So slow, so strong! So sweet, so long! So sweet, so long!	Duggan 1929:37
		I'm a bellbird	Southey 2009
		I'm the best bird	Jan 2009
Bell's Vireo, *Vireo bellii?*	N. America	Cheedle chee chee cheedle chew Respell: chedder che-che-chedder chew	Feith 2003a
Berrypicker and Longbill family (species?), Wasio (Kaluli), *Melanochartiidae (family)*	PNG	Wa wasio, ugufɔ oga genelɔ (Kaluli) Ugufɔ and genelɔ = redness; oga = pandanus/berries; so, I interpret it as "time to pick the berries"	Feld 2012:79
Black and White Warbler, *Mniotilta varia*	N. America	Wheezy, wheezy, wheezy, wheezy	Feith (n.d.)
		Wheezy, wheezy, . . .	Feith 2003a
		Wee see, wee see, wee see Respell: we see	Jonas 1999:11
		Wheezy, wheezy, wheezy	Schmalz n.d.
Black-Backed Forktail, *Enicurus immaculatus*	SE Asia	Wheat, wheat	King & Dickinson 1975:342 citing Mason
Black-Breasted Wood Quail, *Odontophorus leucolaemus*	Costa Rica	Where are you? Where are you?	Young 2003:3

English Name, Other Name (language) *Binominal name*	Location	Warblish (Language); Translation (Explanation)	Source Author YEAR: page #
Black-Capped Chickadee, *Poecile atricapillus?* *Penthestes atricapillus?*	N. America	Hi sweetie	Chadd & Taylor 2016:215
		Hey sweetie	LesleytheBirdNerd 2013
		Cheeseburger Chickadee-dee-dee	Feith 2003a
Black-Chinned Honeyeater, *Melithreptus gularis*	Australia	Chee, chee, creep, creep, creep	Higgins et al. 2001:902 citing Morgan 1922
Black-Collared Barbet, Isinagogo (Xhosa), *Lybius torquatus*	South Africa	Two-pudley, two-pudley, two-pudley	Barnes & Behrens 2017:109
		Radebe! Mashwabadi! Mthimkulu! Nosele! (Xhosa) (clan names)	Wainwright 1983:301
Black Cuckoo, Ngechechangu (Wakami), Unontan' Ofayo (Xhosa), *Cuculus clamosus*	Tanzania / Tanganyika	(missing in text) (Wakami) Bring me my cooking pot	Koopman 2018a:19
		Ngechechangu (Swahili?) Bring my cooking pot	A. J. Moreau 1940:55
		Ngechechangu (Wakami?) Give me my cooking pot	R. E. Moreau 1942:1002
	South Africa	I'm so saaaaad	Barnes & Behrens 2017:89

English Name, Other Name (language) *Binominal name*	Location	Warblish (Language); Translation (Explanation)	Source Author YEAR: page #
... Black Cuckoo ... continued ...	Southern Africa	*Ndina mntan' ufayo / Ndiba ndiya mbika / Kanti akabikeki* (Xhosa) I have a dying child / I am reporting him / Whereas he cannot be reported (unclear if warblish or poetry)	Wainwright 1983:298
Black Currawong, *Strepera fuliginosa*	Australia	Kar-week, week-kar Respell: car-week, weak-car	Pizzey 1980:400
Black-Faced Monarch, Black-Faced Flycatcher, *Monarcha melanopsis*	Australia	Why-you, which-you Which-a-where Which-a-where you Why, you witch	Pizzey 1980:257
Black-Faced Woodswallow, *Artamus cinereus*	Australia	Chiff chiff	Pizzey 1980:395
Black Fantail, Jolbeg (Kalam), *Rhipidura atra*	PNG	Chap chap	Pizzey 1980:395
Black Grouse, Терентио-Тетереву [Terentiyu-Teterevu] (Russian), Orre (Swedish), *Lyrurus tetrix*	Sweden	*Mor koka gröten, blörrelöppen, själv åt ho öppen, blörrelöppen* (Swedish) Mother cooked the porridge, she ate it herself, she walked around	Norudde 2009
	Russia	*Куплю шубу! Куплю шубу!* [Kuplyu shubu! Kuplyu shubu!] (Russian); Will buy a fur coat! Will buy a fur coat!	Bianki 2013:13

English Name, Other Name (language) *Binominal name*	Location	Warblish (Language); Translation (Explanation)	Source Author YEAR: page #
... Black Grouse ... *continued* ...	Russia	*Чу-шшь! Чушь! Продам шубу, продам шубу, куплю . . .* [Chu-shsh'! Chush'! Prodam shubu, prodam shubu, kuplyu . . .] (Russian) Gibberish! Gibberish! I'm selling a fur coat, selling a fur coat, I'll buy—	Bianki 2013:13
		Удрал! Удрал! [Udral! Udral!] (Russian) Run away! / Get out!	Bianki 2013:9
		Проспал, пропал, пропал! [Prospal, propal, propal!] (Russian) I overslept! All is lost! All is lost!	Bianki 2013:6
		Чу-шшь! Чушь! Куплю балахон, балахон, балахон! [Ču-šš! Čuš! Kupliu balachon, balachon, balachon!] (Russian) Gibberish! Gibberish! I will buy a robe, robe, robe.	Bianki 2013:9
		Балахон, балахонб балахон! [Balachon, balachon balachon!] (Russian) A robe, robe! Robe!	Bianki 2013:7
		Чушь! Продам балахон продам куплю— [Chush'! Prodam balakhon prodam balakhon kuplyu—] (Russian) Gibberish! I will sell a robe, sell a robe, and buy—	Bianki 2013:8

English Name, Other Name (language) *Binominal name*	Location	Warblish (Language); Translation (Explanation)	Source Author YEAR: page #
Black Guillemot, *Cepphus grille*	N. America	Swweeeeer Respell: swear	Burrows 2002:172
Black-Headed Oriole, Usibombothi (Zulu), *Oriolus larvatus*	South Africa	Cock: *We! bafana, niye kweluseni, ziphi izinduku? Abafana bazokunishaya ekhanda balithi Nte! Nte! Nte!* (Zulu) Cock: Hello! (I say you) Boys! Are (you really) going out to herd (the cattle), where are (your) sticks? The (other) boys will strike you on the head and cause it (your head) to sound Nte! Nte! Nte!	Dunning 1946:49
		"In order to give the full meaning or sense of this cry, it should be translated to read as follows: Hello! I say, you Boys! Surely you are not going out to herd (the cattle) without your sticks? Are you not aware that if you do so, the (other) boys at the herding grounds, who are armed with sticks on their heads will cause it to sound Nte! Nte! NB: The latter part of the above translation, namely, "the boys will strike you on the head and cause it to sound Nte! Nte! Nte!, being idiomatic, is liable to cause confusion, for the reason that those liable to be so struck number more than one whereas the singular forms of "head" and "it" are used. Therefore its equivalent is:—The boys will strike (all or as many of) you (as they can manae to, each) on the head (and thus) they will cause it to sound Nte! Nte! Nte!"	
Black Laughing Thrush, *Garrulax lugubris*	S.E. Asia	Queer-queer-hoop	Smythies et al. 1999:511; 1960:421
		Queer-queer-hoop-hoop-hoop	
		Hoop-hoop-hoop	

English Name, Other Name (language) *Binominal name*	Location	Warblish (Language); Translation (Explanation)	Source Author YEAR: page #
Black-Masked White-eye, Mindanao White-eye, *Lophozosterops goodfellowi*	Philippines	Tu-pik chu-beer Respell: to-pick two-beer	Kennedy et al. 2000:338
		Su si deer Respell: sushi dear	Kennedy et al. 2000:339
Black Monarch? Ñyolelegp (Kopon), *Symposiachrus axillari?*	PNG	Ñyolelegp (Kopon) A man is dying (bird is a message-bearer of the Kopon people)	Majnep & Bulmer 1977:103
Black Rail, *Laterallus jamaicensis*	N. America	Kitty-go	Jonas 1999:6
Black Stilt, Kaki (Māori), *Himantopus novaezelandiae*	NZ	Yep yep yep	Chambers 2007:32
Black-Tailed Godwit, *Limosa limosa*	UK, Africa	Wick-a WICK-a	Thomas 2019:172
Black-Tailed Treecreeper, , *Climacteris melanura*	Australia	Pee, peepeepeepeepeepee, pee, pee	Pizzey 1980:313
Black-Throated Blue Warbler, *Setophaga caerulescens*	N. America	Tip	Burrows 2002:258
		I am lazy	Feith 2003b
		I am laa-zyyyy	Mosco 2017a
		I am lazeee	Schmalz n.d.
		I'm so la-zy	Young 2003:2
		I am soo lay-zeee	Burrows 2002:258
		Please please please squeeze	Lorenzin 2011

English Name, Other Name (language) Binominal name	Location	Warblish (Language); Translation (Explanation)	Source Author YEAR: page #
...Black-Throated Blue Warbler ... continued	N. America	Beer beer beeeer	Schmalz n.d.
		Beer beer beer beeee	Young 2003:2
		Beer beer beer	Feith 2003b
Black-Throated Green Warbler, *Setophaga virens/Dendroica virens*	N. America	I'm so laa-zyyyy	Mosco 2017a
		1, 2, 3, I'm lazy	Legris n.d.
		See-see-see SUZY!; zoo zee zoo zoo zee	Burrows 2002:260
		Zay zay zoo zee, Respell: say say say Suzy	Schmalz n.d.
		See see see see see sah say	Saunders 1951:185
		Trees trees, murmuring trees	Feith 2003b, Mosco 2017a, Young 2003:2
		Trees trees, murm'ring trees	S. Mathews 1921:191
		'Tis 'tis 'tis sweet here	S. Mathews 1921:192
		Cheese, cheese, a little more cheese!	S. Mathews 1921:194
		Sleep, sleep, pretty one, sleep	S. Mathews 1921:194
		Lar-board watch a-hoy! (Larboard is an old term for the port side of the ship. Last line in each stanza of 'Larboard Watch')	S. Mathews 1921:193
Black-Throated Warbler, Tifɛn (Kaluli), *Melanocharitidae (family)?*	PNG	(missing in source) (Kaluli) (the bird "may help Kaluli locate stray pigs with warblish announcements of their whereabouts.")	Feld 1982:79 & cited in Sarvasy 2016:777
Gerygone palpebrosa?		Siyo gogo bayo (Kaluli) Oink I'm staying right here	Feld 2012:79

English Name, Other Name (language) *Binominal name*	Location	Warblish (Language); Translation (Explanation)	Source Author YEAR: page #
Black-Throated Whipbird, *Psophodes nigrogularis*	Australia	Let's scratch teacher	Pizzey 1980:267
		Pick it up	Pizzey 1980:267
Black-Winged Stilt, *Himantopus himantopus*	Southern hemisphere	Kik-kik-kik Respell: kick-kick-kick	King & Dickinson 1975:147
Blue Duck, *Whio* (Māori), *Hymenolaimus malacorhynchos*	NZ	*Whio* (Māori) Whistle	Keane-Tuala 2015
		Where? (wailing, despairing)	L. Moon et al. 2011:4
Blue Jay, *Cyanocitta cristata*	N. America	Jeer jeer jeer	Clark 2017; Schlitz Audubon Nature Center 2017
		Jay jay	Feith 2003a
		Tweedle-dee	Feith 2003a
		Thief! Thief! Thief!	Jonas 1999:10
Blue-Billed Duck, *Oxyura australis*	Australia	Dunk, dunk, dunk-dunk-dunk	Wheatbelt 2018:50
Blue-Headed Vireo, Solitary Vireo, (*Vireo solitarius, Vireo plumbeus, Vireo cassinii,* were all once considered one bird) *Vireo solitarius*	N. America	See you, be-seeing ya, so long	Feith 2003a
		Come here Jimmy quickly	Roth 2012:79; South Bay Birders n.d.
		Come here … Jimmy … Quickly	Rothenberg 2005:14
		Teeyahtoway. Respell: the other way	Saunders 1951:166
		Look up, over here, see me, up here	Schmalz n.d.

English Name, Other Name (language) *Binominal name*	Location	Warblish (Language); Translation (Explanation)	Source Author YEAR: page #
Blue-Throated Barbet, Indian Blue-Throated Barbet, *Megalaima asiatica*	Asia, Burma	Took-a-rook, took-a-rook	Smythies 1953:313; 2001:299
	Asia	Please; please; please squeeeeze	South Bay Birders n.d.
Blue-Winged Kookaburra, *Dacelo leachii*	Australia	Klock, klock, klock, klock Respell: clock clock clock clock	Pizzey 1980:214
Blue-Winged Parrot, *Neophema chrysostoma*	Australia	Chappy-chappy-brrt-chippy-chippy-brrt (chippy = small sparrow; chappy is a chap = man)	Pizzey 1980:190
Blue-Winged Warbler, *Vermivora cyanoptera*	N. America	Bee buzz	Feith 2003a
		Bee-buzzzz	Mosco 2017a
		Blue winged!	Lorenzin 2011
Bobolink, *Dolichonyx oryzivorus*	N. America	Bob-o-lincoln	Artuso 2018
		Bob o'Lincoln	Quinion 2016
		Pink	Burrows 2002:298
		Bobolink bobolink spink spank spink	Burrows 2002:298
		Bob-o'-link, Bob-o'-link, Spink, spank, spink	S. Mathews 1921:51 citing poet Bryant
		Rob, Rob, Lincoln, Lincoln. Lincoln Bobolink, Bobolink, Bobolink, spink-a-wink, link-a-jink, tink-a-bink, a sink.	S. Mathews 1921:50
Bobwhite, *Colinus* (genus)	N. America	Too sweet!	Lorenzin 2011

English Name, Other Name (language) *Binominal name*	Location	Warblish (Language); Translation (Explanation)	Source Author YEAR: page #
Bonaparte's Gull, *Larus philadelphia*	N. America	Ear ear	Burrows 2002:153
Boreal Chickadee, *Poecile hudsonicus*	N. America	Check the day	Feith 2003a
		Check the day day	Feith 2005
Brewer's Blackbird, *Euphagus cyanocephalus*	N. America	Whiskey	Feith 2003a
Bridled Honeyeater, *Bolemoreus frenatus*	Australia	We-are	Pizzey 1980:329
Bright-Rumped Attila, *Attila spadiceus*	Tropical America	Beat-it, beat-it, beat-it now	Young 2003:3
Broad-Winged Hawk, *Buteo platypterus*	N. America	Tee-teeeeee Respell: tea-tea-----	Feith 2003a
Bronze Cuckoo, Sayeikia (Shambaa,Wasamba) *Lampromorpha klaasi*	Africa	Sayeikia (Shambaa? Wasambaa) Famine will come	R. E. Moreau 1942:1002
Brown Creeper, American Treecreeper, *Certhia americana*	N. America	Pee pee	Brown Creeper 2020
		Willow wee	Brown Creeper 2020
		Trees-trees-trees see the trees	Burrows 2002:226
		Trees, trees, pretty little trees	Mosco 2017b
		See all the big trees, see, see	Feith 2005
		See-see-see-sisi-see	Schmalz n.d.

English Name, Other Name (language) *Binominal name*	Location	Warblish (Language); Translation (Explanation)	Source Author YEAR: page #
Brown Cuckoo-Dove? *Macropygia phasianella?*	Australia	Didja walk? Didja walk? (Respell: did you walk?)	Young 2003:2 citing Glen Threlfo
Brown Falcon, *Falco berigora*	Australia	Yeah-cook Yeah-cook-uk-uk	Wheatbelt 2018:86 Wheatbelt 2018:86
Brown Gerygone, *Gerygone mouki*	Australia	Which-is-it-is-it Diddle-it-did-dit Which-is-it, which-is-it	Pizzey 1980:298 Pizzey 1980:298 Pizzey 1980:298
Brown Hill Warbler, Himalayan Prinia, *Prinia crinigera crinigera*	Burma	Chew-it, chew-it	King & Dickinson 1975:372 citing Smythies
Brown Honeyeater, *Lichmera indistincta*	Australia	Sweet-sweet-quarty-quarty Sweetie-sweetie	Pizzey 1980:343 Wheatbelt 2018:68
Brown Oriole, (also see New Guinea Friarbird as the Kaluli people consider these two birds as the same bird), Bɔlɔ (Kaluli), *Oriolus szalayi? Philemon buceroides novaeguineae*	PNG	*Dowo, nɔwo* (Kaluli) Mother, father (this bird and Brown Oriole both say this because they are the dead children calling their parents) *Hɛ gɔ fɔn* (Kaluli), Where are my feathers? (bird is bald around the head and neck)	Feld 2012:77

English Name, Other Name (language) *Binominal name*	Location	Warblish (Language); Translation (Explanation)	Source Author YEAR: page #
... Brown Oriole ... *continued* ...	PNG	*Ku genelɔ!* (Kaluli), Red cock!	Feld 2012:78
		Ku halaidɔ (Kaluli), Hard cock!	
		Hɔ, hɔ, Gigio ku genelɔ! (Kaluli), Gigio has a hard cock (where Gigio is an interchangeable name) Kaluli men reply to taunts about their genitalia with "*wefio, kɔm!*" = "shut up, retard!" Or "*towɔ dabɛno mobiakɛ!*" = "we're unwilling to listen to your talk."	
	PNG	*Ninɛli monowo id alu nagalakɛ-o hɔɔ!* (Kaluli), I just ate and my asshole really hurts, ha! (bird calls in late afternoon and dinnertime)	Feld 2012:78-79
		Ninɛli monowo 'kufɔ hɔsulowo hɔɔ (Kaluli), I just ate and my belly is really full, ha! (bird calls in late afternoon and dinnertime)	Feld 2012:79
Brown Prinia, Brown Hill Warbler, *Prinia polychroa*	Burma	Chew-it, chew-it	Smythies 1953:192
Brown Quail, *Coturnix ypsilophora*	Australia	Be quick be quick	Souter 2004:90, Wheatbelt 2018:72
		Not faair, not faair	Young 2003:3

English Name, Other Name (language) *Binominal name*	Location	Warblish (Language); Translation (Explanation)	Source Author YEAR: page #
Brown Thrasher, *Toxostoma rufum*	N. America	Hello, hello, yes, yes, yes. Who is this? Who is this? Who is this? Well, well, well, I should say, I should say, How's that?, I don't know, I don't know, What did you say? What did you say? Certainly, Certainly, Well, well, well, Not that I know of, Not that I know of, Tomorrow? Tomorrow? I guess so, I guess so, All right, All right, Goodbye, Goodbye	Bent 1948:370 citing Cook 1929
		Dig-it dig-it, hoe-it hoe-it, pull-it-up, pull-it-up	Burrows 2002:245
		Drop it, drop it, pick it up, pick it up	Feith 2003a
		Drop it, drop it, cover it up, cover it up, pull it up, pull it up	Feith 2003b; South Bay Birders n.d.
		Drop it, drop it—cover it up, cover it up—pull it up, pull it up, pull it up	Bent 1948:369 citing Thoreau Walden Pond
		Plant a seed, plant a seed, bury it	Kawasaki 2018:7
		Shuck it, shuck it; sow it, sow it; Plough it, plough it; plough it; hoe it, hoe it	S. Mathews 1921:213; & cited by Bent 1948
		Turkey	Jonas 1999:9
Brown-Crested Flycatcher, *Myiarchus tyrannulus*	N. America	Come HERE, come HERE	Brown-Crested Flycatcher 2020
		Whit-will-do, whit-will-do	
		Quit-quit-quit-quit	Dormon 1969:25

English Name, Other Name (language) *Binominal name*	Location	Warblish (Language); Translation (Explanation)	Source Author YEAR: page #
... Brown-Crested Flycatcher ... *continued* ...	Argentina	PLEASE, put-it-HERE..put-it-HERE....DEAR, put-it.HERE	Kawasaki 2018:13 citing Pieplow p. 266
Brown-Eared Bulbul, *Microscelis flavala/amaurotis?*	Burma	Kick me, when-do-we-go Keep, keep it going	Smythies 1953:87
Brown-Headed Cowbird, *Molothrus ater*	N. America	Bubble zee, Respell: bubble tea Bubble, bubble, zee, Respell: bubble, bubble tea	Feith 2003a Schmalz n.d.
Brown-Headed Honeyeater, *Melithreptus brevirostris*	Australia	Chip, click, chick	Higgins et al. 2001:921
Brush Cuckoo, Square-Tailed Cuckoo, *Cacomantis variolosus* (previously *Cuculus variolosus*)	Australia	Weep weep . . . . Wheet to wheet; Respell: week to week Where's-the-tea Fear-fear-fear-fear Where's the pippy Where's-the-tea-Pete	Kennedy et al. 2000:165 Pizzey 1980:195
Buff-Breasted Paradise Kingfisher, White-Tailed Kingfisher, *Tanysiptera sylvia*	Australia	Chop chop Chap, chap, chap, chap, chap Jab!	Buff-Breasted Paradise Kingfisher 2025 Pizzey 1980:216
Buff-Breasted Babbler, *Trichastoma tickelli*	Asia	Pit-you, pit-you	King & Dickinson 1975:295
Bulbul, *Ngilikilajako (Kikami), Pycnonotidae* (family)	Tanzania	*Ngilikilajako* (Kikami) Warthog, your tail!	Koopman 2018a:19 citing Moreau

English Name, Other Name (language) *Binominal name*	Location	Warblish (Language); Translation (Explanation)	Source Author YEAR: page #
Burchell's Coucal, Fukwe (Bantu?), *Centropus burchellii*	Africa, Sub-Saharan & South Africa	*Wafa baba, wafa mame, ngafa, isizunqu—nqu—ngu* (Zulu?) My father is dead, my mother is dead, and now I die of loneliness	Bulpin 1966:26
Burrowing Owl *Athene cunicularia*	N. America	Quick! Quick!	Mosco 2017b
Bush Wren, Mātuhituhi or Mātuhi (Māori), *Xenicus longipes (extinct)*	NZ	*Tuia, tuia* (Māori) Keep together, stay united (from the song 'Ki kō, ki kō)'	Archer 2020 citing Te Māreikura Hori Enoka
California Quail, *Callipepla californica*	NZ	Tomato	Anne-Marie (Personal communiation)
		Otago	Helen Mae Innes
		Call Margo	
		Watch Fargo	
		Embargo	
		Dick-vercoe (man's name)	Winter 2020
		Tobacco	Leary 2016
		McPherson	
		Qua-quergo	
		Ki kuu kuu & chicago	Chambers 2007:91
	Australia	¡Sí señor! (Spanish) Yes sir	CoEDLang 2017

English Name, Other Name (language) *Binominal name*	Location	Warblish (Language); Translation (Explanation)	Source Author YEAR: page #
...California Quail ... *continued* ...	N. America	Chicago	N. Allen 2012:141, Leary 2016, Young 2003:2
		Where are you?	Fugl 2014
Canada/ N. America Warbler, *Cardellina canadensis* (previously *Wilsonia canadensis*)	N. America	Chip	Burrows 2002:273
		Check	Burrows 2002:274
		Chip chip dippety chipety dip Respell: chip chip dippity chippity dip	Feith 2003a
Cape Eagle-owl? Hooting Owl, isiKova (Zulu), uMabengwane (Zulu), *Bubo capensis*	South Africa	*Vuk' ungibule!* (Zulu) Get up and whack me!	Koopman 2018b:265 citing Bryant 1905:321
Cape May Warbler, *Dendroica tigrina*	N. America	See see see see	Burrows 2002:257
		Seat seat seat	Feith 2003a
Cape Parrot, Isikhwenene (Zulu & Xhosa), *Poicephalus robustus*	Southern Africa	Haha! Haha! / *Ndinabo nam abantwana* / Haha (Xhosa?) Haha! Haha! / I too have children / Haha!	Wainwright 1983:298
Cape Wagtail, Willie Wagtail, Umvemve (Zulu), *Motacilla capensis*	South Africa	Cock: *Sawuɓona, sawuɓona, sawuɓona. Yeɓo sawuɓona.* ×3 Cock: I behold you, I behold you, I behold you. Yes, I behold you. . ×3	Dunning 1946:55–56

English Name, Other Name (language) *Binominal name*	Location	Warblish (Language); Translation (Explanation)	Source Author YEAR: page #
Carolina Chickadee, *Penthestes carolinensis*	N. America	My watcher key, my watcher key	S. Mathews 1921:233 citing Chapman
Carolina Wren, *Thryothorus ludovicianus*	N. America	Sweet heart sweet heart	Bent 1948:228
		Sweet William, sweet William	
		Come to me, come to me	
		Jew-Pet-er, Jew-Pet-er	
		Tree- double-tree double-tree double-tree	
		Sugar to eat, sugar to eat, sugar to eat, sugar	
		Which jailer, which jailer	
		Richelieu, richelieu, richelieu (a French name)	
		Witchery witchery witchery	Dormon 1969:61
		Secret, secret, secret	
		Cheerily cheerily cheerily	Feith 2003a
		Chewy chewy chewy	
		Tea-kéttle, tea-kéttle, tea-kéttle	Bent 1948:228
		Teakettle, teakettle, teakettle	Dormon 1969:61; Mosco 2017a; Schmalz n.d.; Young 2003:2
Cerulean Warbler, *Setophaga cerulea*	N. America	Beer beer beer si si zee	Feith 2003
		Respell: beer beer beer see see see	

English Name, Other Name (language) Binominal name	Location	Warblish (Language); Translation (Explanation)	Source Author YEAR: page #
Cetti's Warbler, Cettia cetti	UK	Me? Cetti? If you don't like it - fuck off!	Strandman 2006 citing Simon Barnes
		What's my name? Cettis! Cettis! Cettis! That's it!	Mrpjdavis 2006
		Hey! What do-you want? What do-you want?	Skatebirder 2008
		What's the day today?	The Octagon 2008:1
		That's the way to do it!	The Octagon 2008:10
		Chet! Chet-tee! I'm a little chettee, I'm a little chettee (Cetti's is pronounced chettiz)	Thomas 2019:128
		Chip! Chip-pee! Chippy-chip-shop chippy-chip-shop	
		Chippy chip shop	Thomas 2019:129
		Chip, chip shop, chippy chip shop chippy chip shop	Thomas 2019:33
Changeable Hawk Eagle, Spizaetus cirrhatus	Asia	Quick quick quick quick quick quick	Smythies et al. 1999:197-8
		Yeep yip yip, yeep yip yip yip (slang for yes)	
Chanting Scrubwren, Nene (Kaluli), Crateroscelis murina	PNG	Kalu yabɛ (Kaluli) A person is coming	Feld 2012:79
		Ne mayabɛ (Kaluli) I'm hungry	Feld 2012:79
		Sei yabɛ (Kaluli) A witch is coming	Feld 2012:79
Chestnut-Headed Tesia, Tesia castaneocoronata	Asia	Sip, sip-it-up	King & Dickinson 1975:373

English Name, Other Name (language) Binominal name	Location	Warblish (Language); Translation (Explanation)	Source Author YEAR: page #
Chestnut-Backed Scimitar-babbler, *Pomatorhinus montanus*	S. E. Asia	Poop-poop Poop-poop-poop	King & Dickinson 1975:298
Chestnut-Cheeked Starling, *Agropsar philippensis*	Philippines	Check check	Kennedy et al. 2000:317
Chestnut-Crowned Laughingthrush, *Trochalopteron erythrocephalum*	Asia	Walk to work	King & Dickinson 1975:317 citing Smythies
Chestnut-Sided Warbler, *Dendroica pensylvanica, Setophaga pensylvanica*	N. America	So pleased, pleased, pleased to MEET-CHA!	Burrows 2002:255
		Pleased pleased pleased to meet cha	Feith 2003b
		Pleased pleased pleased to meet ya	Feith n.d.
		I wish, I wish, I wish, to see Miss Beecher	S. Mathews 1921:184
		Tsee, tsee, tsee, Happy to meet you!	S. Mathews 1921:186
		Please, please, please to meet'cha	Schmalz n.d.
		See-see-see-miss-beech'er	South Bay Birders n.d.
		See see see Miss Beech-er	Young 2003:2
		Pleased pleased pleased to meet you	Mosco 2017a
Chestnut-Tailed Siva, *Siva singula*	Burma	Too-sweet-sweet	Smythies 1953:67
Chestnut-Winged Babbler, *Cyanoderma erythroptera*	S. E. Asia	Poop-poop-poop-poop	King & Dickinson 1975:307

English Name, Other Name (language) *Binominal name*	Location	Warblish (Language); Translation (Explanation)	Source Author YEAR: page #
Chicken, *Gallus gallus domesticus*	Fiji	*Pak pak* (Fiji Baat) Chatterbox	Vicki (Personal communication)
	Russia	*Kyда? Kyд-kyда? Kyда?* [Kuda? Kud-kuda? Kuda?] (Russian) Where? Where to? Where?	Bianki 2013:4
	Ireland	*Mac na hōghe slān* (Irish) The son of the Virgin is safe	Cocker 2013:69
	Finland	Female: *Plock upp stickor och kast upp på tak*; Male: *Upp alla nu nu, klockan är sju, sju* (Finnish) Female: Pick up sticks and throw up on the roof. Male: Up all now now, the clock is seven, seven (translated by Mikaela Nyman)	Norudde 2009 n.d.
		Kukko krekuu (Finnish) Rooster crows	Mikaela Nyman (Personal communication)
		Koka kaffe! (Finnish?) Cook coffee! (translator: Mikaela Nyman)	Norudde 2009
	Sweden	*Ägg, ägg, upp i tak* (Finnish) Eggs, eggs, up in the ceiling	
		Female: *Ägg, ägg, upp i tak* (Swedish) Egg, egg, up in the ceiling (with rising pitch)	Abelin 2011:15
		Male: *Upp alla nu, klockan är sju* (Swedish) Up everyone now, it's seven o'clock	Abelin 2011:16

English Name, Other Name (language) *Binominal name*	Location	Warblish (Language); Translation (Explanation)	Source Author YEAR: page #
... Chicken ... *continued* ...	Switzerland	*Güggerüggü* (Swiss German) Rooster *(gugger)* crowing *(uugguu)*	Lena Tichy (Personal communication)
	German	*Kikkeri ki* (German) (chirpish)	Cocker 2013:69
	Somalia	*Waa-Na-Soo-gaaaaadh* (Kisomali) Dawn has arrived	Ottó 1901:7
	Hungary	*Ki kotoz itt?* (Hungarian) Who is it? (who is poking around looking for something?) (translators: Daisy Coles & Balint Koller)	
	N. America, Nebraska	Don't you have work to do?	Cocker 2013:69
	Israel	*Koo koo ri koo* (Hebrew?) Looney	
	NZ	I don't believe you Whatcha gonna do? Hey you I told you Don't go Ah well	Helen Mae Innes
	Southern Africa	You're a fool too	Cocker 2013:69

English Name, Other Name (language) Binominal name	Location	Warblish (Language); Translation (Explanation)	Source Author YEAR: page #
... Chicken ... continued ...	South Africa	*Woza la! Si lapha* (Zulu) Come over here! This is where we are!	Adjaye 1994:132
	Vietnam	Male: *Ba co nha khong.* Female: *Co, co, co* (Vietnamese) Male: Wife at home or not? Female: Yes, yes, yes, yes.	Cocker 2013:69
Chiming Wedgebill, *Psophodes occidentalis*	Australia	But did you get drunk	Hannah Tysoe (Personal communication)
Chinese Francolin, Pusong Tsina (Pilopino), *Francolinus pintadeanus*	Philippines Asia	Come to the peak, ha-ha More beer hah	King & Dickinson 1975:100
	Burma	Do-be-quick-papa	Smythies 2001:178
Chinspot Batis, *Batis molitor*	South Africa	Three blind mice (descending notes)	Barnes & Behrens 2017:128
Chipping Sparrow, *Spizella passerina*	N. America	Chip chip	Frances & Burnie 2007:477
Chirruping Wedgebill, *Psophodes cristatus*	Australia	But did you get drunk? Sit 'n cheer (answered by female with r-e-e-e-t CHEER!)	Pizzey 1980:266 Pizzey 1980:267
Chuck Will's Widow, *Antrostomus/Caprimulgus carolinensis*	N. America	CHIP fell out of the white OAK (emphasis mine) Chuckwuts-widow	Dormon 1969:55 Cleere 2010: Appendix 2

English Name, Other Name (language) *Binominal name*	Location	Warblish (Language); Translation (Explanation)	Source Author YEAR: page #
... Chuck Will's Widow, ... *continued* ...	N. America	Chuck will's widow	Frances & Burnie 2007:290; Wells 2002:83; Saunders 1951:286;
Cinnamon-Breasted Wattle-Bird, Golyad (Kalam), *Melidectes torquatus*	PNG	*Gol nak, gol yad* (Kalam) Your exposed brightly coloured skin, my exposed brightly coloured skin	Majnep & Bulmer 1977:62
Coal Tit, *Periparus ater*	UK	Itsy witsy teeny weeny	Compare the Marsh Tit 2012
		Ouija Ouija	Thomas 2019:33
Common Blackbird, *Turdus merula*	NZ	Well a day	Andersen n.d.
		I'm such a pretty bird	Helen Mae Innes
		What are you talking about?	
		What do you wanna do?	
		What a pretty	
		What are you?	
		What are you looking at?	
	Sweden	*Jophejdi* (Swedish) Yodel(?)	Norudde 2009
Common Bulbul Top-Knot, Iphothwe (Zulu) *Pycnonotus barbatus*	South Africa	Doctor-quick doctor-quick be-quick be-quick.	Common Bulbul, 2025

English Name, Other Name (language) *Binominal name*	Location	Warblish (Language); Translation (Explanation)	Source Author YEAR: page #
... Common Bulbul ... continued ...	South Africa	Cock: *bafana, bafana, inkomo ziyobuya nin? Niyogcina konke, aniboni ukuthi izwe lifile? Nithathe izagilanje, aniboni ini ukuthi ilanga lishonile, kuyogcina thina?* (Zulu) Cock: Boys! Boys! When are the cattle returning (i.e., when are you returning with the cattle?) Will you (manage to) collect them all (i.e., won't you find that some have strayed and are missing when you start returning home with them? Don't you see that the land (country) is dead? (i.e., that there is drought and famine in the land?) You have actually taken your throw-sticks with you. Can't you see that the sun has set and that we (Bulbus) are the last (to retire of all birds).	Dunning 1946:51
Common Chaffinch, Eurasian Chaffinch, Bofink (Swedish), Bogfinke (Danish?), Pinson (French), *Fringilla coelebs*	UK	Chip-chip-chip-chip tell-tell-tell cherry-erry-erry-erry tissy-che-wee-ooo	Thorpe 1961:12
		Wink (call) Skipping down the stairs (song)	Thomas 2019:70
		Finch	Barnes 2016:67
		Dig dig dig dig (pause) diddly diddly diddly diddly (falls) CHINK (hits water)	Compare the Marsh Tit 2012
	NZ	Pink	Andersen 1926:110

English Name, Other Name (language) Binominal name	Location	Warblish (Language); Translation (Explanation)	Source Author YEAR: page #
...Common Chaffinch ... continued ...	NZ	Pink pinnk (call); chip chip chip tell tell tell cherry-erry-erry tissi cheweeo (song)	Gunson 2011:149
	France	Pinson (French) (French: a name; English: obsolete, a thin shoe)	Andersen 1926:110
	Estonia	Siit-siit sa ei saa mitte üks pirrutikk! (Estonian) You won't get a single splint from here	Bhattacharya 2019:43 citing Jüssi 2007:27
	Denmark	Der er ikke mer wc-papir med tryk på wc (Danish?) There is no more toilet paper in the toilet	Norrude 2009
	Sweden,	Har du nu varit ute och RÅNT IGEN (Swedish) Have you been LOITERING/DRIFTING AGAIN?	
		Per, Per, Per i Östervik – kom hit! (Swedish) Per (boy)', Per, Per in Östervik - come here!	
		Snälla, snälla mamma får jag gå på bio ikväll klockan tio, klockan tio (Swedish) Please, please mom can I go to the movies tonight at ten, at ten	Abelin 2011:13
		Trilla nerför trappan – nu är jag här (Swedish) Fall down the stairs - now I'm here	
		Snälla, snälla (Swedish) Please, please (falling, begging intonation)	Abelin 2011:14
		Si-Si-Si jag är en bolschevik (Swedish) Si-Si-Si I'm a Bolschevik	Norudde 2009

English Name, Other Name (language) *Binominal name*	Location	Warblish (Language); Translation (Explanation)	Source Author YEAR: page #
... Common Chaffinch ... *continued* ...	Sweden	*Trilla nerför trappan - nu är jag här* (Swedish) Fall down the stairs - now I'm here (falling intonation)	Abelin 2011:14
		Mamma, mamma, mamma varför kan inte jag få gå på bio? (Swedish) Mum, mum, mum why can't I go to the cinema	Norrude 2009
		Ååå lilla mamma, kan vi gå på bio idag? (Swedish) Oh little mother, can we go to the cinema today?"	
		Snälla snälla mamma får jag gå på bio ikväll kl 10...kl 10 (Swedish) Please kindly mother, can I go to the cinema tonight at 10 ... 10am	
		Ja ja ja ja jag är från Örnsköldsvik! (Swedish) "Yes yes yes yes yes I am from Örnsköldsvik!"	
		Ett två tre fyra fem sex sju åtta nio tio judiska bud! (Swedish) One two three four five six seven eight nine ten Jewish commandments	
		Ja, ja, ja, ja ä från Jönköping ja (Swedish) Yes, yes, yes, yes I am from Jönköping, yes (other place names can be substituted)	

English Name, Other Name (language) *Binominal name*	Location	Warblish (Language); Translation (Explanation)	Source Author YEAR: page #
... Common Chaffinch ... *continued* ...	Sweden	*Se se se så vacker ja é* (Swedish) See see how beautiful I am	Norudde 2009
		Sitter du, sitter du, sitter du i skogen å skiter du Fritiof lilla? (Swedish) Are you sitting, are you sitting, are you sitting in the woods shitting, little Fritiof? (Fritiof is a masculine given name)	
		Skall du gå ut och springa i kväll igen, va?! (Swedish) Are you going out and running tonight again, huh ?!" (call/response 2/3 call by willow warbler)	
		Du ska då alltid ut och drälla (Swedish) You should always go out and drink	
		Du ska då alltid ut och drälla (Swedish) You always have to go and loiter around (translator: Mikaela Nyman)	
		Snälla lilla mamma kan jag få gå på bio ikväll? (Swedish) Please, little mother, can I go to the cinema tonight?	
Common Chiffchaff, *Phylloscopus collybita*	Sweden	*Salt sill, salt sill, salt sill* Salt herring, salt herring, salt herring	Norudde 2009

English Name, Other Name (language) *Binominal name*	Location	Warblish (Language); Translation (Explanation)	Source Author YEAR: page #
Common Cuckoo, *Cuculus canorus*	Europe	Love you! Love you!	Helen Mae Innes
Common Hawk Cuckoo, *Hierococcyx varius varius*	Burma	Brain-fever	Smythies 2001:246
Common Hill-Partridge, *Arborophila torqueola*	Asia	Poor	King & Dickinson 1975:100
Common House-Martin, *Delichon urbicum*	Norway	*Böigg e bo utan navar utan stavar bara neve deill navar* (Norwegian) Build a nest without a drill without rods just the beak to drill	Norudde 2009
Common Loon, *Gavia immer*	N. America	Call: I'm here, where are you? Response: I'm over here Ha, ha, ha, ha, hoo, hoo, hoo, ha-oo-oo	Bird Academy 2010 Jonas 1999:5
Common Moorhen, *Gallinula chloropus*	N. America	Ticket-ticket-ticket Cup	Burrows 2002:112
Common Murre, *Uria aalge*	N. America	FEED-me-now, feed-me-now, feed-me-now!	Burrows 2002:169
Common Nightingale, *Luscinia megarhynchos*	N. America	Chew-chew chew-chew, cheer-cheer cheer-cheer, cheer-up cheer-up cheer-up, tweet tweet jug jug jug	Preston & Gower 2018:176 citing John Clare
		Twit, twit, twit/ jug, jug, jug, jug, jug, jug/so rudely forc'd / tereu	Preston & Gower 2018:179 citing Eliot

English Name, Other Name (language) Binominal name	Location	Warblish (Language); Translation (Explanation)	Source Author YEAR: page #
... Common Nightingale, ... continued ...	N. America	What? What? What, john? Heart aches and a drowsy numbness pains? - tra-la-la! -tri-li-lilly-lilyly!	Preston & Gower 2018:181 citing D. H. Lawrence
		Chee chew chee chew chee chew - cheer cheer cheer chew chew chew chee – up cheer up cheer up tweet tweet tweet jug jug jug	Rothenberg 2005:25 citing John Clare
Common Pheasant, Ring-Necked Pheasant, *Phasianus colchicus*	NZ	I'm stuck	Anon via website
		Korr-cock	N. Allen 2012:142
	N. America	Cow cat	Feith 2003a
Common Poorwill, *Phalaenoptilus nuttallii*	N. America	Poor-jill	Frances & Burnie 2007:290
		Poor-will	
		Poor-will-ow	
Common Potoo, *Nyctibius griseus*	South America	POO-or me, O, O, O, O	Young 2003:3
Common Quail, Prepeliță (Romanian), Перепел [Perepel] (Russian), *Coturnix coturnix*	UK	Wet my lips	Common Quail 2020
	Romania, Bucovina	*Prind păduchi!* (Romanian) I catch lice!	Puscariu 1920–1921:93
	Russia	Спать пора! Спать пора! [Spat' pora! Spat' pora!] (Russian) Time to sleep! Time to sleep!	Bianki 2013:15
Common Quaker Babbler, *Alcippe poioicephala*	Burma	Chewy-chewy-chewy-chewy-chewy	Smythies 1953:71–72

English Name, Other Name (language) *Binominal name*	Location	Warblish (Language); Translation (Explanation)	Source Author YEAR: page #
Common Redpole, *Carduelis flammea*	N. America	Swe-eet	Burrows 2002:310
	NZ	Chit chit chit chit	Williams 1976:26
		Chew chew chew chew	Bianki 2013:10
Common Redstart, Обыкновенная горихвостка [Obyknovennaya gorikhvostka] (Russian), *Phoenicurus phoenicurus*	Russia	Жить! Жить! [Zhit'! Zhit'!] (Russian) Alive! Alive!	
Common Reed Bunting, *Emberiza schoeniclus*	UK	Hello, hello, hello, piss off!	Norudde 2009
Sävsparv (Swedish),	Germany	*Ich sing immer noch schlecht* (German) I still sing badly	Xenospiza 2014
	Russia	*Никиту видел? Тришку видел?* [Nikitu videl? Trishku videl?] (Russian) Have you seen Nikita? Have you seen Trishka?	Bianki 2013:8
Common Rosefinch, Чечевица краснопёрая [Chechevitsa krasnoporaya] (Russian), Rosenfink (Swedish), *Carpodacus erythrinus*		*В багдаде все спокойно* [V bagdade vse spokoyno] (Russian) Everything is calm in Baghdad	Vadim_mikhaylin 2019
		Витю видел? [Vityu videl?] (Russian) Did you see Victor? (Translator: Vladimir Safonov)	Vadim_mikhaylin 2019
	Sweden	*Köp en video* (Swedish) Buy a video	Norudde 2009

English Name, Other Name (language) *Binominal name*	Location	Warblish (Language); Translation (Explanation)	Source Author YEAR: page #
... Common Rosefinch ... *continued* ...	Sweden	*Se video* (Swedish) Watch video	Norudde 2009
		Skit I de du (Swedish) Don't you worry about that / don't give a damn / don't give a shit / let it go (translator: Mikaela Nyman)	Abelin 2011:15
		Se video, Köp en video, Skit I de du (Swedish) Watch video, Buy a video, You shit you (Google Translate)	Norudde 2009
	UK	Nice to see you Pleased to meet you	Abelin 2011:15; Norudde 2009
		Glad to see you Pleased to see you	Abelin 2011:15
Common Snipe, Enkelbeckasin (Swedish), *Gallinago gallinago*	Sweden	*Herrarna, herrarna, herrarna* (Swedish) The men/boys *Grebba lilla, grebba lilla* (Swedish) Little women/girls Call: *Herrarna, herrarna, herrarna*. Response: *Grebba lilla, grebba lilla* (Swedish) Call: Gentlemen, gentlemen, gentlemen (or boys, boys). Response: Little girls, little girls	Norudde 2009
	N. America	Wheat wheat wheat wheat	Burrows 2002:141

English Name, Other Name (language) *Binominal name*	Location	Warblish (Language); Translation (Explanation)	Source Author YEAR: page #
Common Starling, *Sturnus vulgaris*	Australia	Dick!	Pizzey 1980:380
Common Whitethroat, Törnsångare (Swedish), Sylvia communis *Curruca communis?*	Europe/Africa Sweden	Oh hear me dear ….	S. Mathews 1921:100
		Tycker du det, tycker du (Swedish) Do you think so, do you think?	Norudde 2009
		Backa och kör in i garaget (Swedish) Back and drive into the GARAGE	
Common Wood Pigeon, Ring Dove, Ringduvan (Swedish), Ijuba, Ihobe (Zulu) *Columba palumbus*	Sweden	*Du tog sju för tu, din tjuv* (Swedish) You took seven for two, you thief	Abelin 2011:14
		Ja haar ju en ring (Swedish) I do have a ring (there's a ring-like pattern on dove's neck)	
		Jag vill ha smörgas, jag vill ha smörgas (Swedish) I want a sandwich, I want a sandwich	
		Men gå då, ändå (Swedish) But please go	
		Men gå då, ändå! (Swedish) But please go, anyway!	
		Men gå då, nån gång (Swedish) But please go some time	
		Så kom då, ändå (Swedish) So come then, anyway	

English Name, Other Name (language) *Binominal name*	Location	Warblish (Language); Translation (Explanation)	Source Author YEAR: page #
... Common Wood Pigeon ... *continued* ...	Sweden	*Men jar har ju två, men ja har ju två (ringar)* (Swedish) But I have two, but I have two (rings)	Abelin 2011:14
		Men RING då nån gång, men RING då nån gång (Swedish) But ring me some time, but ring me sometime	
		Min älskling du ä (Swedish) My darling you are	
		Du tog min hustru du (Swedish) You took my wife, you	Abelin 2011:14–15
		Du är tokig, du är dum (Swedish) You are crazy, you are stupid	Abelin 2011:15
		Du steker kokött, du steker kokött, gott (Swedish) You roast beef, you roast beef, good	Norudde 2009
		Du du du du, som tog mina sju sju sju, o la dit de tu tu tu tu (Swedish) You you you you, who took my seven seven seven seven, and placed there the two two two two (translated by Mikaela Nyman)	
		Du tog sju för tu, din tjuv (Swedish) You took seven for two, you thief (translated by Mikaela Nyman)	

English Name, Other Name (language) *Binominal name*	Location	Warblish (Language); Translation (Explanation)	Source Author YEAR: page #
...Common Wood Pigeon ... *continued* ...	Sweden	*Du tog mina tu du* (Swedish) You took my two, you.	Norudde 2009
		Jag vill ha smörgås. Jag vill ha smörgås (Swedish) I want a sandwich. I want a sandwich	
		Men RING då nån gång (Swedish) But ring me sometime	
		Min älskling du ä (Swedish) My darling you are	
		Så kom då, ändå. Så kom då, ändå (Swedish) Then come on, anyway. Then come on, anyway	
		Sju sju mot tu tu (Swedish) Seven seven against two (Google translate)	
		Jag haar ju en ring ... (Swedish) But I have a ring...	
		Men gåå då nån gång (Swedish) But go sometime now / but walk then, sometime soon!	
		Får jag dina sju, sju, får du mina tu, tu ... Du! (Swedish) Do I get your seven, seven, you get my two, two ... You!	

English Name, Other Name (language) *Binominal name*	Location	Warblish (Language); Translation (Explanation)	Source Author YEAR: page #
... Common Wood Pigeon ... *continued* ...	Sweden	*Men ja har ju två, men ja har ju två* (Swedish) But yes you have two, but yes you have two	Norudde 2009
		Du är tokig, du är dum (Swedish) You're crazy, you're stupid	
		Du tog min hustru du (Swedish) You took my wife, you	
	UK	No, you can't have sweeties!	Anon via website
		My toe bleeds Georgie	Rachel Kirkwood (Personal communication)
		I DON'T want to go (punctuation mine)	Thomas 2019:27
		I don't want to go	Thomas 2019:72
		I don't want to go, I don't want to go	RSPB n.d.
		Don't want to go x3	Thomas 2019:74
	Russia	*Кого-с? Кого-с?* [Kogo-s? Kogo-s?] (Russian) Whom! Whom!	Bianki 2013:5
		На дубу сижу, витютень, На красу гляжу, витютень! [Na dubu sizhu, vityuten', Na krasu glyazhu, vityuten'!] (Russian) I'm sitting on an oak tree, coo coo, I'm looking at the beauty, coo coo!	Bianki 2013:8

English Name, Other Name (language) *Binominal name*	Location	Warblish (Language); Translation (Explanation)	Source Author YEAR: page #
… Common Wood Pigeon … *continued* …	South Africa	*Avuthiwe, amtokwe* x3 (Zulu) It (the mabele corn) is ripened, it is reddening x3	Dunning, 1946: 32
		Gu-gu, ngadenzima, a vutiwe amatulwa, ngadenzima. Gu-gu (Zulu?) Coo-coo, 'Ngadenzima; the wild medlars are ripe, 'Ngadenzima. Coo-coo.	Callaway 1868:140
Common Yellowthroat, Maryland Yellow-Throat, *Geothlypis trichas*	N. America	Which is it? Which is it? Which is it?	Young 2003:3
		Witchety witchety witchety-witch	Burrows 2002:272
		Twichety twichety twichety twich	Common Yellowthroat 2020
		Witchety, witchety, witchety Witchity, witchity, witchity	Feith n.d.; Feith 2003b Mosco 2017b
		Which is it? Which is it?	Kawasaki 2018:7
		Get a penny, get penny	Roth 1998:54
Connecticut Warbler, *Oporornis agilis*	N. America	Whip, whip-it-up, whip-it-good Or tip tupa teepo tupa teepo	Feith 2003b; Feith n.d.
		Beecher beecher	Saunders 1951:294
Coppersmith Barbet, *Megalaima haemacephala*	Burma	Took OR tonk ('Like the tap of a small hammer on metal, hence the name of coppersmith')	Smythies 2001:301
Corn Bunting, *Emberiza calandra*	UK	Pit pit pit pit pit	Thomas 2019:116

English Name, Other Name (language) *Binominal name*	Location	Warblish (Language); Translation (Explanation)	Source Author YEAR: page #
Cotton Pygmy Goose, Cotton Teal, *Nettapus coromandelianus*	Burma	Fixed bayonets Ka-kalaga Chirpish	Smythies 1953:541; 2001:127
Crane, Журавлик [Zhuravlyk] (Russian), *Gruidae* (family)	Russia	*Трогай, трогай! В поход! За горы, за моря: Летим не зря, Мы да орлы - Курлы! Курлы!* [Trogay, trogay! V pokhod! Za gory, za morya: Letim ne zrya, My da orly - Kurly! Kurly!] (Russian) Let's go! Let's go! On a tour, on a trip! Over the mountains, over the seas, we're flying decisively us and the eagles craney, craney! *Ут-рро! Ут-рро!* [Ut-rro! Ut-rro!] (Russian) Morning! Morning!	Bianki 2013:12 Bianki 2013:6
Crescent Honeyeater, *Phylidonyris pyrrhopterus*	Australia	Egypt	Pizzey 1980:344
Crested Fireback, *Lophura ignita*	Asia	Sleep	Smythies et al. 1999:225
Crested Francolin, (previously *Dendroperdix sephaena*) *Francolinus sephaena*	Tanzania; Kami, north Uluguru, Tanganyika	*Ngilikilajako* (Kikami) Warthog your tail! (insult)	A. J. Moreau 1940:59

English Name, Other Name (language) *Binominal name*	Location	Warblish (Language); Translation (Explanation)	Source Author YEAR: page #
Crested Shriketit, *Falcunculus frontatus*	Australia	Knock-at-the-door	Pizzey 1980:247
		Knock-at-the-door-whack!	Pizzey 1980:247; Young 2003:3
Crimson Chat, *Epthianura tricolor*	Australia	Dik-it, dik-it; Respell: dick-it dick-it	Pizzey 1980:354
		Check, check	Pizzey 1980:354
Crow, Ворона [Vorona] (Russian), Corvidae *(family)*	Russia	*Харч! Харч!* [Xarc! Xarc!] (Russian) Grub! Grub!	Bianki 2013:12
	Sweden	*Vará, vará, vará* (Swedish) Where, where, where?	Norudde 2009
		Jag har ont, jag har ont, jag har ont (Swedish) I'm in pain, I'm in pain, I'm in pain (translator: Mikaela Nyman)	
		Där bak, där bak, där bak (Swedish) Back there, back there, back there	
	Hungary	*Jakab pap hat vak bak. Vadgalamb ül* (Hungarian) Pope Jacob, six blind he-goats. The wild pigeon sits (translator: Daisy Coles)	Ottó 1901:7
		Kár! Kár! (Hungarian) What a pity!	Daisy Coles (Personal communication)

English Name, Other Name (language) *Binominal name*	Location	Warblish (Language); Translation (Explanation)	Source Author YEAR: page #
Curlew Sandpiper? Ithendele, Intendele (Zulu) *Calidris ferruginea?*	South Africa	Cock: *Sinegaqa* ×3 Hen: *Sophakelwa, uɓani* ×3 Cock: We have assegai (wooden spear) ×3 Hen: Who will serve us out with food? ×3	Dunning 1946:36
Dark-Capped Bulbul, *Pycnonotus tricolor*	South Africa	Quick chop to quick Respell: quick chop too quick	Barnes & Behrens 2017:118
D'Arnaud's Barbet, Barbet, Mhokeuta (Wazigua/Tanzanian), Lolenzoka (Tanzanian), *Trachyphonus d'arnaudii*	Tanzania (Tanganyika) Kami, north Uluguru	*Mhokeuta* (Wazigua/Zigula?) Draw the bow *Lolenzoka* (Wazigua/Zigula?) Look at the snake *Mhokeuta* (Wazigua/Zigula?) Draw the bow	R. E. Moreau 1942:1002 Koopman 2018a:19; Moreau 1940:51
Diamond Firetail, *Stagonopleura guttata*	Australia	P-a-i-r-r (birds are seen in pairs)	Pizzey 1980:369
Dickcissel, *Spiza americana*	N. America	Dick dick dick-cissel (Scandinavian name) Dick dick sisisis; clip clip sisisis Dick, dick, sizzle, sizzle	Burrows 2002:297 Saunders 1951:300 Soper 2019
Diederik/Didric Cuckoo, Jan-Diederik (Afrikaans?), Ngolankuchange (Tanzanian), *Chrysococcyx / Lampromorpha caprius*	Southern Africa, Tanzania	*Jan-Diederik* (Afrikaans?) (person's name) *Ngolankuchange* (Xhosa?) Knife for gashing	Koopman 2018a:19

English Name, Other Name (language) *Binominal name*	Location	Warblish (Language); Translation (Explanation)	Source Author YEAR: page #
... Diederik Cuckoo ... *continued* ...	Tanzania	*Ngolankuchanje* (Bantu?) Knife for gashing	A. J. Moreau 1940:55
	Sudan Baggara	*Eed-i-inkaserat, eed-i-inkaserat* (Chadian Arabic?) My arm is broken	Owen 1947:194
		Eed-i-biriat (Chadian Arabic?) Eat and drink (Google translate)	
Dimorphic/Rufous Fantail, Jolbeg (Kalam), *Rhipidura brachyrhyncha*	PNG / Kalam	*Joley-boley* (Kalam) Alight in one place, alight in another, call and call again	Majnep & Bulmer 1977:85
Doves (includes Stockdove (*Columba oenas*), Eurasian Collared Dove (*Streptopelia decaocto*), Ring Dove,	Sweden	*Skogsduvan: Gå då! Turkduvan: Men gå då! Ringduvan: Men gå då, ändå!* (Swedish) Stock Dove: Go!" Collared dove: But go then! Ring dove: But so go then! (# of syllables = beats in bird's call)	Norudde 2009
		Skogsduva: Så kom, så kom Turkduva: Så kom då, så kom då Ringduvan: Så kom då, ändå. Så kom då, ändå (Swedish) Stock Dove: Then come, come. Collared Dove: Then come, then come. Ring Dove: Then come on, anyway. Then come on, anyway.	

English Name, Other Name (language) *Binominal name*	Location	Warblish (Language); Translation (Explanation)	Source Author YEAR: page #
...Doves ...*continued* ...	Sweden	*Skogsturken ringer* (Swedish) The forest pigeon rings / the woods call / the forest turkey is calling (Google translate)	Norudde 2009
Downy Woodpecker, *Dryobates pubescens*	N. America	Pick Keep, keep, keep	Feith 2003a Saunders 1951:77
Drongo Cuckoo, *Surniculus lugubris*	Asia	One, two, three, four, five, six	King & Dickinson 1975:186
Duck, Утка (Russian), *Anas* (genus)	Russia	*Bpa-aa! Bpa-aa! Bpa-aa!* [Vra-ag! Vra-ag! Vra-ag!] (Russian); Enemy! Enemy! Enemy!	Bianki 2013:5
	Hungary	*Csak csapra! Csak csapra!* (Hungarian) Only on tap! Only on tap! (translator: Daisy Coles); (response to Rock Pigeon saying "we have wine")	Ottó 1901:7
	Southern Africa	Duck call: *Isifuba sam sithe. Gaa gaa gaa! Drake* response: *Uzithi, tshwe tshwe tshwe!* (Xhosa) (Duck) My chest goes: gaa gaa gaa! (Drake reply) You should say, tshwe, tshwe, tshwe!	Wainwright 1983:298
Dusky Myzomela, *Myzomela obscura*	Australia	See see see	Pizzey 1980:353
Eagle-owl? *Bubo* (genus)	Africa, Sudan / Baggara	*Kozi, -mmmm, Kosi, - mmmm* (Chadian Arabic?) (Brooding over daughter's (named Kozi) death	Owen 1947:194
Eastern Barn Owl, *Tyto alba delicatula*	Australia	Sk-air OR skee-air OR skee-aarr Respell: scare	Wheatbelt 2018:91

English Name, Other Name (language) *Binominal name*	Location	Warblish (Language); Translation (Explanation)	Source Author YEAR: page #
Eastern Bluebird, *Sialia sialis*	N. America	Cheer, cheerful charmer	Feith 2003a; Schmalz n.d.; Sarvasy 2016:774
		Purity . . . Purity	Roth 1998:54
Eastern Crowned Warbler, *Phylloscopus coronatus*	S. E. Asia	Swee-eet	King & Dickinson 1975:362 citing Nisbet
Eastern Kingbird, *Tyrannus tyrannus*	N. America	Cheer, cheerful charmer	Feith 2003a
		Kit-kit-kitter-kitter	Jonas 1999:6
Eastern Meadowlark, *Sturnella magna*	N. America	This is the year	Burrows 2002:300
		See-you at school-today	Feith 2003a
		Spring of the year	
		See you at school! Soon!	Kawasaki 2018:7
		Eas-tern mea-dow-lark	Lorenzin 2011
		But I DO love you	South Bay Birders n.d.
Eastern Phoebe, *Sayornis phoebe*	N. America	Feebe peebe pireet; Respell: Phoebe's a pirate	Saunders 1951:77
		Phoe-be	Schmalz n.d.
Eastern Towhee, Rufous-sided Towhee (previously Eastern Towhee & Spotted Towhee), *Pipilo erythrophthalmus*, *Epthianura tricolor*	N. America	Drink your tea	Feith 2003a; Young 2003:2
		Drink your teeeee	Burrows 2002:276, Schmalz n.d.
		Towhee	Feith 2003a
		Drink you teeeeea!!	Mosco 2017a

English Name, Other Name (language) *Binominal name*	Location	Warblish (Language); Translation (Explanation)	Source Author YEAR: page #
Eastern Wattled Honey Eater, Iao (Samoan), , *Foulehaio carunculata*	Samoa	*Alu ese! Alu ese!* (Samoan) Get away! Get away! (this bird warns the chicken that the Lulu (barn owl?) Is coming to eat them)	Sharron Udy & Joe Polu (Personal communication)
Eastern Whip-Poor-Will, Goatsucker, Whippoorwill, (*Caprimulgus vociferus*) *Antrostomus vociferus*	N. America	Whip-poor-will	Burrows 2002:187
		Whip poor will	Dormon 1969:54
		Whip it good	Helen Mae Innes
		Whip poor Will!	Sarvasy 2016:774
		Whiter-wee	Saunders 1951:63
		Whip Will's widow	Wells 2002:82
		Whipper will	Wells 2002:83
		Chip flew out of White Oak (name of a stream nearby his home where farmers went to chop wood)	Cowser 1969:43
Eastern Wood-Pewee, *Contopus virens*	Central America	*Jo-se Ma-RI-a* (Spanish) Joseph Mary	Young 2003:2
	N. America	Pee-a-wee	Young 2003:2
Eurasian Blue Tit, *Cyanistes caeruleus*	Hungary	*Nincs, nincs, itt sincs!* (Hungarian) There's none, there's none; here either! (said when looking for food; translator: Daisy Coles)	Ottó 1901:7

English Name, Other Name (language) *Binominal name*	Location	Warblish (Language); Translation (Explanation)	Source Author YEAR: page #
... Eurasian Blue Tit ... *continued* ...	Hungary	*Kicsit ér, kicsit ér!* (Hungarian) It's not worth much! It's not worth much! (said when finds food; translator: Daisy Coles)	Ottó 1901:7
	UK	I'm a blue tit	Barnes 2011:67
		P diddy diddy diddy; P P P diddy diddy diddy	Compare the Marsh Tit 2012
Eurasian Bullfinch, *Domherren* (Swedish), Снегирь [Snegir'] (Russian),*Pyrrhula pyrrhula*	Sweden	*Jul, jul, jul. Snö, snö, snö* (Swedish) Christmas x3. Snow, snow, snow.	Abelin 2011: 14
	Russia	Жуть! Жуть! [Zhut'! Zhut'!] (Russian) Terrible! Terrible!	Bianki 2013:10
Eurasian Collared Dove, *Turkduvan* (Swedish) *Streptopelia decaocto*	Sweden	*Så kom då* (Swedish) So come then	Abelin 2011:14
		Så kom då, så kom då (Swedish) Then come, then come	Norudde 2009
		Så gå då (Swedish) So please go	Abelin 2011:14
		Så gåå då.. Så gåå då (Swedish) So go then . . . So go then	Norudde 2009
		Men gå då! (Swedish) But please go!	Abelin 2011:14
		Kom Josef, kom Josef (Swedish) Come Joseph, come Joseph	Abelin 2011:14 citing Norudde 2009

English Name, Other Name (language) *Binominal name*	Location	Warblish (Language); Translation (Explanation)	Source Author YEAR: page #
Eurasian Collared Dove ... *continued* ...	Sweden	*Turkiet, turkiet, turkiet* (Swedish) Turkey, turkey, turkey	Abelin 2011:14 citing Norudde 2009
	UK	*Airrrrrrr* (said as they land)	Thomas 2019:39&73
		U-ni-ted (said like a football chant)	Thomas 2019:73
		Be careful, be careful	Compare the Marsh Tit 2012
Eurasian Golden Oriole, *Oriolus oriolus*	Serbia	*Crvljiva gljiva* (Serbian) Worm-infested mushroom (By the time rioles start singing in late spring, the mushrooms are no longer very fresh, so it's a warning for mushroom-pickers.)	Zheljko 2014
	Belarus	Пить [Pit] (Russian) Rain / I want rain / it must rain; drink (dictionary)	Eugene Baranovsky (Personal communication)
	Finland	*Kuha kiehuu* (Finnish) Pike (fish) boils? / The goose is boiling?	Norudde 2009
Eurasian Hoopee, Common Hoopee, Пёстрый Хохлатый Удод [Postryy Khokhlatyy Udod] (Russian), *Upupa epops*	Russia	Худо тут! Худо тут! Худо тут! [Khudo tut! Khudo tut! Khudo tut!] (Russian) Bad here, bad here, bad here.	Bianki 2013:10
	Belarus	Худо тут [Khudo tut] (Belarusian) Bad here/bad sound here/bad omen here	Eugene Baranovsky (Personal communication)
	Burma	Hoop-hoop-hoop	Smythies 1953:358

English Name, Other Name (language) *Binominal name*	Location	Warblish (Language); Translation (Explanation)	Source Author YEAR: page #
Eurasian Oystercatcher, Strandskata (Swedish), *Haematopus ostralegus*	UK	W-weep	Thomas 2019:
	Sweden	*Tre ägg, tre ägg* (Swedish) Three eggs, three eggs (it always lays 3 eggs)	Norudde 2009
Eurasian Siskin? Чиж [Chizh] (Russian), Чижике [Chizhike] (Russian) *Spinus spinus*	Russia	*Kuubik, kuubik, kuubik, …* (Swedish) Cubic, cubic, cubic, ... Чулки, чулки, валенки! Чулки, чулки, варежки! [Chulki, chulki, valenki! Chulki, chulki, varezhki!] (Russian) Stockings, stockings, felt boots! Stockings, stockings, mittens!	Bianki 2013:13
Eurasian Tree Sparrow, Pilfink (Swedish), *Passer montanus*	Sweden	*Sällvik, sällvik* (Swedish)	Norudde 2009
Eurasian Woodcock, Morkulla (Swedish), *Scolopax rusticola*	Sweden	*Erk, Erk, Erk … Jovisst!* (Swedish) Erk, erk, erk … Sure!	Norudde 2009
Eurasian Scops Owl, Сплюшка [Splyushka] (Russian), *Otus scops*	Russia	*Сплю! Сплю! Когда же ночь? Когда же мышей-то ловить? Тьмы* [Splyu! Splyu! Kogda zhe noch'? Kogda zhe myshey-to lovit'? T'my] (Russian)	Bianki 2013:10

English Name, Other Name (language) *Binominal name*	Location	Warblish (Language); Translation (Explanation)	Source Author YEAR: page #
... Eurasian Scops Owl ... continued	...	I'm sleeping! I'm sleeping! When is the night? When to catch mice? There is no darkness. All is light! I am sleeping! I am sleeping!	...
European Goldfinch, *Carduelis carduelis*	UK	Tickle it	Thomas 2019:77
European Greenfinch, *Carduelis chloris*	NZ	Chrr Respell: chur (NZ slang)	Marler 1956:57
European Pied Flycatcher, Svartvit Flugsnappare (Swedish), *Ficedula hypoleuca*	Sweden	20-21-21-21 Kiwi kiwi chips kiwi kiwi chips kiwi kiwi	Norudde 2009
European Robin, Redbreasted Robin, Красногрудая Заряночка (Russian), *Erithacus rubecula*	Russia	*Терентий! Терентий! Проснись! Проснись! С ружьём идут - убьют, убьют, убьют!* [Terentiy! Terentiy! Prosnis'! Prosnis'! S ruzh'yom idut - ub'yut, ub'yut, ub'yut!] (Russian) Terence! Terence! Wake up! Wake up! They're coming with a gun - they'll kill you, they'll kill you, they'll kill you!	Bianki 2013:6
Fan-Tailed Cuckoo, Ash-Coloured Cuckoo, *Cacomantis flabelliformis*	Australia	Peeeeer Respell: peer	Pizzey 1980:196
		Get-work	
		Get-woorrk	Wheatbelt 2018:119

English Name, Other Name (language) *Binominal name*	Location	Warblish (Language); Translation (Explanation)	Source Author YEAR: page #
Fawn-Breasted Bowerbird, *Chlamydera cerviniventris*	Australia	Churr-r-r-r	Pizzey 1985:96 citing John Macgillivray
Feral Pigeon *Columba livia domestica*	NZ	Move	Helen Mae Innes
Fernbird, Kōtātā, Mātātā (Māori), Poodytes punctatus (*Megalurus punctatus*)	NZ	Tick tick tick	Chambers 2007:140
		Utik Respell: you dick	Crowe 2001:54
		U-tick Respell: you tick, or you dick	N. Allen 2012:161
		Uu-tik uu-tick	Chambers 2007:140
Field Sparrow, *Spizella pusilla*	N. America	Nel-l-l-l-ly-ly-ly-ly Bly-y-y-y-y-y Respell: Nelly Bly	S. Mathews 1921:104
Fierynecked Nightjar, Afrikaanse Naguil (Afrikaans), *Caprimulgus pectoralis*	South Africa	*Jaag weg die wewenaar* (Afrikaans) Chase away the widower (translator: Google)	Koopman 1990:81 citing MacLearn 1985:355
		Good Lord deliver us	
		Koo-WEEU, koo-Wiriri (Zulu)	
		Zavolo, Zavolo, sengel abantabakho (Zulu) Zavolo, Zavolo, milk for your children (this bird is believed to suck teats of cattle at night)	
		God deliver us	Barnes & Behrens 2017:208
Firebird? *Monarcha leucotis?*	Australia	You-GET-awaaay	Pizzey 1980:259

English Name, Other Name (language) *Binominal name*	Location	Warblish (Language); Translation (Explanation)	Source Author YEAR: page #
Flame Robin, *Petroica phoenicea*	Australia	You may come, if you will, to the sea	Pizzey 1980:239
Flat-Billed Flycatcher, Black Monarch? Ñyolelegp (Kopon), *Tohnomyias sulphur escens?*	PNG	*Ñyolelegp* (Kopon) A man is dying	Majnep & Bulmer 1977:103
Fluffy-Backed Tit-Babbler, *Macronous ptilosus*	S. E. Asia	Poop poop poop poop poop	King & Dickinson 1975:308
Fork-Tailed Drongo? Large Drongo Shrike, Intengu (Zulu), *Dicrurus adsimilis?*	South Africa	Cock: *Wonqamula, qede Mantaba. Woncomboza ungayithola intandane.* (Zulu) Cock: (You had better) make haste and finish your preparations (i.e., wash your feet, etc.) for the journey, Mantaba. (Be sure) you announce your intention (insistently and brazenly enough) of getting (adopting) an orphan and you will succeed in getting (possession of) one. (These are instructions to a wife to procure a second wife for the husband.)	Dunning 1946:56–58
Fox Sparrow *Passerella iliaca*	N. America	All I have is what's here dear, won't you won't you take it?	Burrows 2002:282

English Name, Other Name (language) *Binominal name*	Location	Warblish (Language); Translation (Explanation)	Source Author YEAR: page #
Francolin, *Ngilikilajako* (Kikami), *Francolin sephaena*	Tanzania	*Ngilikilajako* (Kikami) Warthog, your tail!	R. E. Moreau 1942:1002
Freckled Duck, *Stictonetta naevosa*	Australia	See-you	Wheatbelt 2018:42
Friendly Fantail, White-eared Fantail, *Ttmñ* (Kalam), *Rhipidura albolimbata*	PNG	*Byn jwyn, byn jwyn jwyn, kab aglep, kab agln agln, smen agyn, smen agyn agyn* (Kalam) I'm off now and attracting all the girls to follow me: I'm getting the over stones hot and cooking food; I'm paying bride wealth	Majnep & Bulmer 1977:85
Galah, *Cacatus roseicapilla*	Australia	Chill, chill	Pizzey 1980:166
		Sip-sip	Higgins 1999:118-9
Giant Nuthatch, *Sitta magma*	China, Burma	Get-it-up, get-it-up	Smythies 1953:19
Gibberbird, *Ashbyia lovensis*	Australia	Dip, dip	Pizzey 1980:356
Glossy Black-Cockatoo, *Calyptorhynchus lathamii*	Australia	Tarr-red . . . Tarr-red	Higgins et al. 1999:61
Glossy Swiftlet, *Mmañp* (Kalam), *Collocalia esculenta*	PNG	Sjweywey bird: *Dede-cy-o, dede-cy-o, laplap ceg-o.*	Majnep & Bulmer 1977:87

English Name, Other Name (language) *Binominal name*	Location	Warblish (Language); Translation (Explanation)	Source Author YEAR: page #
... Glossy Swiflet ... *continued* ...	...	Mmañp bird [smaller swiftlets, especially Collocalia esculenta] replies: *wog gy mañban, waty gy mañban, tap sy ok nep ñban*. Warbler bird calls back: *sy wey wey, sy wey wey wey*. (Kalam) Sjweywey bird: Keep (your food) hidden (in the rocks where Swiflets nest), keep it hidden, your skin is big, your skin is big (but your body underneath all those feathers is very small)". Mmañp/Swiflet replies: You don't make gardens, you don't make fences, you just steal food and eat it. Warbler called back: Secretly you eat, eat, secretly you eat, eat	...
Goldcrest,	UK	Sicily sicily	Thomas 2019:
Kungsfågel (Swedish), *Regulus regulus*	Sweden	*Lidl-Lidl, Lidl-Lidl, Lidl-Lidl, Lidl är så billigt* (Swedish) Lidl-Lidl, Lidl-Lidl, Lidl-Lidl, Lidl is so cheap (name of discount supermarket chain)	Norudde 2009
		Det går upp, det går upp, det går upp, och sen går det ner (Swedish) It goes up, it goes up, it goes up, and then it goes down (lower pitch at end)	

English Name, Other Name (language) *Binominal name*	Location	Warblish (Language); Translation (Explanation)	Source Author YEAR: page #
Goldcrest ... *continued* ...	Sweden	*Jag är minst, jag är minst, jag är minst i hela Sverige* (Swedish) I'm the smallest, I'm the smallest, I'm the smallest in all of Sweden	Norudde 2009
Golden Babbler, *Stachyris chrysaea*	S. E. Asia	Sweep, sweep-sweep-sweep-sweep	King & Dickinson 1975:306 citing Darnell
Golden-Crowned Kinglet, *Regulus satrepa*	N. America	Tsee-tsee-tsee-tsee, why do you shilly-shally?"	Burrows 2002:231
Golden-crowned Sparrow's *Zonotrichia atricapilla*	N. America	I'm so tired	Mosco 2017b
Golden-Headed Cisticola, *Cisticola exilis*	Australia	Pillek Respell: pillock	Pizzey 1980:276
Golden-Throated Barbet, *Megalaima franklinii*	Nepal, China	Look-'igh-up, look-'igh-up (The word high is higher in pitch)	Smythies 1953:314–315
	Burma	Look-'igh-up	Smythies 2001:300
Golden-winged Warbler, *Vermivora chrysoptera*	N. America	Bee buzz buzz buzz	Feith 2003a
Goose, *Anatidae (family)*	Russia	Га-ад! Гад! [Ga-ad! Gad!] (Russian) Bastard! Bastard!	Bianki 2013:6
Gould's Bronze-Cuckoo, *Chrysococcyx minutillus russatus*	Australia, New Guinea	See-see-see	Kennedy et al.2000:167

English Name, Other Name (language) Binominal name	Location	Warblish (Language); Translation (Explanation)	Source Author YEAR: page #
Grasshopper Sparrow, Ammodramus savanarum	N. America	Tic-tac to see	Feith 2003a
		X-Y-Zee-e-e-e-e-e-e!	S. Mathews 1921:90
Gray/Grey Catbird, Dumetella carolinensis	N. America	Meow (interspecies mimicry)	Mosco 2017a; Burrows 2002:243
		Check-check	Burrows 2002:243
Gray/Grey-Cheeked Fulvetta, Alcippe morrisonia	Asia	Sweet sweet Georgie	Young 2003:2
Great Argus, Argusianus argus argus	Burma	How-how	Smythies 2001:165
Great-Crested Flycatcher, Myiarchus crinitus	N. America	Creep, creep	Feith 2003a
Great Eared Nightjar, Eurostopodus macrotis	Burma	Too-too-we-go	Symthies 2001:269 citing Davidson
Great Horned Owl, Bubo virginianus	N. America	Eat-my-food, I'll-eat you	Burrows 2002:178
		Hoo, hoo-hoo, hoo Respell: who, who-who, who	Feith 2003a
		Pátkwatana tanínšin + (person's name) (Sahaptin) Arrowhead has eaten + (person's name)	Hunn 1991:140 & cited in Sarvasy 2016:775
		Who's awake? Me too!	Sarvasy 2016:774
Great Kiskadee, Pitangus sulphuratus	Caribbean	Ques-que'll-dit (French) What does it say?	Mona Williams (Personal communication)

English Name, Other Name (language) *Binominal name*	Location	Warblish (Language); Translation (Explanation)	Source Author YEAR: page #
Great Knot, *Calidris tenuirostris*	Americas	Chucker-chucker-chucker	King & Dickinson 1975:140 citing Wells
Great Tit, Talgoxe (Swedish), *Parus major*	UK	Pink pink	Thomas 2019:70
	Sweden	*Vintern tö, vintern tö* (Swedish) Winter thaw (bird appears in spring)	Abelin 2011:14
		Tittut-tittut-tittut-tittut I (Swedish) Peekaboo-peekaboo-peekaboo-peekaboo	Norudde 2009
		Var är du? (Swedish) Where are you?	Abelin 2011:14
		Whiskey, whiskey, whiskey	
		Här ska sååås, här ska sååås (Swedish) We're going to seed, we're going to seed (I would translate as "gonna seed, gonna seed" to mimic the syllable count)	Abelin 2011:14
		Edit (Swedish), Edit	Norudde 2009
		Kiss a shit!	Abelin 2011:14
		Kyss en skit! (Swedish) Kiss a shithead! (or kiss a useless bastard) (translated by Mikaela Nyman); *Just här* (Swedish) Right here!	Norudde 2009

English Name, Other Name (language) *Binominal name*	Location	Warblish (Language); Translation (Explanation)	Source Author YEAR: page #
... Great Tit ... continued ...	Sweden	*Titta hit titta hit, jag är gul och svart och vit* (Swedish) Look here look here, I am yellow and black and white	Abelin 2011:14
		Här ska såås, här ska såås, här ska såås ... (Swedish) Here will be sown, here will be sown, here will be sown ...	
Greater Coucal, *Centropus sinensis?*	India / Asia	Hoop hoop hoop hoop hoop	Kennedy et al. 2000:171
Greater Green-Billed Malcoha, *Phoenicophaeus tristis*	Burma	Cook ... Cook ... Cook	Smythies 1953:328
Greater Honeyguide, *Indicator indicator*	South Africa	VIC-tor, VIC-tor, VIC-tor	Barnes & Behrens 2017:111
Greater Racket-Tailed Drongo, *Dicrurus paradiseus*	Borneo	Tinkle-doo, tinkle-doo	Smythies et al. 1999:622
Greater Yellowlegs, *Tringa melanoleuca*	N. America	Dear dear dear Whew, whew, whew. Dear! Dear! Dear!	Feith 2003a Jonas 1999:6
Green Bee-Eater, *Merops orientalis*	Burma	Tree-tree-tree-tree (said while flying)	Smythies 2001:286
Green Catbird, *Ailuroedus crassirostris*	Australia	Here-I-are Heeere I aaaare	Pizzey 1980:390 Young 2003:3

English Name, Other Name (language) *Binominal name*	Location	Warblish (Language); Translation (Explanation)	Source Author YEAR: page #
Green Heron, *Butorides virescens*	N. America	Skew!	Feith 2003a
Green Pigeon, *Treron (genus)*	Congo	Oh well. Very well, getting rich, getting rich, that's so, that's so	Koopman 2018a:16 citing McLachlan & Liversidge 1978:233
Green Sandpiper, Черныш-кулик [Chernysh-kulik] (Russian), *Tringa ochropus*	Russia	Жгите сено, жгите сено, жгите сено! Новое поспело! [Zhgite seno, zhgite seno, zhgite seno! Novoye pospelo!] (Russian) Burn the hay, burn the hay, burn the hay! Newly ripened! (burn the old hay because the new hay is ready)	Bianki 2013:9
Green Willow Warbler, Пеночка-теньковка (Russian), *Phylloscopus nitidus*	Russia	Тё-тень-ка! Пе-ноч-ке День-день-ской Тень! [To-ten'-ka! Pe-noch-ke Den'-den'-skoy Ten'!] (Russian) Aunty! Give me all day-day shade!	Bianki 2013:10
		Тё-тень-ка! Пе-ноч-ке День-день-ской Тень! Тень! Тень! [To-ten'-ka! Pe-noch-ke Den'-den'-skoy Ten'! Ten'! Ten'!] (Russian) Aunty! Give me all day-day shadow! Shadow! shadow!	Bianki 2013:13
Green-Billed Malkoha, *Phaenicophaeus tristis*	Burma	Cook … cook … cook … co-co-co-co	Smythies 2001:252

English Name, Other Name (language) *Binominal name*	Location	Warblish (Language); Translation (Explanation)	Source Author YEAR: page #
Green-Faced Parrotfinch, *Erythrura viridifacies*	Philippines	Day day day; grey-grey-grey-ray-day-lay-grey	Kennedy et al. 2000:340
Grey-Backed Camaroptera Uboi (Zulu) Grey-Backed Bush Warbler *Camaroptera brevicaudata Camaroptera sundevalli* (old)	South Africa	Cock: *Boi, boi, boi baxaɓene, boi, boi, boi.* Hen: *baxaɓen* ×3 Cock: *Deda* ×6 (Zulu) Cock: *Boi, boi, boi,* they have quarrelled, *boi, boi, boi.* Hen: They have quarrelled ×3 Cock: Get out of the way ×3	Duning 1946:37
Grey Butcherbird, *Cracticus torquatus*	Australia	And if that's not lovin' me (like melody of the song Little Green Apples)	Young 2003:3
Grey Fantail, Guri Djugi (Kattang?), Djuri Djuri (Kattang) *Rhipidura albiscapa*	Australia	*Guri djuri, guri djuri, guri djuri* (Kattang) A black fellow is coming *Ju(wa)ng ju(wa)ng jalawalinj* (Kattang) Over there he is sitting *Djubinj bijai* (Kattang) You are deaf *Guri barai* (Kattang) A black fellow will come from . . . *Guri bara, guri bara, guri djuri* (Kattang) A man in the west, a man in the west, a man is coming soon	Holmer & Holmer 1969:38

English Name, Other Name (language) *Binominal name*	Location	Warblish (Language); Translation (Explanation)	Source Author YEAR: page #
... Grey Fantail ... *continued* ...	Australia	(Missing in source)	Holmer & Holmer 1969:38
		You are deaf, you don't listen to me. There is a spirit, a spirit is moving (if you ignore the bird this is what it says)	
		Gin buru, gin buru (Kattang) A woman from the north, a woman from the north	
Grey Go-Away Bird, *Corythaixoides concolor*	South Africa	Guuu-waaaay Respell: go-away	Barnes & Behrens 2017:86
Grey Jay, *Perisoreus canadensis*	N. America	Chuck chuck	Feith 2003a
Grey Partridge, *Perdix perdix*	N. America	Kuta-kut-kut-kut-kut Respell: cutter-cut-cut-cut	Burrows 2002:103
	Scotland?	Quick! Quick! Quick!	Sewell 2013:52
	UK	Ear-yuk	Thomas 2019:124
Grey Peacock Pheasant, *Polyplectron bicalcaratum bicalcaratum*	Burma	Trew-tree Respell: true-tree	Smythies 2001:166
Grey Wagtail *Motacilla cinerea*	UK	Zit-zit	Thomas 2019:87
Grey Warbler, Riroriro (Māori), *Gerygone igata*	NZ	You, you; you, you	Andersen 1926:51
		Cherrily, oh ye oh; ye oh; cherrily oh ye oh Cherrily, oh ye oh; ye oh; cherrily oh ye oh	Andersen 1926:55

English Name, Other Name (language) *Binominal name*	Location	Warblish (Language); Translation (Explanation)	Source Author YEAR: page #
... Grey Warbler ... *continued* ...	NZ	*Riro riro riro riro* (Māori) Gone gone gone gone	Andersen 1926:58-59
		I. Don't. Like. You.	Helen Mae Innes
		4, 3, 2, 1, hic!	
		Why don't you go get the fish and chips now and I'll go get the drinks and snacks now?	
		What are you doing sit-sit-sitting there?	
		What are you do-ing-ing-ing-ing-ing?	
		De.ar de.ar de.ar tee de.ar de.ar	Andersen 1926:51
Grey Whistler, *Pachycephala simplex*	Australia	One two three four five	Pizzey 1980:252
		Catch a fish alive	
		Tic tac toe	Young 2003:3
Grey-Headed Bush-Shrike, Ghost Bird, *Malaconotus blanchoti*	South Africa	Whhooooooo Who (sung sorrowfully)	Barnes & Behrens 2017:135
Grey-Headed Canary Flycatcher, *Culicicapa ceylonenis*	Asia	*Veni, vidi, vici* (Latin) I came, I saw, I conquered (Google translate)	King & Dickinson 1975:392 citing Smythies
		Silly billy	Smythies et al.1999:537
	Borneo	Sil-ly-bil-ly-me	
	Burma	Silly-billy	Smythies 1953:151

English Name, Other Name (language) *Binominal name*	Location	Warblish (Language); Translation (Explanation)	Source Author YEAR: page #
Grey-Headed Woodpecker, *Picus canus*	Eurasia	Too too too too	Bhattacharya 2019:82
Greylag Goose, Дикие Гуси [Dikiye Gusi] (Russian), *Anser anser?*	Russia	*Го-лод-но! Хо-лод-но!* [Go-lod-no! Kho-lod-no!] (Russian) Nothing to eat! Too cold!	Bianki 2013:12
Grey-Sided Laughingthrush, *Garrulax caerulatus*	Asia	Oh dear dear	King & Dickinson 1975:313 citing Smythies
Guan, *Penelopinae* (subfamily)?	Brazil	*Niri-niri-niri* (Guanano) (unclear exactly what the words are but the children turn into Guans then complain that their mother scolds them with these words)	Aikhenvald 2003:46 & 123
Guineafowl, *Numididae* (family)	Sudan Baggara	*El shamis iza kuwirat, el nuğum iza inkaderat ...* (Chadian Arabic?) (From the Koran? Warning of the/a day of doom)	Owen 1947:193
		Suraj, suraj (Chadian Arabic?) (name of king; Baggara tribe; they tired of their king and sent him away, but after ruling themselves they decided they wanted their king back and went through the forest calling his name)	

English Name, Other Name (language) *Binominal name*	Location	Warblish (Language); Translation (Explanation)	Source Author YEAR: page #
Hadada Ibis, Black Ibis, Hadadah (Afrikaans?), iNkankane (Zulu), *Bostrychia hagedash*	South Africa	*Ngahamba, ngahamba, ngahamba* (Zulu) I travel, I travel, I travel	Bulpin 1966:27
		Cock: *Ngahamba, ngahamb, ngahamba* ×3 (Zulu) Cock: I (have) travelled, I (have) travelled, I (have) travelled. ×3	Dunning 1946:52
Hairy Woodpecker, *Dryobates villosus*	N. America	Peck	Feith 2003a
		Keep, keep, keep	Saunders 1951:76
Hamerkop (Afrikaans?), Hammerhead Crane/Stork, uThekwana (Zulu), Utekwane (Zulu), *Scopus umbrette*	South Africa	*Nga ngi ba ngi muhle; ng'oniwa I loku na loku* (Zulu) I should be beautiful, but I am spoiled by this and by this (bird points at the ugly parts of its body)	Callaway 1868:140
	South Africa	*Thekwane, Thekwana, nganqimuhle kodwa ngoniwa yilokhu nalokhu* (Zulu?) *Thekwane, Thekwane,* I would have been a handsome chap but I am spoilt by this and that and that	Bulpin 1966:26–27
Helmeted Friarbird, *Philemon buceroides*	Australia	Poor devil, poor devil	Higgins 2001:534 citing Campbell & Barnard 1917
		Poor-devil	Pizzey 1980:318, 1997:372; Young 2003:3

English Name, Other Name (language) *Binominal name*	Location	Warblish (Language); Translation (Explanation)	Source Author YEAR: page #
Helmeted Friarbird, *Philemon buceroides*	Australia	Watch out, watch out	Higgins et al. 2001:534 citing Deignan 1964, Parker 1971
		Whack-a-where	Pizzey 1980:318, 1997:372
Hermit Thrush, *Catharus guttatus*	N. America	Chuck	Burrows 2002:240
		Treee	Field 2003a
		Why don't you come to me	Lorenzin 2011
		Why don't you come to me? Here I am right near you	
Herring Gull, *Larus smithsonianus*	N. America	Hiyah, hiyah, hiyah, hiyah	Jonas 1999:4
Hodgson's Hawk-Cuckoo, Horsfield's Hawk-Cuckoo, *Cuculus fugax*	Asia	Wheet wheet wheet wheet tu Respell: wheat wheat wheat wheat too	Kennedy et al. 2000:163
		Fe-ver OR gee-whiz (repeated) OR gee-whiz OR pee-weet	King & Dickinson 1975:182
	Asia, Burma	Gee-whizz, gee-whiu (repeated)	Smythies 1953:323
Honeyguide (family), *Indicatoridae* (family)	Southern Africa	Quick! Quick! Quick! Honey! Quick! Look! Look! Look! Oh! Person with wings, Look! Here I come!	van der Post 1961:64

English Name, Other Name (language) *Binominal name*	Location	Warblish (Language); Translation (Explanation)	Source Author YEAR: page #
Hooded Cuckooshrike, Kmn nmwd (Kalam) *Coracina longicauda*	PNG	*Namwd ymdŋ-o! Namwd kagm-o!* (Kalam) (The bird is warning the ymdŋ and kagm (local ring-tailed possums) that hunters are about.)	Majnep & Bulmer 1977:82
Hornbill, Kaywl (Kalam), *Aceros plicatus*	PNG	Female: *yad…yad…yad* (Kalam) Mine…mine…mine Male: *nak … nak … nak* (Kalam) Yours…yours…yours	Majnep & Bulmer 1977:132
Horsfield's Babbler *Malacocincla sepiarium*	Borneo	Tip, top, tiu	Smythies et al.1999:498
House Finch (Brown?) *Haemorhous mexicanus*	N. America	Which year is the year of the witch, which year?	Feith 2005
House Sparrow, Воробей [Vorobey] (Russian), *Passer domesticus*	Russia	Чуть жив! Чуть жив! [Chut' zhiv! Chut' zhiv!] (Russian) Just alive! Just alive!	Bianki 2013:10
	N. America	Chill-up	Burrows 2002:315
	NZ	Cheer up!	McEwen 2017
		Ouch /au/	Helen Mae Innes
		Out! Out! Out!	
	UK	What a distinguished stranger	Wilde 1909:13
	Australia	Cheerup; Respell: cheer up	Tracey et al. 2007:195

English Name, Other Name (language) *Binominal name*	Location	Warblish (Language); Translation (Explanation)	Source Author YEAR: page #
Hudsonian Godwit, *Limosa haemastica*	N. America	God-WIT!	Burrows 2002:127
Imbangaqhwe (Zulu) *Binomial?*	South Africa	Cock: *Mayebabo! Mayebabo; ngafa, ngafa, ngafa, iqhwa!* ×3 Cock: Oh my father! Oh my father! I died, I died, I died (with the) cold! (i.e., I am dying (perishing) with the cold!) ×3	Dunning 1946:48
Inca Dove, *Columbina inca*	N. America	No hope	Young 2003:3
Indian Cuckoo, Chinese Cuckoo, Vishupakshi (Malayalam), *Cuculus micropterus,*	China	豌豆包谷 [Wāndòu bāogǔ] (simplified Chinese) Pea and maize corn	Indian Cuckoo 2025
		快快割麥 [Kuài kuài gē mài] (simplified Chinese) Go to cut wheat	Indian Cuckoo 2025
		豌豆八哥 [wāndòu bāgē] (simplified Chinese) Myna of pea	Indian Cuckoo 2025
		不如归去 [Bùrú guī qù] (simplified Chinese) You should go home (evokes homesickness in hearer)	He et al. 2016:xv
		不如歸去 [Bùrú guī qù] (traditional Chinese) You should go home	Nic Wynne (Personal communication)
		不如歸去 [Bùrú guī qù] (simplified Chinese) Why not go home	Indian Cuckoo 2025

English Name, Other Name (language) *Binominal name*	Location	Warblish (Language); Translation (Explanation)	Source Author YEAR: page #
... Indian Cuckoo, ... *continued* ...	China	光棍好苦 [guānggùn hǎo kǔ] (simplified Chinese) Single, lonely	Indian Cuckoo 2025
		光棍好过 [guānggùn hǎoguò] (simplified Chinese) Single, happy	
		家婆打我 [jiāpó dǎ wǒ] (simplified Chinese) Mother-in-law beats me	
		阿公阿婆，割麦插禾 [āgōng ā pó, gē mài chā hé] (simplified Chinese) Grandpa, Grandma, cut wheat, transplant rice	
		滑哥煲粥 [huá gē bāo zhōu] (simplified Chinese) Catfish congee	
	India	*Ke:ta satto, makka keṭṭo* (Sholaga) *Ke:ta* died, his children cried (lit. Things were bad for his children).	Agnihotri & Si 2012:124, Indian Cuckoo 2025
		One more bot-tle! One more bot-tle!	Barnes 2004:76
		(original missing in source) Where is my sheep? (uttered by the soul of a dead shepherd)	Indian Cuckoo 2025
		Kallan chakkayittu Malayalam Thief stole jackfruit	

English Name, Other Name (language) *Binominal name*	Location	Warblish (Language); Translation (Explanation)	Source Author YEAR: page #
... Indian Cuckoo, ... continued	Vietnam, Mảng tribe	*Bắt cô trói cột* (Vietnamese) Take a woman and tie her to a post	Indian Cuckoo 2025
Indian Nightjar, *Caprimulgus asiaticus*	Burma	Took-took-took-irr-r-r-r	Smythies 2001:267
Indian Peafowl / Peacock, *Pavo cristatus*	NZ	Come back! Come back! Fuck off! Fuck off! Watch out! Watch out!	Helen Mae Innes
	N. America	May-awe!	Preston & Gower 2018:95 citing Carver
Indigo Bunting, *Passerina cyanea*	N. America	Spit	Burrows 2002:296
		Blue-blue, where-where, here-here, see-it, see-it	Kawasaki 2018:6
		Fire-fire, where-where, here-here, see-it, see-it	Burrows 2002:296
		Fire, fire, where, where, here, here	Sarvasy 2016:774
		Fire! Fire! Where?? Where??	Mosco 2017a
		Fire, fire, where, where, here, here	Feith 2003a
		Bean porridge hot, bean porridge cold, bean porridge in the pot, nine days old.	Roth 2012:81 citing Saunders 1951:244
Indochinese/Lesser Cuckooshrike, *Coracina / Lalage polioptera*	Burma	Three blind mice (same tune as Three Blind Mice)	Smythies 1953, 2001:365
Inornate Warbler, *Phylloscopus inornatus*	Asia	West	King & Dickinson 1975:360

English Name, Other Name (language) *Binomial name*	Location	Warblish (Language); Translation (Explanation)	Source Author YEAR: page #
Insindaphi (Zulu) Binomial nomenclature?	South Africa	Cock: *Nsindaphi, Nsindaphi, Duma, Duma, Duma.* ×3 (Zulu) Cock: *Nsindaphi, Nsindaphi*, sound (our fame) abroad, sound (our fame) abroad, sound (our fame) abroad. ×3	Dunning 1946:39
Jackdaw, *Coloeus (genus)*	UK	Jack! Jack!	Barnes 2016:63
Jacky Winter, *Microeca fascinans,*	Australia	Peter Peter-Peter	Pizzey 1980:245
Kaka, Kākā (Māori), *Nestor meridionalis*	NZ	Get out! Ge' ou' (sounds like a glottal stop instead of a "t" sound)	Helen Mae Innes
Kakapo?, Kākāpō? (Māori), *Strigops habroptila*	NZ	*Kia iro! Kia iro koe!* (Māori) Remember! Remember! Be you remembering your thrashing [Be patient! Be patient!: Google translate]	Andersen 1926:28 citing Colenso
Kentish Plover, *Charadrius alexandrinus*	Asia	Pick pick pick	Smythies et al. 1999:227
Kentucky Warbler, *Geothlypis formosa*	N. America	Here, here, here, turtle, turtle, turtle	Jonas 1999:13
Killdeer, *Charadrius vociferus*	N. America	Kill-dee kill-dee kill-deer	Burrows 2002:119
		Deer-deer	
		Killdeer killdeer	Feith 2003a

English Name, Other Name (language) *Binominal name*	Location	Warblish (Language); Translation (Explanation)	Source Author YEAR: page #
King Rail, *Rallus elegans*	N. America	Hip hip hurrah!	Young 2003:3
Klaas's Cuckoo, Meidjie (Afrikaans), *Chrysococcyx klaas?*	Tanzania	*Sayeika* (Wasambaa? Shambala?) Famine is coming	Koopman 2018a:19 citing Moreau 1940:55
Knysna Loerie, Golomi, *Tauraco corythaix*	Southern Africa	*Golomi, linda! Linda!* (Xhosa?) Lourie, wait, wait!	Wainwright 1983:298
Large-Billed Leaf-Warbler *Ohylloscopus magnirostris*	Asia	Dir-tee Respell: dir-ty	King & Dickinson 1975:361 citing Ticehurst
Large Hawk-Cuckoo, Hierococcyx sparverioides / *Cuculus sparverioides*	Asia, Philippines	Pi-peea (chirpish) Brain-fever	Kennedy et al. 2000:162
	Asia	Pi-pee-ha (chirpish; accent on 2nd note) Brain fe-ver	King & Dickinson 1975:181
	Asia, Burma	Brain-fever	Smythies 2001:246
Large-tailed Nightjar, N?kalo (Kaluli), *Caprimulgus macrurus*	PNG	*Nu de uu* (Kaluli) Grandmother bring firewood (sung in the evening when it's cooler)	Feld 2012:79
	Burma	Chock-a-chock	Smythies 2001:267
Lark, *Galerida* (genus)	Hungary	*Kicsi csűr!* (Hungarian) Little beak! (translator: Daisy Coles)	Ottó 1901:7

English Name, Other Name (language) *Binominal name*	Location	Warblish (Language); Translation (Explanation)	Source Author YEAR: page #
Laughing Dove, *Spilopelia senegalensis Stigmatopelia*	Kami, north Uluguru	*Kasongolela katuri* (Bantu?) Little have-a-*kinu*-carved (*kinu* = wooden mortar for pounding corn)	A. J. Moreau 1940:56
Laughing Gull, *Larus atricilla*	N. America	Ha-ha-ha-ha-ha-ha Ha-ha-ha-ha-ha-haah-haah	Burrows 2002:151 Jonas 1999:5
Leach's Petrel, *Oceanodroma leucorhoa*	UK	I'm a little Leach's, and I'm in my hole	Thomas 2019:
Leaden Flycatcher, *Myiagra rubecula*	Australia	See-hear, see-hear, see-hear	Pizzey 1980 :260
Leaf Warbler, Peñbyn, Majabyn, Najabyn (Kalam), *Phylloscopus trivirgatus*	PNG / Kalam	*Pen ñbyn-pen ñban-e* (Kalam) I give you (something), you give (something) back to me! *Maj-abyn-nep* (Kalam) I only go to the sweet potato plots	Majnep & Bulmer 1977:87
Least Bittern, *Ixobrychus exilis*	N. America	Poopoopoopoo	Feith 2003a
LeConte's Sparrow, *Ammospiza leconteii*	N. America	Crackers and cheese	Feith 2005
Lesser Coucal, *Centropus bengalensis*	Philippines	Hoop Tu-dut OR tu-dut-dut Respell: do-that or true-dat	Kennedy et al. 2000:171–172

English Name, Other Name (language) *Binominal name*	Location	Warblish (Language); Translation (Explanation)	Source Author YEAR: page #
Lesser Cuckoo, *Cuculus poliocephalus (intermedius)*	Africa, Asia	Pot-pot chip-chip-to-you Who-who-whar-who-who-wha	King & Dickinson 1975:184
		Play with me, play with me!	David Safonov-Innes (Personal communication)
Lesser Green Leafbird, *Chloropsis cyanopogon*	Sumatra Borneo	Mer-ry Christ-mas	King & Dickinson 1975:261
Lesser Grey Hornbill, Abu Mangur (Arabic?), *Lophoceros nasutus?*	Sudan / Baggara tribe	Call: *Şeif wa kharif ma dugtu ferik* (Chadian Arabic?) All summer and rains I've never had a ripe dura-head	Owen 1947:193
Lesser Yellowlegs, *Tringa flavipes*	N. America	You you	Feith 2003a
Levaillant's Cuckoo, Inkanku (Zulu), *Coccystes caffer* (old), *Clamator levaillantii*	South Africa	Cock: *Phezukwomkhono, phezukwomkhono, phezukwomkhono.* (Zulu) Cock: (Up) Above the arms (with the hoe). (Up) Above the arms (with the hoe). (Up) Above the arms (with the hoe). (i.e., he is announcing that it is time for everyone to commence sowing)	Dunning 1946:53
		Cock: *Khaula, khaula, khaula.* Cock: Terminate, terminate, terminate (i.e., finish off the work in the fields; the bird changes its cry in Autumn to this.)	Dunning 1946:54

English Name, Other Name (language) *Binominal name*	Location	Warblish (Language); Translation (Explanation)	Source Author YEAR: page #
Lewin's Honeyeater, *Meliphaga lewinii*	Australia	Week-week-week	Higgins et al. 2001:91 citing Eades
Little Bee-Eater, *Merops pusillus*	South Africa	S-lip	Barnes & Behrens 2017:98
Little Blue Penguin? Kororā (Māori), *Eudyptula minor*	NZ	Why?	L. Moon 2011:9
Little Crow, *Corvus bennetti*	Australia	Nark, nark, nark, nark Nark nark nark nark	Pizzey 1980:409 Tracey et al. 2007:140
Little Friarbird, *Philemon citreogularis*	Australia	Che-weep-will, che-weep-wil, che-weep-wil, che-weep. Respell: she-weep-will, she-weep-will, she-weep-will, she weep	Higgins et al. 2001:568
		I've-got-red-hair-air	Pizzey 1980:321 1997:372
		Ow, ow, don't pull my hair-air	Young 2003:3
Little Grey-Winged Partridge Inswepe (Zulu) Coqui Partridge, Francolin *Binomial?*	South Africa	Cock: *Khona ngigodola koɓa nani.* ×3 Hen: *Shesha nenja* ×3 (Zulu) Cock: Even if I am chilled (shivering) with the cold, what does it matter? ×3 Hen: Make haste with dogs ×3	Dunning 1946:35

English Name, Other Name (language) *Binominal name*	Location	Warblish (Language); Translation (Explanation)	Source Author YEAR: page #
... Little Grey-Winged Partridge ...*continued* ...?	South Africa	Cock: *Masishoshe* ×9 Hen: *Masilele KwaMtengele kunani?* ×3 (Zulu) Cock: Let us get along (i.e., get a move on with our journey) ×9 Hen: (Well) Even if we (have to) sleep at Mtengele's what will it matter? (*Ukushosha* means to go stooping. Or running along the ground as a bird)	Dunning 1946:35
		Cock: *Nswempe! Nswempe! Siyagodola, siyagodola. Siyolala kwaɓa? Siyolala kwaɓa.* ×3 (Zulu) Cock: Nswempe, nswempe, we are chilled with cold, we are chilled with cold. Whose place shall we sleep at? Whose place shall we sleep at? ×3	Dunning 1946:36
Little Owl, *Athene noctua*	UK	Hullooo Respell: hello (will say this as a greeting if you bid him 'Good day')	Sewell 2013:47
Little Raven, *Corvus mellori*	Australia	Car, car, car, car	Pizzey 1980:408
Little Ringed Plover, *Charadrius dubius*	Burma	Pink pink pink	Smythies 2001:194

English Name, Other Name (language) Binominal name	Location	Warblish (Language); Translation (Explanation)	Source Author YEAR: page #
Little Spiderhunter, Arachnothera longirostra	Philippines	Cheek-cheek-cheek	Kennedy et al. 2000:327
	S. E. Asia	Cheek-cheek	King & Dickinson 1975:419
Little Tern, Sternula albifrons	N. America	Kitty-kitty-kitty	Jonas 1999:7
Little Wattlebird, Anthochaera chrysoptera	Australia	Cooked-apple cooked-apple	Higgins et al. 2001:496 citing Keast 1993
		Get-up, get-up, wak, wak, keik-kewick, keik-kewick	Higgins et al. 2001:496 citing Mathews
		Clock	Higgins et al. 2001:497
		Fetch the gun, fetch the gun	Pizzey 1980:316; Young 2003:3
		Fetch the gun	Pizzey 1997:370
Long-Billed Corella, Cacatua tenuirostris	Australia	Cadillac, Cadillac	Higgins 1999:132 citing Tembly
Long-Tailed Cuckoo, Koekoeā (Māori), Urodynamis taitensis	NZ	*Ko o o e* (Māori) You(?); (also its name)	Andersen 1926:26
Long-tailed Manakin, Chiroxiphia linearis	Central America	*Toledo* (Spanish)	Young 2003:2

English Name, Other Name (language) *Binominal name*	Location	Warblish (Language); Translation (Explanation)	Source Author YEAR: page #
Louisiana Waterthrush, *Parkesia motacilla*	N. America	See you see you see you nice to meet you, chao	Feith 2005
MacGillivray's Warbler *Geothlypis tolmiei*	N. America	Sweeter, sweeter, sweeter, sugar, sugar	Mosco 2017b
MacLeay's Honeyeater, *Xanthotis macleayanus*	Australia	A free TV	Young 2003:3
Magnolia Warbler, *Dendroica magnolia*	N. America	Pretty pretty lady Sweeter, sweeter, sweetest	Burrows 2002:256 Feith 2003a
Magpie, *Gymnorhina tibicen*	Australia NZ	Waddle giggle gargle paddle poodle What I said to him, what I said was this. Quite a lot of artists want to doodle Quardle oodle ardle wardle doodle (chirpish)	P. Allen 1996:7 Helen Mae Innes Glover, 1964
Major Mitchell's Cockatoo, *Cacatua leadbeateri*	Australia	Creek-ery-cree	Higgins et al. 1999:159
Many-Coloured Barbet, *Megalaima rafflesi*	Asia	Took-took-took took-took	Smythies 1960:323
Marsh Tit, *Poecile palustris*	UK	Bee-bee-bee	Thomas 2019:
Masked Finch, *Poephila personata*	Australia	Twat, twat	Pizzey 1980:372
Masked Woodswallow, *Artamus personatus*	Australia	Chap chap	Pizzey 1980:393

English Name, Other Name (language) *Binominal name*	Location	Warblish (Language); Translation (Explanation)	Source Author YEAR: page #
Meadow Pipit, *Anthus pratensis*	UK	Sip sip sip sip sip sip Sip sip sip	Thomas 2019:121 Thomas 2019:52
Meadowlark, Eastern Meadowlark? *Sturnella* (genus)	N. America	[missing in source] (Sioux?); ("it would say an objectionable expression in bird talk/ say things to us that we did not care to hear") [missing in source] (Sioux?); ("it would call out a boy's name and say his mamma wanted him")	Standing Bear 1928:39
Merlin, *Falco columbarius*	N. America	Kikikikiki Respell: key key key key key	Feith 2003a
Mindanao Lorikeet, *Trichoglossus johnstoniae*	Philippines	Chick, chick-it OR twick-it (I think it sounds like bird swearing.)	Kennedy et al. 2000:154
Mistle Thrush, *Turdus viscivorus*	UK	You want to go? I let you go. So, go, go now go …	Thomas 2019:89
Mistletoebird, *Dicaeum hirundinaceum*	Australia	Swizit-swizit, weet-weet-switzit Respell: visit, visit, next week visit Wait-a-bit, wait-a-bit, zhipp! Wait-a-bit Pretty-sweet!	Pizzey 1980:357 Wheatbelt 2018:214
Mlele (Zulu) (A very small dove) *Binomial?*	South Africa	Cock: *Bengilele kwaSokhulu* (Zulu) ×3 Cock: I have been sleeping at Sokhulu's ×3 Cock: *Ngivela kwaCekwane* (Zulu) ×3 Cock: I have (just) arrive from Cekwane's. ×3	Dunning 1946:39

English Name, Other Name (language) *Binominal name*	Location	Warblish (Language); Translation (Explanation)	Source Author YEAR: page #
... Mlele ... *continued* ...	...	(Cekwane is a district in the Ixopo Division not far from Creighton and the Upper Umzimkulu River, called after a man of olden days of that name.)	...
Moorhen, *Rallidae (family)*	UK	Brook!	Thomas 2019:
Morepork, Boobook, Mopoke, Ruru (Māori), *Ninox novaeseelandiae*	Australia	More pork	Pizzey 1980:202
		Boo-book	
		Yo-yo-yo-Mor-mor-mor	
	NZ	More more more	Chambers 2007:114
		Morepork	Gunson, 2011:140
		Tut, tut	Marler 1956:53
		Ow, ow; Respell: how how	Marler 1956:54
Mountain Chickadee *Poecile gambeli*	N. America	Cheeseburger	Mosco 2017b
Mountain Mouse-Warbler, Kosp (Kalam), *Crateroscelis robusta*	PNG	We cc ye, we cc yeye (Kalam) (telling the game animals to go and hide; the hunters will shoot it if it sings this)	Majnep & Bulmer 1977:95
		Ñ-o ped-ok-ey ped-ok-ey (Kalam) Son, something is close by (i.e., telling people that there is a game mammal somewhere near)	

English Name, Other Name (language) *Binominal name*	Location	Warblish (Language); Translation (Explanation)	Source Author YEAR: page #
... Mountain Mouse-Warbler ... *continued* ...	PNG	Ñ-o mdp-ey mdp-ey (?) (kalam) Son, something is close by (i.e., telling people that there is a game mammal somewhere near)	Majnep & Bulmer 1977:95
		Ñ-o py-ok-ey py-ok-ey (Kalam) Son, something is close by (bird tells the hunter if game is nearby)	Majnep & Bulmer 1977:95; cited in Sarvasy 2016:776-777
		Ñ-o yj pls gp-ey, ñ-o yj pls gp-ey (Kalam) Son, now something is caught (bird tells hunter if something is in his traps)	
Mourning Collared Dove? Common Black-Collared Little Dove? *Streptopelia decipiens?*	Sudan / Baggara tribe	Bwodkarou, bwodkarou (Dinka/Thuɔŋjän?) 200 of 'em (litigant neighbours boast about having 200 cows in a dowry case)	Owen 1947:194
		Kheir gabl, kheir gabl, kheir gabl (Chadian Arabic?) It was better in the past	
Mourning Dove, *Zenaida macroura*	N. America	Oh-woe-woe-woe (sad, slow song)	Burrows 2002:175
		Hoo-la-hoop, hoop, hoop	Feith 2003a
		Where ARE you, you you? (exasperated tone of voice)	Helen Mae Innes
Mourning Warbler, *Geothlypis philadelphia*	N. America	Cheree cheree to meet you ("ya" not "you" on recording)	Feith 2003a
		Chury chury to meet you	Feith website version

English Name, Other Name (language) *Binominal name*	Location	Warblish (Language); Translation (Explanation)	Source Author YEAR: page #
Mugimaki Flycatcher, *Ficedula mugimaki*	Philippines	Chat chat chatter chat	Kennedy et al. 2000:292
Mulga Parrot, *Psephotellus varius*	Australia	Sweet-sweet	Wheatbelt 2018:115
Namaqua Dove Inkombose (Zulu) Long-Tailed Dove *Oena capensis*	South Africa	Cock: *Nkombose kababa! Majuba niyizithutha, ngoba ningena phansi kwetshe limi ngothi, angaze ngilibone itshe limi ngothi.* (Zulu) Cock: Nkombose, the son of my father, must say that you (other varieties of) pigeons are (an utter brainless set of) simpletons, because you enter under (beneath) a stone which stands supported by a twig. I have never seen a stone which stands supported by a twig (ordinarily, unless it has been designedly set and so supported, as a trap to catch one with). (The Inkombose is the only variety of pigeon dove family, which is not to be caught by the sort of trap described above, whereas most, if not all the other varieties of pigeons, dove and other birds are; hence his admonishing them for their stupidity and lack of caution.)	Dunning 1946:49
Nashville Warbler, *Vermivora ruficapilla*	N. America	Ti-ti-ti-ti Respell: tea	Burrows 2002:252

English Name, Other Name (language) *Binominal name*	Location	Warblish (Language); Translation (Explanation)	Source Author YEAR: page #
... Nashville Warbler, ... *continued* ...	N. America	See-it see-it see-it Seebit seebit seebit seeseesee Respell: see-a-bit see-a-bit see-a-bit see see see Dear, dear, too true!	Burrows 2002:251 Feith 2003a Jonas 1999:12
Natal Bush Partridge (old), Isikhwehle (Zulu), Coast Partridge, *Binomial?*	South Africa	Cock: *Siluthuli, siluthuli, siyaqumbisa, siqhub'uthuli Wawa.* ×3 (Zulu) Cock: We are dust, we are dust (as numerous as the dust. We cause (the stomachs) to swell (i.e., cause disturbances in the stomachs of those who kill us and eat us for food). We (raise the dust and) carry it along (before us as we go). He fell. ×3	Dunning 1946:37–38
Natal Grass Warbler, Uvusa (Zulu), *Binomial?*	South Africa	Cock: *Sahlupheka, sahlupheka, sahlupheka, ukuba kazijishona-nje, njengoba seɓeshis'isikhotha, thina esingenabafazi siyolalaphi?* ×3 (Zulu) Cock: We (have) suffered, We (have) suffered, We (have) suffered. As it (the sun) has not yet set (and also) because they (the people) have burned the grass on the Veld), we who have no wives (having lost them as well as the rest of our families and our nest through that cause) where are we to sleep?	Dunning 1946:50–51

English Name, Other Name (language) *Binominal name*	Location	Warblish (Language); Translation (Explanation)	Source Author YEAR: page #
New Guinea Friarbird, Bɔlɔ (Kaluli), *Philemon buceroides novaeguineae*	PNG	*Hɛ gɔ fɔn* (Kaluli) Where are my feathers? (bird is bald around the head and neck)	Feld 2012:77
		Dowo, nɔwo (Kaluli) Mother, father (this bird and Brown Oriole (Oriolus szalayi) both say this because they are the dead children calling their parents)	Feld 2012:79
		Ninɛli monowo id alu nagalakɛ-o hɔɔ! (Kaluli) I just ate and my asshole really hurts, ha! (bird's call is in the late afternoon and dinner time; rude version)	Feld 2012:78-79
		Ninɛli monowo 'kufɔ hɔsulowo hɔɔ (Kaluli) I just ate and my belly is really full, ha! (bird's call is in the late afternoon and dinner time; polite version)	Feld 2012:79
		Hɔ, hɔ, Gigio ku genelɔ! (Kaluli) Gigio has a red cock! (other names can be substituted)	Feld 2012:78

English Name, Other Name (language) *Binominal name*	Location	Warblish (Language); Translation (Explanation)	Source Author YEAR: page #
... New Guinea Friarbird ... *continued* ...	PNG	*Ku genelɔ!* (Kaluli) Red cock! (Kaluli men reply "wɛfɪo, kɔm!" = "shut up, retard!" Or "towɔ dabɛno mobiakɛ!" = "we're unwilling to listen to your talk.")	Feld 2012:78
		Ku halaidɔ (Kaluli) Hard cock! (The Kaluli men reply "wɛfɪo, kɔm!" = "shut up, retard!" Or "towɔ dabɛno mobiakɛ!" = "we're unwilling to listen to your talk".)	
New Zealand Fantail, Pīwakawaka, Piwaiwaka (Māori), *Rhipidura fuliginosa*	NZ	Tip te ti ti ti tip te tia tia tia Respell: tip the tea tea tea, tip the tier tier tier	Andersen 1926:26
		Tei! Tei! Tei! (Māori warblish or English chirpish?) If Māori then could refer to Pāteke (*Anas chlorotis*) or could translate as "to be".	
		Ti! Ti! Respell: Tea! Tea! Twee_dle_a twee_dle_a	Andersen 1926:27 citing Colenso
		Fi fi fi Respell: fee fee fee, or free free free Pretty creature, pretty creature	Andersen 1926:23

English Name, Other Name (language) Binominal name	Location	Warblish (Language); Translation (Explanation)	Source Author YEAR: page #
... New Zealand Fantail ... continued	NZ	Cheet Respell: cheat	G. Moon 1967:12
		I'm gonna catch you catch you catch, catch you catch you catch; (in flight, while hawking insects) Stranger come! Stranger; stranger! Stranger! Strangler! Strangler! Strangler! Strangler! Gurgle! (silence) (sounds like its being strangled)	Helen Mae Innes
Nightingale? Thrush Nightingale? Соловей [Solovey] (Russian), *Luscinia megarhynchos* (Common Nightingale)? or *Luscinia luscinia* (Thrush Nightingale)?	Russia	*Мужик, мужик. Сало. Пёк, пёк, пёк! Тянул, тянул - тррр! Ешь, ешь, ешь, Гор-рячо!* [Muzhik, muzhik. Salo. Pok, pok, pok! Tyanul, tyanul - trrr! Yesh', yesh', yesh', Gor-ryacho!] (Russian) Man, man. Fat. Pek, Pek, Pek! He pulled, pulled - trrr! Eat, eat, eat, Wow!	Bianki 2013:8
Nightjar, uZavolo, Savolo (Zulu), Night Hawk, Whip-poor-will, Goatsucker, *Caprimulginae* (subfamily)?	South Africa	*Ndakhe ndaya! / Ndakhe ndaya! / Ndee tyibilili! / Ndadlula, nde thendele! / Yiza nengubo leyo, sambathise le ntothololo! / Ethe induku leyo, ndibethe le ntothololo!* (Zulu) I once went / I once went / And I slipped - *tyibilili!* / I passed by and I slipped - *thendele!* / Bring that blanket and let's wrap this useless thing up! / Bring that stick so that I can thrash this little rubbish!	Wainwright 1983:301

English Name, Other Name (language) *Binominal name*	Location	Warblish (Language); Translation (Explanation)	Source Author YEAR: page #
... Nightjar ... *continued* ...	South Africa	Cock: *Savolo, Savolo, sengel'abantabami* ×3 (Zulu)	Dunning 1946:42
		Cock: Savolo, Savolo, milk (the cows) for my (i.e., our) family ×3	
		Zavolo, Zavolo, sengel' abantabakho (Zulu?) Zavolo, Zavolo, milk for your children	Bulpin 1966:27
		Zavolo! Sengela abantu bakho! (Zulu) Nightjar! Milk for your people!	Wainwright 1983:300
Noisy Friarbird, *Philemon corniculatus*	Australia	Yodelchuck	Higgins et al. 2001:553 citing McFarland 1994
		Keyhole	Hannah Tysoe (Personal communication)
		Keyhole, keyhole	Pizzey 1980:320
		More soldier	
		Poor soldier	Hannah Tysoe (Personal communication); Pizzey 1997:372
		Tobacco	
		Tobacco, tobacco	Pizzey 1980:320
		Four o'clock	Pizzey 1980:320; Tracey et al. 2007:155
Noisy Miner, *Manorina melanocephala*	Australia	Pee, pee, pee	Pizzey 1980:323

English Name, Other Name (language) *Binominal name*	Location	Warblish (Language); Translation (Explanation)	Source Author YEAR: page #
… Noisy Miner … *continued* …	Australia	Weedidit Respell: we did it Shrill!	Pizzey 1980:323 Pizzey 1985:90 citing Richard Howitt
Noisy Pitta, *Pitta versicolor*	Australia	Walk-to-work (heard in spring and summer, not winter) Walk to work	Higgins et al. 2001:97 citing Beruldsen & Uhlenhut 1995 Pizzey 1980:219; Young 2003:2
Northern Bobwhite, *Colinus virginianus*	N. America	Come-right-here … Come-right-here (birds call this until the flock is back together)	Young 2012:36
Northern Cardinal, *Cardinalis cardinalis*	N. America	What cheer! What cheer! Birdie-birdie-birdie what cheer What cheer, what cheer, cheer cheer cheer	Burrows 2002:293 Feith 2003a
Northern Flicker, *Colaptes auratus*	N. America	Kick-kick-kick-kick-kick-kick Rapid, loud laughing Flicka flicka; Respell: Flicker	Burrows, 2002:196 Dormon 1969:64 Burrows 2002:244
Northern Mockingbird, *Mimus polyglottos*	N. America	Chair (mimicking other birds) Pretty, pretty, pretty Eat-it-all, eat-it-all, eat-it-all	Jonas 1999 Jonas 1999:8

English Name, Other Name (language) *Binominal name*	Location	Warblish (Language); Translation (Explanation)	Source Author YEAR: page #
Northern Parula, Parula, Northern Warbler, *Setophaga americana*	N. America	Zip	Burrows 2002:253
		Da-da-da-that's all folks	Feith n.d.
		Da-da-da-da-that's all folks	Roth 2012:79
Northern Rough-Winged Swallow, *Stelgidopteryx serripennis*	N. America	Trip trip	Feith 2003a
		Trip trip trip trip trip trip	Feith 2003b
Northern Waterthrush, *Parkesia noveboracensis / Seiurus noveboracensis*	N. America	Nice old ladies don't chew chew	Feith 2003b
		Nice old ladies don't chew	Feith n.d., Sarvasy 2016:774
		Sweet sweet sweet, swee wee wee, chew chew chew chew	Burrows 2002:270
Olive-Sided Flycatcher, *Contopus cooperi*	N. America	Quick, three beers (courtship song)	Burrows 2002:198; Young 2003:2
		Quick, three beers!	Feith 2003a; Sarvasy 2016:774
		Quick! Three beers	Young 2012:22; Mosco 2017b
		Quick, free beer	Young 2003:2
		Pick up the beer check quick	
		Quit whee deeah Respell: quit VCR	Saunders 1951:92

English Name, Other Name (language) *Binominal name*	Location	Warblish (Language); Translation (Explanation)	Source Author YEAR: page #
Olive Whistler, *Pachycephala olivacea*	Australia	Pee-sweet Respell: pea-sweet	Pizzey 1980:249
		Peee-pooo; Pooo-peee	
		Tu-wee-e-tchow Respell: so we eat chow	
Orange-Breasted Bushshrike, *Chlorophoneus sulfureopectus*	South Africa	What-to-toooo-dooo	Barnes & Behrens 2017:134
Orchard Oriole, *Icterus spurius*	N. America	When the green gets back in the tre-ees	Dormon 1969:39
Oriental Pratincole, *Glareola maldivarum*	Burma	To-wheel, to whee	Smythies 2001:217
Ovenbird, Golden-Crowned Thrush, *Seiurus aurocapilla*, *Seiurus aurocapillus*	N. America	Teacher, teacher	Mosco 2017a
		Teacher teacher teacher	Feith 2003a
		Teacher, teacher, teacher, teacher	Jonas 1999:14
		Teacher, TEACHER, TEACHER	Young 2003:3
		Teacher, teacher, TEACHER, TEACHER, TEACHER	S. Mathews 1921:199 citing Burroughs
		Tea-cher tea-cher tea-CHER tea-CHER	Burrows 2002:269
Owl, Strigiformes (order)	Russia	Сплю! Сплю! Солнца нет, а свет - не люблю! Всё сплю, сплю ... [Splyu! Splyu! Solntsa net, a svet - ne lyublyu! Vso splyu, splyu ...] (Russian)	Bianki 2013:6

English Name, Other Name (language) Binominal name	Location	Warblish (Language); Translation (Explanation)	Source Author YEAR: page #
... Owl ... continued ...	Russia	Sleeping, sleeping! No sun, but I don't like the light! I sleep all the time.	Bianki 2013:6
		Шубу-у! [Shubu-u!] (Russian) Fur coat!	Bianki 2013:9
	N. America,	O-ko'-ko-ko-o' (Ojibwe or Chippewa?) Afraid	Cooke 1884:246
Painted Finch, Painted Firetail, *Emblema pictum*	Australia	Chek-dod-did-dit Respell: check-dog-did-it	Pizzey 1980:389
Painted Honeyeater, *Grantiella picta*	Australia	Geor-gie OR Georg-EEE OR sue-see Respell: Suzy	Higgins et al. 2001:994
Palm Warbler, *Dendroica palmarum*	N. America	Check	Burrows 2002:264
		Sup (slang: short for "what's up?")	Burrows 2002:264
Paradise Riflebird, *Ptiloris paradiseus*	Australia	Y-a-a-ss Or yass yass	Pizzey 1980:391
Paradise Shelduck, Pūtangitangi (Māori), *Tadorna variegata*	NZ	I knooooooow! I knoooooow!	Helen Mae Innes
Pearl Spotted Owlet? Nkovana (Zulu), Owl, *Glaucidium perlatum*	South Africa	*Woza, woza, woza ngikubone* (Zulu) Come, come, come that I may see you	Adjaye 1994:132

English Name, Other Name (language) *Binominal name*	Location	Warblish (Language); Translation (Explanation)	Source Author YEAR: page #
Pheasant-Tailed Jacana, *Hydrophasianus chirurgus*	Burma	Sewn, sewn, sewn	Smythies 2001:191
Philadelphia Vireo, *Vireo philadelphicus*	N. America	Look-up way-up tree-top see-me	Burrows 2002:209
Pied Avocet, *Recurviostra avosetta*	Africa, Asia	Chuck, chuck, chuck, hawy	King & Dickinson 1975:147 citing Smythies
Pied Chat, Wlmeñ (Kalam), *Saxicola caprata*	PNG / Kalam	*B nak ok asaw nep yj yj wkñ?* (Kalam) This man of yours is coming, shall I tell him your name or not?	Majnep & Bulmer 1977:81
		"You answer the bird, '*Mnm nak apan yk manŋbyn-o, kab Kon kab ptg pwg-gp yj yj wkaŋ*' [yes, you speak but I don't hear, speak again and say his name properly and I shall hear the big River Kon (Jimi) pounds noisily on the rocks and I don't hear, say the name again and I shall hear.' Then the bird tells you the name. If it calls out the name of a distant relative who live in the Asai or the Simbai, it means that person is coming, so you tell your family to prepare food. But if it just calls the name of a rock or a tree, you may bring it is warning you of a witch. However, there are times when it will clearly call the name of an enemy, for example the name of the leader of an enemy group. And if you are travelling away from home, *wlmeñ* may bring messages about you, to your family. A bird will tell my mother in Kaironk when i get back to Port Moresby, from this trip. / It is the ghost of a dead father or dead brother who appears as this bird and gives you messages." you should not kill or eat this bird. Majnep & Bulmer 1977:112	

English Name, Other Name (language) Binominal name	Location	Warblish (Language); Translation (Explanation)	Source Author YEAR: page #
Pied Currawong, Strepera graculina? or Strepera versicolor? or Strepera fuliginosa?	Australia	Crik crik bewair!	Pizzey 1980:400
		Currar-awok-awok-currar Respell: hurrah-a-wok, a-wok, hurrah	
		Crook crook beware	Pizzey 2000:59
Pied Wagtail, Motacilla alba yarrellii	UK	Chiswick flyover (flight call)	Thomas 2019:83
Pied-Billed Grebe, Podilymbus podiceps	N. America	Cow, cow, cow, cowp, cowp Respell: cow, cow, cow, kelp, kelp	Feith 2003a
		Kuk-kuk-cow-cow-cow-cowp-cowp. Respell: cook-cook-cow-cow- kelp-kelp	Pied-Billed Grebe 2025 citing Fisher & Morlan 1996:19
Pigeon, Wild Pigeon, Pigeon, Dove, Bush Dove, iJuba (Zulu?), isiKhombazane (Zulu?) Columbidae (family)	South Africa	*Amdokwe avuthiwe* (Zulu?) The kaffir corn is ripe (this bird described as "enemy of the African corn-wife")	Bulpin 1966:27
		Ngibe ngiyazalele lapho, ngithathelwe; ngibe ngiyazalele lapho, ngithathelwe, ngize ngiwe inhliziyo yami ithi to-to-to-to- (Zulu?) Whenever I lay eggs I get robbed of them; whenever I lay eggs I get robbed of them, until my heart goes to-to-to-to- (wistful call)	
Pink-Footed Goose, Anser brachyrhynchus	UK	Wink-wink	Thomas 2019:

English Name, Other Name (language) Binominal name	Location	Warblish (Language); Translation (Explanation)	Source Author YEAR: page #
Plaintive Cuckoo, Cacomantis merulinus	Philippines	Way-to-weep (followed by) pee pee pee pee . . . Pee pee pee pee . . .	Kennedy et al. 2000:165
Pomarine Jaeger, Stercorarius pomarinus	N. America	Which-yew Weak, weak	Burrows 2002:148
Prong-Billed Barbet?, Semnornis frantzii	Costa Rica	Ha ha	Young 2003:5
Prothonotary Warbler, Protonotaria citrea	N. America	[text missing in source] (speaks language of Chitimacha Indians of Southwest Louisiana)	Dormon 1969:43
		Sweet sweet sweet	Feith 2003a
Ptarmigan, Lagopus (genus)	UK	Here comes the bride (lyrics to song)	Thomas 2019:27
Puff-Throated Babbler, Pellorneum ruficeps	India, China	To meet you	King & Dickinson 1975:294
		Pretty dear	Symthies 1953:21-22,
Purple Martin, Progne subis	N. America	Chew	Feith 2003a
Purple-Gaped Honeyeater, Lichenostomus cratitius	Australia	Twit-twit	Wheatbelt 2018:153
		Too-whip	Wheatbelt 2018:154
Quail, Coturnix pectoralis	Philippines	Wet my lips	Chadd & Taylor 2016:58
Quail? or Brown Quail? Coturnix ypsilophora	N. America	Rise and run	Dormon 1969:76

English Name, Other Name (language) Binominal name	Location	Warblish (Language); Translation (Explanation)	Source Author YEAR: page #
Quail, Isigwaca (Zulu), Binomial?	South Africa	Cock: *bobodla, bobodla, bobodla* ×3 (Zulu) Cock: You must roar, you must roar, you must roar.	Dunning 1946:55
Rainbow Pitta, *Pitta iris*	Australia	To-walk-to-work Walk-to-work	Higgins et al. 2001:121
		Want-a-whip	Higgins et al.2001:121 citing MacDonald 1973
Raven, Common Raven? *Corvus corax*	N. America	Nevermore; (from the poem The Raven)	Poe 1898
Razorbill, Lesser Auk, *Alca torda*	N. America	Hey Al!	Jonas 1999:5
Red-Backed Shrike? Red-Winged Bush Shrike Umngquphane (Zulu) *Lanius collurio?*	South Africa	Cock: *Uyitshitshi ini na Tshovo?* ×3 (Zulu) Cock: Are you then a young girl Tshovo? ×3	Dunning 1946:37
Red-Bellied Pitta (now 10 species),*Pitta erythrogaster, Philippine pitta, Erythropitta erythrogaster?*	Australia	Walk-to-work	Higgins et al.2001:98 citing Beruldsen & Uhlenhut 1995
Red-Bellied Woodpecker, *Melanerpes carolinus*	N. America	Sure	Feith 2003a

English Name, Other Name (language) *Binominal name*	Location	Warblish (Language); Translation (Explanation)	Source Author YEAR: page #
Red-Billed Hornbill (Maybe Northern Red-Billed Hornbill?) *Tockus erythrorhynchus?*	Sudan / Baggara tribe	Response: *T'akul um batn, t'akul um batn* (Chadian Arabic?) All you'll get is gripes (Response to call by African Grey Hornbill/Lesser Grey Hornbill: '*Şeif wa kharif ma dugtu ferik*' [All summer and rains I've never had a ripe dura-head])	Owen 1947:194
Red-Breasted Nuthatch, *Sitta canadensis*	N. America	Yank-yank-yank	Burrows 2002:224; Jonas 1999:12
		Ink, ink, ink	Feith 2003a; Mosco 2017b
Red-Browed Pardalote, Kwarlpatelkalyelkalye (Kaytetye) *Pardalotus rubricatus*	Australia	*Artweyetherre apelaperrane* (Kaytetye; an Arandic language) Two ritual avengers are walking past	Turpin et al. 2013:26
		(Missing in source) Stranger coming (or similar phrase)	Turpin et al. 2013:26 & in Sarvasy 2016:775
Red-Capped Parrot, *Purpureicephalus spurius*	Australia	Getacheck OR checkacheck Respell: get-a-check OR check-a-check	Wheatbelt 2018:112
Red-Capped Plover, *Charadrius ruficapillus*	Australia	Poo-eet Respell: poet	Wheatbelt 2018:32
Red-Capped Robin, *Petroica goodenovii*	Australia	*Guniibuu* (Yuwaalaraay Gamilaraay) Mum the testicles / mum the balls ... *continued* ...	Giacon 2013:258

English Name, Other Name (language) Binominal name	Location	Warblish (Language); Translation (Explanation)	Source Author YEAR: page #
... Red-Capped Robin ... continued ...		... continued ... Call sounds like name. 'Name means "mum the testicles" there's a story to go with it. Author questions the accuracy of the onomatopoeia: "It may be that onomatopoeic accuracy suffers when the name has to be analysable, entertaining or memorable, as well as onomatopoeic." The young bird asks for the kangaroo testicles his mum is cooking saying "gunii-buu" glossed "mum-the balls"'. Giacon 2013, p. 270.	
Red-Chested Cuckoo, iNkanku (Zulu?) Piet-My-Vrou (Afrikaans) *Cuculus solitarius*	South Africa	Piet-my-wife (According to internet Piet can be a nickname for a Boer, or a magpie, or a gossip/talkative person)	Barnes & Behrens 2017:87
		It will rain	
		Piet-my-vrou (Afrikaans) Red-chested woman	Michael Weber (Personal communication)
		Phezukomkhono (Zulu?) On your shoulder (announced the approach of spring with ... thus telling the tribesmen to put their hoes on their shoulders and be off to the fields)	Bulpin 1966:27
		Khawula, khawula (Zulu?) End the word, end the work (with the approach of autumn the same bird changed its cry to ...)	
	Tanzania, , Pangani	*Semchocho* (Bondei, a Bantu language) Deluge chap (calls in heavy rain i.e., *chocho*)	A. J. Moreau 1940:56

English Name, Other Name (language) *Binominal name*	Location	Warblish (Language); Translation (Explanation)	Source Author YEAR: page #
... Red-Chested Cuckoo ... *continued* ...	Kenya	*Ngwikia ku* (Gikuyu: a Bantu language) Where do I sow the seed?	Muiruri & Maundu 2010:287 in Sarvasy 2016:777
		Mbaikia ku (Meru: a Bantu language) Help me put the load of firewood onto my back [to take home]	
Red-Eyed Vireo, *Vireo olivaceus*	N. America	Here I am! Don't you see me? Well, why don't you?	Dormon 1969:33
		Fish'll bite today-ee!	Dormon 1969:34
		Here I am, over here, vireo	Feith 2003b
		Here I am, over here, in the tree, look up, vireo, at the top, where are you?	
		You see it, you hear it, you know it, you feel it, what of it?	Jonas 1999:12
		Fat worms ... plenty to eat ... Gobble 'em up ... they're sweet ... Come dear ... don't delay ... Fly this way ... I'm here!	S. Mathews 1921:152
		Tom-Kelly ... whip-Tom-Kelly!	S. Mathews 1921:152 citing Wilson Flagg
		Where are you? And here I am	South Bay Birders n.d.
		Here I am. Where are you?	Young 2003:3
		Where are you? Here I am. I am here.	Mosco 2017a

English Name, Other Name (language) *Binominal name*	Location	Warblish (Language); Translation (Explanation)	Source Author YEAR: page #
Red-Headed Honeyeater? Or Red-Headed Myzomela? *Myzomela erythrocephala*	Australia	Chewy chewy	Hannah Tysoe (Personal communication)
Red-Headed Woodpecker, *Melanerpes erythrocephalus*	N. America	Queer!	Feith 2005
	N. America	Queer, queer	Young 2003:3
Red Knot, Lesser Knot, Huahou (Māori), *Calidris canutus*	N. America	Knut. Respell: Canute	Burrows 2002:129
	S. E. Asia	Knot	King & Dickinson 1975:138
	NZ	Poor-me poor-me	Chambers 2007:251
Red-Legged Crake, *Ralina fasciata*	Philippines	Gogogogogo (loud staccato)	Kennedy et al. 2000:70
Red-Lored Whistler, *Pachycephala rufogularis?*	Australia	See-saw-sik Respell: see-saw-sick See saw	Pizzey 1980:249
Red-Necked Stint, *Calidris ruficollis*	Burma	Week-week-week	Smythies 2001:205
Redthroat, Red-Throated Scrubwren, *Pyrrholaemus brunneus*	Australia	A-pitta-pitta-pit Respell: a-bit-a-bit a-bit	Pizzey 1980:296
Red-Throated Woodpecker Quarrler, Usibagwebe (Zulu) *Binomial?*	South Africa	Asibagwebe, asibagwebe, asibagwebe, sithathe amathunjwana, siwathi khahla, badlele ogageni. ×3 (Zulu) ... continued ...	Dunning 1946:34

English Name, Other Name (language) *Binominal name*	Location	Warblish (Language); Translation (Explanation)	Source Author YEAR: page #
… Red-Throated Woodpecker Quarrler *… continued …*	…	*… continued …* Let them try them, let them try them, let them try them (the grasshoppers, etc.) and take (their) little bowels (including the heart, liver, lungs, etc.) and throw them down with a clattering sound (so that) they (other birds) may eat (that meat) from the carcase. ×3	…
Red Wattlebird, *Anthochaera carunculata*	Australia	Cook	Higgins et al. 2001:474
		Yak	Pizzey & Knight 1997:370
		Chock	Pizzey & Knight 1997:370; Tracey et al. 2007:166
		Tobacco box	Souter 2004:90; Tracey et al. 2007:166; Wheatbelt 2018:74
		What's o'clock	Tracey et al. 2007:166
		Chock-a-lock	Wheatbelt 2018:074
Red-Wattled Lapwing, *Vanellus indicus*	Burma	Did he do it, pity to do it	Smythies 2001:197
Red-Winged Blackbird, *Agelaius phoeniceus*	N. America	Check!	Jonas 1999:15
		Gonhorrheaaa, gonhorrhea (from a poem)	Budhwar 2019:50

English Name, Other Name (language) *Binominal name*	Location	Warblish (Language); Translation (Explanation)	Source Author YEAR: page #
... Red-Winged Blackbird ... *continued* ...	N. America	*O-ka-lee, kong-quer-ree, You-choo tea, Oolong tea! Gl-oogl-eee, Conk-a-ree, Quang-se tea, Shoo-chong tea!* (Chinese & English) (Mathews combines warblish from Thoreau, Emerson, Mr Chapman, Gibson, etc. into one call. According to Nic Wynne (Personal communication) from Taiwan, these are ALL names of types of tea	S. Mathews 1921:54
		Okalee, conkaree, youchoo tea, oolong tea (Chinese & English)	Roth 1998:54
Red-Winged Parrot, *Aprosmictus erythropterus*	Australia	*Ching ching*	Pizzey 1980:174
		Chink chink	Pizzey 1980:175
Redwing Partridge, Indendele (Zulu & Xhosa), Redwinged Francolin? *Scleroptila levaillantii*?	Southern Africa	*Nkwenkwe, yinja! Thafa lenkciyo! Gaga lenkciyo! Eli thafa lenkciyo! Dadadethu! Gogo lenqilo! Nqilo! Nqilo! Gogo lenqilo!* (Xhosa & Zulu) Boy, it's a dog! / Click here! / Gaga sentence! / This plateau! / My sister! / Granny bitch! Stop! / Granny bitch! (Google Translate)	Wainwright 1983:302
Red-Winged Tinamou, *Rhynchotus rufescens*	Brazil	*Eu, nunca mais* (Portuguese) Me, never again	Cocker 2013:13 citing Sick 1993:100
		Call and response. The two birds had been best friends but after an argument the red-winged went to the "open sunlit grasslands" and the undulated tinamou went to the dark forest. The undulated tinamou later regretted their falling out and ... *continued* ...	

English Name, Other Name (language) *Binominal name*	Location	Warblish (Language); Translation (Explanation)	Source Author YEAR: page #
... Red-Winged Tinamou *... continued ...*	*... continued ...*	said mournfully, *vamos-fazer-as-pazes* (shall we make peace?) (4 notes) The red-winged tinamou responded with *Eu, nunca mais* (me, never again).	
Reichenow's Melidectes, Nol (Kalam), *Melidectes rufocrissalis*	PNG / Kalam	*Ss kyan kyan* (Kalam) Urine you-pass you-pass	Majnep & Bulmer 1977:61
		Two birds with same call - see *Belford's melidectes* 'when we hear this, we think rain will soon be comin'; 'they are very noisy birds'; 'These two are very similar, and their calls are the same, but you can tell them apart' by the bill's colour and length. Their names are their calls. The warblish is one of their other calls. Interestingly it is the second bird to call in the morning, which makes me think the urine call is apt as people urinate when they wake in the morning.	
Rifleman, Titipounamu (Māori), *Acanthisitta chloris*	NZ	Zit zit zit zit	Chambers 2007:107
Ring-Necked Dove, Cape Turtle/Half-Collared Dove, Ijuba (Zulu), *Streptopelia capicola*	Africa (?)	*Werk stadig, werk stadig* (Dutch) Work steadily, work steadily	Koopman 2018a:16 citing McLachlan & Liversidge 1978:228
		How's father, how's father	
	South Africa	*Makhulu ngiphe isidudo* ×3 (Zulu) Grandmother give me (an) inspiration ×3	Dunning 1946:38–39
		(Isidudo/inspiration = encouragement or advice & she is asking her grandmother to dip into the vast store of knowledge and experience of her girlhood days, and to give her advice and inspiration which will enable her to outshine other women and girls in attractiveness to marry a chief or man of distinction or eminence)	

English Name, Other Name (language) *Binominal name*	Location	Warblish (Language); Translation (Explanation)	Source Author YEAR: page #
Riverside Wren, *Cantorchilus semibadius*	Costa Rica	Male: victory / we-do-it / victory / we-do-it; 'the slashes represent places where the male slows down to allow the female to join in a duet'	Young 2003:3
Rock Pigeon, *Columba livia*	NZ	Bruuu brruu brruuu brruu Respell brew brew brew brew	Chambers 2007:93
	Hungary	*Van borunk! Van borunk!* (Hungarian) We have wine! We have wine! (Call is answered by duck "only on the tap" x2.)	Ottó 1901:7 (translated by Daisy Coles)
Rockwarbler, Cataract-Bird, Cavebird, *Origma solitaria*	Australia	Goodbye, goodbye, goodbye (melancholy)	Pizzey 1980:291; Souter 2004:90
Rose Robin, *Petroica rosea*	Australia	Dick dick did it	Hannah Tysoe (Personal communication)
		Dick, dick-didit-deer-deer Respell: dick did it, dear dear	Pizzey 1980:238
Rose-Breasted Grosbeak, *Pheucticus ludovicianus*	N. America	Chink (metallic sound)	Feith 2003a
		Cheer-up; cheer-a-lee; cheer-ee-o Respell cheer up, cheerily, cheerio	South Bay Birders n.d.
Ruby-Crowned Kinglet, *Regulus calendula*	N. America	Tea-tea-tea-tew-tew look-at-Me, look-at-Me, look-at-Me	Burrows 2002:232

English Name, Other Name (language) *Binominal name*	Location	Warblish (Language); Translation (Explanation)	Source Author YEAR: page #
Rufous Shrikethrush, Little Shrikethrush, *Colluricincla rufogaster (Colluricincla megarhyncha)*	Australia	Eeee, butch-butch-butcher Cup of tea, wot-wot-wot	Pizzey 1980:254
Rufous Treepie, *Dendrocitta vagabunda*	Burma	Bob-a-link	Smythies 2001:355
	Indian subcontinent & S. E. Asia	টাকা চোর [*Taka chor*] (Bengali) Coin thief / money thief	Ali & Ripley 1983:216-221
Rufous-Browed Peppershrike, *Cyclarhis gujanensis*	Costa Rica	I'm-a-ru-fous-pep-per-shrike	Young 2003:3
Rufous-Sided Towhee (now Eastern & Spotted Towhee), *Pipilo erythrophthalmus & Pipilo maculatus*	N. America	Drink your teeee Respell: drink your tea	Schmalz n.d.
Rufous-Tailed Tailorbird, *Orthotomus sericeus*	Philippines	To-wee-to-wee-to-wee	Kennedy et al. 2000:281
	S. E. Asia	Kon-ti-ki, kon-ti-ki	King & Dickinson 1975:370
Sacred Kingfisher, Kōtare (Māori), *Halcyon sancta / Todiramphus sanctus*	NZ	Ki-ki-ki-ki Respell: key-key-key-key	Chambers 2007:71
		Weet-weet-weet-weet Weet - archaic 'to know'	Crowe 2007:28

English Name, Other Name (language) *Binominal name*	Location	Warblish (Language); Translation (Explanation)	Source Author YEAR: page #
Sanderling, *Calidris alba*	N. America	Kip (said in flight, perhaps when tired?) Quit kit!	Burrows 2002:130 Jonas 1999:6
Sandstone Shrikethrush, *Colluricincla woodwardi*	Australia	Peter!	Pizzey 1980:254
Satin Flycatcher, Satin Sparrow, Shining Flycatcher *Myiagra cyanoleuca*	Australia	Weir-to-weir-to-weir (weir = dam)	Pizzey 1980:261
Savannah Sparrow, *Passerculus sandwichensis*	N. America	Tea tea tea teeeeea today Take, take, take it easy	Burrows 2002:282 Feith 2003a
Scaled Quail, *Callipepla squamata*	N. America	Paark! Pe-cos; Pe-cos; Pe-cos Respell: park! Because because because	South Bay Birders n.d.
Scaly-Crowned Babbler, *Malacopteron cinereum*	Borneo	Zip, zip, zip-zip OR wit, wit-wit, wit-wit-wit	Smythies et al.1999:500
Scarlet Robin, *Petroica multicolor*	NZ	Pee...pee...pee Plink! ... Plink! ...plink! Respell: blink!	Williams 1976:92
Scarlett-Rumped Trogon, *Harpactes duvanaucelii*	Burma	Too-too-too	Smythies 2001:278
Schlegel's Whistler, Konds (Kalam), *Pachycephala schlegeli*	PNG / Kalam	*Tw pc pc* Axe chop chop (this is a sign of good weather; he is telling people to work at clearing their gardens.)	Majnep & Bulmer 1977:84 (via Sarvasy)
Sedge Wren, *Cistothorus stellaris*	N. America	Chat chit chat chachachachacha	Feith 2003a

English Name, Other Name (language) *Binominal name*	Location	Warblish (Language); Translation (Explanation)	Source Author YEAR: page #
Semipalmated Plover, *Charadrius semipalmatus*	N. America	Chewy, chewy	Feith 2003a
Semipalmated Sandpiper, *Calidris pusilla*	N. America	Cherk Respell: jerk	Burrows 2002:131
Sharp-Tailed Sandpiper, *Calidris acuminata*	Australia, Asia	Chew /Wheep Respell: weep	King & Dickinson 1975:141 citing Keith 1967:196-200
Sharp-Tailed Sparrow (now 2 species: Nelson's S.T.S. & Saltmarsh S.T.S.), *Ammodramus nelsoni* & *Ammodramus caudacutus*	N. America	Please hush	Feith 2005
Shining Cuckoo, Shining Bronze-cuckoo, Pipi-wharauroa (Māori), *Chrysococcyx lucidus*	NZ	*Kui, kui, whiti whiti ora!* (Māori) (demigoddess' name), Live, live, life! (from a story; Google translate)	Andersen 1926:26
Short-billed Dowitcher, *Limnodromus griseus*	N. America	Toodulu Respell: toodeloo (bye) / (toodeloo is possibly from French à tout à l'heure "see you soon")	Burrows 2002:140
Short-Billed Pigeon, Dos Tontos Son (Spanish), *Patagioenas nigrirostris*	Central & South America	Who-COOKS-for-YOU *Dos TON-tos SON* (Spanish) They are two fools	Young 2003:2

English Name, Other Name (language) *Binominal name*	Location	Warblish (Language); Translation (Explanation)	Source Author YEAR: page #
Silver-Crowned Friarbird, *Philemon argenticeps*	Australia	More tobacco, uh, more tobacco, uh	Higgins et al. 2001:542; Pizzey 1980:319
Silvereye, Tauhou (Māori), *Zosterops lateralis*	NZ	Why-ey-ey-ey	Marler 1956:46
Singing Honeyeater, *Lichenostomus virescens*	Australia	Cr-rook, cr-rook Put, put	Higgins et al. 2001:745
Slaty Monarch, Slaty Flycatcher, *Mayrornis lessoni*	Fiji	Ratch-tatch-tatch-tatch-tatch Respell: catch-catch-catch-catch-catch (a better call for a flycatcher)	Clunie 1984:100
Small Natal Bush Dove, Usikombazana (Zulu), *Binomial?*	South Africa	*Ngabengazalele, babathatha abantabami, ngezwa inhlizizyo yami ithi Ndo, Ndo, Ndo, Ndo, Ndo,Ndo,Ndo, Ndo.* (Zulu) And it happened (eventually that) I bore them (children) and they took (them) my children (away and) I felt my heart say (saying), *Ndo, Ndo, Ndo, Ndo, Ndo, Ndo, Ndo.* Hen: *Ngazalwa ngingedwa kwasekufa uɓaɓa, kwasekufa umami, inhlizyo yami waseyithi To, To, To, To, To, To, To.* (Zulu) Hen: I only was born (i.e., only child) then (my) father died then (my) mother died (and) my heart (then began to cry) To, To, To, To, To, To.	Dunning 1946:51

English Name, Other Name (language) *Binominal name*	Location	Warblish (Language); Translation (Explanation)	Source Author YEAR: page #
Smith's Fantail-Warbler?, Ungceda, (Zulu), Inncethe (Zulu), *Cisticola aberrans?*	South Africa	Cock: *Qashi lami* ×9 (Zulu) Cock: My Tick ×9 (This bird when killed by the herd-boys is always found to have a live tick on the top of its head and in the above cry, he is singing the praises of his inseparable companion, the tick, who not only shares all his joys, but his sorrows as well.	Dunning 1946:38
Snipe, Бекас [Bekas] (Russian), *Gallinago genus*	Russia	Пеки, пеки, пеки, пеки - Бз-зз-ззз! [Peki, peki, peki, peki - Bz-zz-zzz!] (Russian) Bake, bake, bake, bake bzzz	Bianki 2013:12
		А ну купи купи купи Бз-зз-ззз! [A nu kupy kupy kupy be-ee-eee!] (Russian) Well, buy, buy, buy, b-b-b-b-b	Bianki 2013:13
		Теки, теки, теки, теки, ручей, ме-елень-кий! [Teki, teki, teki, teki, ruchey, me-yelen'-kiy!] (Russian) Trickle, trickle, trickle, trickle, creek, shallow!	Bianki 2013:8
Sombre Greenbul, Sombre Bulbul, *Andropadus importunus*	South Africa	Willie! Come out and play with me, sca-a-ared	Barnes & Behrens 2017:170
	Southern Africa	Willie, come and have a fight, sca-a-a-a-red	Koopman 2018a:16; Maclean 1985:501

English Name, Other Name (language) *Binominal name*	Location	Warblish (Language); Translation (Explanation)	Source Author YEAR: page #
Song Sparrow, *Melospiza melodia*	N. America	Maids maids maids pick up the tea kettle kettle kettle	Young 2003:2 citing Richard Walton
		Maids, maids, maids, put on your tea kettle-ettle-ettle	Feith 2003b; Sarvasy 2016:774
		Maids put on your teakettle	Feith 2003a
		Sweet, sweet, sweet, towee	Burrows 2002:284
		Welcome to Campton, tra-la-la-la-la lay	S. Mathews 1921:112
		Welcome to Campton's flow'ring meadows gay	S. Mathews 1921:113
		God be with you 'til me meet a—	S. Mathews 1921:114
		Call: Wail, wail, fickle wife is she, flown away and left me! Response 1: Sad, sad, what a tale of sorrow, she may return tomorrow; Response 2: True, true, very true you see, she's come again to live with me	S. Mathews 1921:117–118
		Fitz! Fitz! Fitz! Wee sir-wee sir-wits wits!	S. Mathews 1921:118
	Australia	Pres-pres-pres-by-ter-ri-an	Lobb 2019:80
Song Thrush, Певчий дрозд [Pevchiy drozd] (Russian), Taltrast (Swedish), *Turdus philomelos*	NZ	Go back, go back, is it him, is it him, is it him …? Who-dunnit, who-dunnit Respell: who done it, who done it?	N. Allen 2012:161 Frame 1957:7
		Did you do it? Did you do it? I saw you. I saw you	Crowe 2007:29

English Name, Other Name (language) Binominal name	Location	Warblish (Language); Translation (Explanation)	Source Author YEAR: page #
... Song Thrush ... continued ...	UK	Bob bob bob bob bob ... jennifer jennifer jennifer jennifer ... nigel nigel nigel ... bob bob bob	Compare the Marsh Tit 2012
		Can you see me? Can you see me? Up here, up here, up here high, high, high, high, high I'm very high indeed in the tree	Thomas 2019:88
	Russia	Пришла весна! Всем, всем, всем! Ликуй, ликуй, ликуй! Все! [Prishla vesna! Vsem, vsem, vsem! Likuy, likuy, likuy! Vse!] (Russian) Spring came! Everyone, everyone, everyone! Rejoice, Rejoice, Rejoice! All!	Bianki 2013:10
	Sweden, Jämtland	Ta e 'kaku, ta e 'kaku sputt ti koppen o bryt i', bryt ii (Swedish) Take a cookie, take a cookie, spit in the cup and dunk it, dunk it (translator: Mikaela Nyman)	Norudde 2009
	Sweden	En tjyv, en tjyv, en tjyv.... (Swedish) "A thief, a thief, a thief ..."	Norudde 2009
		Tramp på du, du har långt hem ×2 (Swedish). Pedal on you, you have a long way home ×2	Norudde 2009
Karl worked as a boy a few miles from Ölme in Värmland (Sweden). The year could have been 1920. The last week in April the farmer was away over the weekend, so Karl was responsible for the cows being milked. After arranging everything in the barn on Saturday ... continued ...			

English Name, Other Name (language) *Binominal name*	Location	Warblish (Language); Translation (Explanation)	Source Author YEAR: page #
... Song Thrush ... *continued* ...		*... continued ...* evening, Karl cycled to his fiancée in Väse. As it got late, Karin thought it was as good that he stayed to get a few hours of sleep. Karl woke up awake and found that he had overslept by an hour. Of hell! Quick on with the clothes and on the bike. After a while, he was both sweaty and needed to piss, so jumped into a grove to relieve himself. That's when it happened. A bloody bird sat talking to him, "pedal on you, you have a long way home, pedal on you, you have a long way home". Karl was both cursed and (?). He threw some stones at the bird, and then continued on. (He told me this when I was 13 years old, in 1958. It wasn't until a few years later that I realized that the song thrush had sung to him)	
	Sweden, Norsjö, Västerbotten	1. *Kniv-tjuv, knivtjuv*. 3. *Bene-vitt, bene-vitt* (Swedish) 1. (bird) knife-thief, knife thief". 2. (boy) What colour was the shaft? 3. (bird) bone-white, bone-white A boy had stolen a knife. On the way home, a song thrush was stubborn by saying "knife-thief, knife thief". The boy started to get annoyed and asked, "What color did the shaft have?" And the bird continued "bone-white, bone-white". The boy then thought it best to turn around and put the knife back.	Norudde 2009
	Sweden	*Ja' ha' tappe en njiv; ja' ha' tappe en njiv. Hure sjein skjafte? Hure sjein skjafte? Bejnevitt, bejnevitt* (Swedish dialect from Vindeln, Västerbotten) I've dropped a knife, I've dropped a knife. What did the shaft look like? What did the shaft look like? Bone white, bone white.	Norudde 2009

English Name, Other Name (language) *Binominal name*	Location	Warblish (Language); Translation (Explanation)	Source Author YEAR: page #
... Song Thrush ... *continued* ...	Sweden	*Jag har tappat en kniv, Jag har tappat en kniv. Hur såg skaftet ut? Hur såg skaftet ut? Benvitt, benvitt* (translation of above dialect into standard Swedish I've dropped a knife, I've dropped a knife. What did the shaft look like? What did the shaft look like? Bone white, bone white.	Norudde 2009
		Är du skitnödig gå och skit, är du skitnödig gå och skit (Swedish) If you need to shit go and shit (translator: Google)	
		Är du skitnödig gå och skit, är du skitnödig gå och skit (Swedish) If you have the urge to poo, take a dump, if you have the urge to poo take a dump/shit (translator: Mikaela Nyman)	
		Metar du Ola, metar du Ola? Dra upp, dra upp, dra upp (Swedish) Are you fishing, Ola? Are you fishing, Ola? Pull it up, pull it up, pull it up! (translator: Google)	
		Metar du Ola, metar du Ola? Dra upp, dra upp, dra upp (Swedish) Are you angling, Ola, are you angling Ola? Pull it up, pull it up, pull it up!" (translator: Mikaela Nyman; refers to fishing with rod and line)	

English Name, Other Name (language) *Binominal name*	Location	Warblish (Language); Translation (Explanation)	Source Author YEAR: page #
... Song Thrush ... continued ...	Sweden	*Petter Erik, Petter Erik, Ska du meta fisk, ska du meta fisk? Fick du inget? Fick du inget? Tvitt fick du! Tvitt fick du!* (Swedish) Petter Erik are you going to angle fish, are you going to angle fish? Did you get nothing? Did you get nothing! You got nothing! (translator: Mikaela Nyman) / "Petter Erik are you going fishing, are you going fishing? Did you get nothing? Did you get nothing! You got nothing!" (translator: Google)	Norudde 2009
		Call: *Spänn för två, spänn för två.* Response: *Klyv'en, klyv'en* (Swedish) Call: Harness two (horses), harness two Response: Split it/him, split it/him (into two) (translator: Mikaela Nyman)	
		The farmer drove home timber in the spring forest. He had loaded on a lot and on an uphill the horse could not cope. Then came the song thrush with advice "harness two, harness two" i.e. Horses. The farmer had only one horse and he talked about it. The answer came lightning fast, "split him, split him!" i.e. Split the horse into two. Norudde 2009	
Sooty Terns, *Onychoprion fuscatus*	N. America	Wide-a-wake	Jonas 1999:3

English Name, Other Name (language) *Binominal name*	Location	Warblish (Language); Translation (Explanation)	Source Author YEAR: page #
South African Coly Mousebird inDhlazi (Zulu) *Colius Capensis*	South Africa	Nginonele pakati njengendhlazi (Zulu) I am fat inside like a mousebird (i.e., my feeling, thoughts, anger, or revenge, is [sic] not seen by you, but you may come to feel it – may be used as a threat, or of a person with a brooding, ill-feeling.)	Koopman 2018b:265 citing Bryant 1905:100
Southern Black-Backed Gull, *Larus dominicanus*	NZ	A ha! (English or Māori? Warblish or Chirpish?) (from a story)	Andersen 1926:26
Southern Fiscal, Fiscal Shrike, Butcher-bird Johnny Hangman, Iqola (Zulu) *Lanius collaris*	South Africa	See below Cock: *Goshi! Goshi! Dadi! Ngigwaz'uɓa? Ngigwaz'uɓa? Ngigwaz'uɓa? Ngigwaza kuɓo laɓo, mpela, mpela.* ×3, *Sanxokwe, Sanxokwe, Ngiyakuloɓola ngenkomo exaka, exaka* ×3, *Athamadoda aphuza utshwala aɓesedakwa, aɓesethath'izagila, azithi xakaxaka, xakaxaka, xakaxaka. Bengiphesheya kwoMdawane, ngudla umgidi omkhuku. Ngayiɓamba intakazana* ngayihlom'otini ekuseni kusasa. Ngaphinda Ngamɓamba Ungceda ekuseni kusasa. Ngamhlom'otini. Ngaliphuza igazi lenyoni ekuseni kusasa, Ngisishaye isiswana saɓomvana ngalelo xeshe, ngoɓa ngiyinkosi yezinyoni. Goshi! Goshi! Dadi! Dadi! Bayede! Bayede! Khuleka! Khuleka! Nkosi! Nkosi!* (Zulu) Cock: Goshi! Goshi! Dadi! Dadi! (Expressions used by this bird to describe the sounds made by the movements of his wings, feet and other parts of his body, as well as by the ejaculation uttered by him at his great displays Who do I (stab) kill? Who do I kill? Who do I kill? I kill the relations ... *continued* ...	Dunning 1946:44

English Name, Other Name (language) *Binominal name*	Location	Warblish (Language); Translation (Explanation)	Source Author YEAR: page #
...Southern Fiscal *... continued ...*		*... continued ...* (those of the kraals) of those (indicating his victims) outright! outright! ×3, (Addressing her Majesty he says) Sanxokwe, Sanxokwe, Sanxokwe, I'll pay your lobola, with a red beast ×3, When men drink beer, they become intoxicated, they take up their sticks and they (the sticks)clashing together sound xaka, xaka, xakaxaka, xakaxaka, xakaxaka, xakaxaka! I have been across (over the other side of) the Umdawene (a fabulous river or place, where) I ate up (the whole of) the big Dance (i.e., completely swept the board of all the prizes there). I caught a small bird (and) I fixed it on the end of a slender twig (or thorn) very early this morning. I repeated this (later) by catching a Fantail Warbler (also) early this morning and fixed it on the end of a slender twig (or thorn). I drank the blood of a bird early this morning, I struck (pierced) its little stomach (so that) it became red with blood at that very moment, because I am the King of Birds. Goshi! Goshi! Dadi! Dadi! Salute me Royally! Salute me Royally! Make obeisance (to me), make obeisance (to me) (Address me as) King! (Address me as) King! (Address me as) King!...	
	South Africa	See below:	Dunning 1946:44
		Cock: *Umfana kaGoloza phambanisa igwele. Nyama ihegazi angiyidli, inyoni ngihlomothini, ngingaze ngidle kusasa. Ngihlezi kaɓi ekhaya, kuyagulwa. Ngithathe izinduku zami ngihambe, Ngifike esangomeni, yathi inyanga umuthi ukusoGoloza, ukuthi ukugasa, ngashaya ngashaya kwathi kwesipansi ngashaya ngashaya kwesiphakathi ngashaya ngashaya kwathi kwesiphesulu ngashaya, ngashaya.* (Zulu) Cock: Son of Goloza (the Starer), mix some mealie-water (with the beer so that it may have a more exhilarating and exuberating effect.) Meat that is dripping (or covered) with blood, I don't eat. (As for) the bird, I fix it on to (the point or end of) a small (slender) *... continued ...*	

English Name, Other Name (language) *Binominal name*	Location	Warblish (Language); Translation (Explanation)	Source Author YEAR: page #
...Southern Fiscal ... *continued* ...		... *continued* ... twig (or thorn) so that I may eat it to-morrow. I am living in trouble (having a bad time), at home there being sickness there (consequently) I took my sticks and set off to divine (i.e., to consult the Diving Doctor). I arrived at his place and he said the right and (proper) medicine (for using in my case) was obtainable from Sogoloza (i.e., Goloza's father, the father of all Starers). I threw (and) I threw (the bones, etc.) and he (the Inyanga) with regard to the (further) concentration on and investigation into my matter, said (I was to proceed), (so) I threw (and) I threw and concerning (those of) of middle part (or the body) I threw (and) I threw; (and lastly) concerning (those of) the upper part of (the body) I threw (and) I threw.	
Southern Ground Hornbill, Ground Hornbill, Turkey-Buzzard iNsinqizi (Zulu), *Bucorvus leadbeateri*	South Africa	Female call: *Ngiyemuka, ngiyemuka, nqiya kwabethu*; Male response: *Hamba, hamba, kad'usho* (Zulu?) Female call: I am going away, going away to my people; male response: Go, go, you have been saying so for a long time (response by male; see call above)	Bulpin 1966:27
		Female call: *sengiyemuka, sengiyemuka; male response: hamba, kad' usho, hamba, kad' usho* (Zulu) Female call: I am going now, I am going now; male response: Go—you have long said so, Go—you have long said so	Koopman 1990:81

English Name, Other Name (language) *Binominal name*	Location	Warblish (Language); Translation (Explanation)	Source Author YEAR: page #
... Southern Ground Hornbill, ... *continued* ...	South Africa	Female call: *Ngi y' emuka, ngi y' emuka, ngi ya kwabetu'* Male response: *Hamba, hamba, kad' u tsho* (Zulu) Female call: I am going away, I am going away to my people Male response: Go, go. You have said so before	Callaway 1868:140
		Vumatiti (language?) (vuma = roar)	A. J. Moreau 1940:61
		Hen: *Iphi'iphi nyama?* ×2 Cock: *Ayikho, isemithini phezulu;* ×2 Hen: *Uphi, uphumsundu?* ×2 Cock: *Awukho, awukh'umsundu* ×2 Hen: *Awukho, awukho ini lapho na?* ×2 Cock: *Au! Saka! Ngizauthathaphi na?* ×2 Hen *Funa, funa khona lapho,* ×2 Cock: *Awukho, awukho lapho;* ×2 Hen: *Ngiyemuka, ngiyemuka, ngiye kwabethu,* ×2 Cock: *Hamba, hamba, kad'usho,* ×2 (Zulu) Hen: Where, where is (the) meat? ×2 Cock: There's none, it's up in the trees above. ×2 Hen: Where, where are the worms? ×2 Cock: There are none, there are no worms. ×2 ... continued ...	Dunning, 1946:32–33

English Name, Other Name (language) *Binominal name*	Location	Warblish (Language); Translation (Explanation)	Source Author YEAR: page #
... Southern Ground Hornbill, *... continued ...*	...	... continued ... Hen: Are there none, are there none over there? ×2 Cock: Oh! Get away with you! Where will I get them from? ×2 Hen: Look for them, look for them over there, ×2 Cock: There are none, there are none over there×2 Hen: I am going, I am going, I am going home to my people (parents) ×2 Cock: Go, go, you have long since said so. ×2	...
Southern Scrub-Robin, *Drymodes brunneopygia*	Australia	Did-you-eat?	Wheatbelt 2018:202
Southern White-Faced Owl? Large Black Owl, Southern uMandubulu (Zulu?) *Ptilopsis granti*	Africa, South Africa	*Vuka, vuka, sekusile* (Zulu) Get up, get up, it has dawned	Bulpin 1966:27; Adjaye 1994:132 citing Samuelson (n.d.)
Sparrow, *Passeridae family*	Russia	Чем? Чем? Чем? [Chem? Chem? Chem?] (Russian) With what? With what? With what?	Bianki 2013:5
Speckled Mousebird, Indlazi (Zulu), Common Coly, Muis-Vogel, *Colius striatus*	South Africa	Cock: *Liph'ibu? Liph'icimbi?* Hen: *Klee! Klee! Klee! Lisemsengeni, solidla kusasa.* (whole conversation ×3) (Zulu) ... continued ...	Dunning 1946:54–55

English Name, Other Name (language) *Binominal name*	Location	Warblish (Language); Translation (Explanation)	Source Author YEAR: page #
Speckled Mousebird, ... continued ...	...	... continued ... Cock: Where are the ibu (berries)? Where are the caterpillars? Hen: Ha! Ha! Ha! They are on the Umsenge (tree). We'll eat them to-morrow (Ibu berries are the berries of the Umsenge tree (*Cussonia spicata*) and are much eaten by the iziNdlazi and are used for catching them. The iCimbi is a large edible caterpillar, of which there are several kinds, all handsome, and is also much eaten by the IziNdlazi and is to be found frequently in the Umsenge tree. That variety of this caterpillar which frequents the Umtholo tree, is the finest and sweetest, with brilliant gold colours on the back.)	...
Spinifexbird, Desertbird, *Eremiornis carteri*	Australia	Cherrywheat (name of an American beer)	Pizzey 1980:275
Spiny-Cheeked Honeyeater, *Acanthagenys rufogularis*	Australia	Give the boy a go Give-the-boy-a-go (in-flight song, repeated, ending in a single abrupt note as bird closes whings and drops) Peer-peer, peer-peer	Hannah Tysoe (Personal communication) Pizzey 1980:317, Pizzey 1997:374 Pizzey 1997:374
Spot-Bellied Bobwhite, Spotted-bellied Bowhite?	N. & Central America	Rob-ert-white	Young 2003:2

English Name, Other Name (language) *Binominal name*	Location	Warblish (Language); Translation (Explanation)	Source Author YEAR: page #
Spotted Eagle-Owl, Iishihuluhulu (Xhosa), Isikhova (Zulu), *Colinus leucopogon*	South Africa	*Vuna! Thutha! / Vuna! Kuya vunwa! / Bulu! Kuya vunwa! / Kusizungu ukusebenza ngobusuku! (Xhosa?)* Reap! Carry away! / Reap! There is reaping being done! / Bulu! There is reaping being done! / It is lonely working by night!	Wainwright 1983:300
		Cock: *Phum'ungibule, Phum'ungibule, Phum'ungibule.* (Zulu) Cock: Come and beat (strike) me; some and beat me, come and beat me (if you consider I am making too much noise and you think you can beat me. I defy you to do so however.)	Dunning 1946:58
Spotted Nutcracker, Eurasian Nutcracker, Кедровка [Kedrovka] (Russian), *Nucifraga caryocatactes*	Russia	*Идём идём охотник идём [Idot idot okhotnik idot]* (Russian) (literal: goes goes hunter goes; figurative: coming coming a hunter's coming; bird warns other creatures; translator: Vladimir Safonov)	Vladimir Safonov (Personal communication)
Spotted Pardalote, Diamond Bird, *Paradalotus punctatus*	Australia	Sleep, deedee Sleepy-baby	Wheatbelt 2018:151
		Sleep-may-be	Pizzey 1980:358
		Tough titty	Young 2003:3
Spotted Sandpiper, *Actitis macularia*	N. America	Eat-wheat, eat-wheat, wheat-wheat-wheat-wheat	Burrows 2002:124

English Name, Other Name (language) *Binominal name*	Location	Warblish (Language); Translation (Explanation)	Source Author YEAR: page #
Spotted Towhee, (previously Eastern & Spotted Towhee), *Pipilo maculatus*	N. America	Drink your teeee	Schmalz n. d.
Stitchbird, Hihi (Māori), *Notiomytis cincta*	NZ	Pek pek pek Respell: peck peck peck	Chambers 2007:112
		See-zip	G. Moon 2018:124
Stock Dove, Skogsduva (Swedish), *Columba oenas*	Sweden	Ove, ove, ove (Swedish) A name	Norudde 2009; Abelin 2011:14
		Gå då! (Swedish) Then go!	Abelin 2011:14
		Du du som tog mina sju sju (Swedish) You, you, that took my two, two	
		Ja tu (Swedish) Me two	
		Du sju (Swedish) You seven	
		Du sju, ja tu (Swedish) You seven, me two (forest pigeon says to magpie)	Norudde 2009
		Skogis, skogis, skogis (Swedish) Woody, woody, woody	Abelin 2011:14

English Name, Other Name (language) *Binominal name*	Location	Warblish (Language); Translation (Explanation)	Source Author YEAR: page #
...Stock Dove, ... continued ...	Sweden	*Skogis, skogis, skogis ...* (Swedish) Forester, forester, forester	Norudde 2009
		Skogsduva = forest pigeon & *skogis* = forest ice, therefore = word play here, *skog* = forest, *is* = ice. Abelin translates as 'woody'; Mikaela Nyman says *lantis* is a person from a rural area so *skogis* might be someone from a forest, so maybe forester, or forest dweller	
	Finland, Helsinki	Du du, som tog mina sju sju, och gav dina tu tu (Swedish? Finnish?) You you, who took my seven seven, and gave your two two	Norudde 2009
		Variation of forest pigeon call from Brutuby in Vantaa outside Helsinki: "You you, who took my seven seven, and gave your tu." Then the pigeon complains about the crow who stole the seven eggs of the pigeon and gave his two instead	
	Sweden	Så kom, så kom (Swedish) Then come, come	Norudde 2009
		Stockdove, Collared Dove, & Common Wood Pigeon say the same thing but the number of repetitions of phrase mimics number of syllables in bird calls	Abelin 2011:14
	Sweden	Så kom (Swedish) Come then	
Striated Babbler, *Turdoides earlei*	Asia	Keep quiet	Smythies 1953:45-46
Striated Grassbird, *Megalurus palustris*	Philippines	Pit chu chu twrup twat-twat-twat-twat Respell: but you you twerp twat-twat-twat-twat	Kennedy et al. 2000:276

English Name, Other Name (language) *Binominal name*	Location	Warblish (Language); Translation (Explanation)	Source Author YEAR: page #
Striated Pardalote, Striated Parrot, *Pardalotus striatus*	Australia	Chip-chip	Castlemaine Bird List
		Pick-pick	
		Pick-it-up	Castlemaine Bird List, Pizzey 1980: 361, Wheatbelt 2018:152
		Pretty-de-Dick	Wheatbelt 2018:152
		Rigby dick	
		Ipenye-petyeme (Arrandic) Stranger coming	Turpin et al. 2013:19; & in Sarvasy 2016:775
Stripe-Breasted Wren, *Cantorchilus thoracicus*	Costa Rica	Male: SEE/me, little me/who's to SEE/me, little me (slashes represent places where the male slows down to allow the female to join in a duet)	Young 2003:3 citing Skutch & Stiles
Striped Honeyeater, *Plectorhyncha lanceolata*	Australia	Wheat peeler peeler	Hannah Tysoe (Personal communication)
		Chirp chirp cherry cherry	Higgins et al. 2001:526 citing North (n.d.)
		Free-wheat-peeler-peeler	Pizzey 1980:317
Stubble Quail, *Coturnix pectoralis*	Australia	Pippy wheat	Pizzey 1958:70
Sultan Tit, *Melanochlora sultanea*	S. E. Asia	Chip-tree-tree	Smythies 1953:16
		Cheery-cheery-cheery	King & Dickinson 1975:286

English Name, Other Name (language) Binominal name	Location	Warblish (Language); Translation (Explanation)	Source Author YEAR: page #
Sunda Bush Warbler, Cettia vulcania	Borneo	Witch-a-wee-cheee-wee	Smythies et al.1999:521
Superb Lyrebird, Menura novaehollandiae	Australia	Whisk whisk	Pizzey 1980:221
Swainson's Thrush, Catharus ustulatus	N. America	Oh, Aurelia will-ya, will-ya, will-yeee	Burrows 2002:239
		Run to your home hear me	Feith 2003a
		Run to your home hear me, hear me	Feith 2003b
Swainson's Warbler, Limnothlypis swainsonii	N. America	Deeta deeta-ship'-poor-will	Schmalz n.d.
		Look look look at me	Young 2003:3
Swallow, Ласточка [Lastochka] (Russian), Hirundinidae family	Russia	Пеки калачи, Жарь на печи Яи-ишенку! [Peki kalachi, Zhar' na pechi Yai-ishenku!] (Russian) Bake the bread, fry the eggs on the stove	Bianki 2013:12
Swamp Sparrow, Melospiza georgiana	N. America	Weet-weet-weet-weet Respell: wheat x4, or wit x4	Burrows 2002:287
Tawny-Breasted Honeyeater, Buff-Breasted Honeyeater, Xanthotis flaviventer	Australia, PNG, Indonesia	Which-witch-is-witch Respell: which witch is which?	Pizzey 1980:326
Temminck's Sunbird, Aethopyga temminckii	Borneo	Sheet, sheet, sheet	Smythies et al.1999:584
Tennessee Warbler, Oreothlypis peregrina	N. America	Take-a take-a take-a, swig swig swig, ch-ch-ch-ch-chug	Feith 2003b
		Take-take-take-a-swig swig swig chchchchug	Feith n.d.

English Name, Other Name (language) Binominal name	Location	Warblish (Language); Translation (Explanation)	Source Author YEAR: page #
Thrush, Turdidae family	Australia	Sweet pretty creature	Hannah Tysoe (Personal communication)
	Hungary	Kell-e dió fiú? (Hungarian) Do you need a nut, son? (translator: Daisy Coles) Szolgabiró! (Hungarian) Judge/magistrate (translator: Daisy Coles) Jó a biró! (Hungarian) The judge is good! (translator: Daisy Coles) Hunczut a biró! (Hungarian) The judge is insolent! (translator: Daisy Coles)	Ottó 1901:8
Thrush Nightingale, Näktergal (Swedish), Luscinia luscinia	Sweden	Coming up, coming up, coming up	Norudde 2009
Tit (family), Синица [Sinitsa] (Russian), Paridae family	Russia	Синь кафтан, синь кафтан! [Sin' kaftan, sin' kaftan!] (Russian) Blue caftan, blue caftan!	Bianki 2013:9
Tomtit, Miromiro (Māori), Petroica macrocephala	NZ	Te-oily-oily-oily-oh Respell: tea Olly Olly Olly oh Willoughby Willoughby	N. Allen 2012:164 Falla, Sibson, & Turbott 1966:200

English Name, Other Name (language) Binominal name	Location	Warblish (Language); Translation (Explanation)	Source Author YEAR: page #
Torresian Crow, Australian Crow, *Corvus orru*	Australia	Uk uk uk uk uk Ok ok ok ok ok	Tracey et al. 2007:140
Towhee, *Passerellidae family*	N. America	Drink your tee-e-e-	Dormon 1969:23
Tree Warbler, Sjweywey (Kalam), Sjwey (Kalam), *Gerygone ruficollis*	PNG / Kalam	*Dede-cy-o, dede-cy-o, laplap ceg-o* (1/3 call/response) (Kalam) Keep (your food) hidden (in the rocks where swiflets nest), keep it hidden, your skin is big, your body underneath all those feathers is very small)	Majnep & Bulmer 1977:87
	PNG / Kalam	*Sy wey wey, sy wey weym* (3/3 call/response) (Kalam) Secretly you eat, eat, secretly you eat, eat	Majnep & Bulmer 1977:87
	"Sjweywey has a number of different calls or songs. One is similar to that of the mmañp [smaller swiflets, especially *Collocalia esculenta*]. There is a story about this. Sjweywey and mmañp insulted each other. Sjweywey sang *"Dede-cy-o, dede-cy-o, laplap ceg-o"*, "keep (your food) hidden (in the rocks where swiflets nest), keep it hidden, your skin is big, your skin is big (but your body underneath all those feathers is very small)" The Swiflet replies, *"wog gy mañban, waty gy mañban, tap sy ok nep ñban"*, "you don't make gardens, you don't make fences, you just steal food and eat it". And the warbler called back, *"sy wey wey ...continued ...*		

English Name, Other Name (language) Binominal name	Location	Warblish (Language); Translation (Explanation)	Source Author YEAR: page #
... Tree Warbler ... continued ...		... continued ..., sy wey wey", "secretly you eat, eat, secretly you eat, eat", which has since been its name - the "j" sound is just put in to make it easier to say. When we hear them call, "dede-cy-o, laplap ceg-o, sy-wey-wey", it is a sign of fine weather."	
Tufted Titmouse, *Baeolophus bicolor*	N. America	Peter, peter, peter, peter	Feith 2003a
		Peter, peter, peter	Kawasaki 2018:8
		Here Peter-Peter-Peter	South Bay Birders n.d.
		Here	
		Here, here	Dunning 1946:53
Trumpeter Hornbill, Double-beaked Toucan, Ikunata (Zulu), *Bycanistes bucinator*	South Africa	Cock: *Kuwe, kuwe, kuwe* ×3 (Zulu) Cock: Towards you, towards you, towards you ×3 (i.e., the game (buck) is running in your direction) (N.B.—In a hunt where the bushes are surrounded by Natives and their dogs each in turn, when a buck of other animal breaks back and runs in another direction, those at the spot where it did so, shout "kuwe" (to you) in te direction of those to where it is running, to warn them to intercept and kill it.)	
Tui, Tūī (Māori), *Prosthemadera novaeseelandiae*	NZ	Yak-yak-yak, *ko ka ko* (is it saying "kōkako", the name of another bird?)	Marler 1956:52
		Nut-cracker	Andersen 1926:128
		Sweet, a longed boon (warblish or description?)	

English Name, Other Name (language) *Binominal name*	Location	Warblish (Language); Translation (Explanation)	Source Author YEAR: page #
...Tui ... continued ...	NZ	What I said was, I love you (The tui is a mimic and the warblish here and below seem to be the Tui mimicking the Bellbird.)	Helen Mae Innes
		What I said was, I won't go	
		What I said was, I hate you	
		I told you; I won't go! Shan't go!	
		This is the pits, the pits! Told you!	
		I. Will. Sing. Now. Sing now! Sing loud!	
		The time is now. To sing! Sing loud!	
		Sing slow. Then fast. Down low! Up high!	
		The tune is clear. Sing low! Up high!	
		I. Want. To. Sing. Down low! Up high!	
		Gawd .... I'm so bored	
Tundra Swan, *Cygnus columbianus*	N. America	Clue!	Feith 2005
Turkey, *Meleagris gallopavo?*	Russia	Hen: *А у меня шубы нет, нет, нет, нет!* [A u menya shuby net, net, net, net!] (Russian) And I don't have a fur coat, no, no, no!	Bianki 2013:4
Turkey, *Meleagris gallopavo?*	Russia	Hen: *Далеко-о идём!* ×2 [Daleko-o idom! ×2] (Russian) We are going far away! We are going far away!	Bianki 2013:4

English Name, Other Name (language) *Binominal name*	Location	Warblish (Language); Translation (Explanation)	Source Author YEAR: page #
... Turkey *... continued ...*	Russia	Poult: *И все босы!* ×2 [I vse bosy! ×2] (Russian) And all of us barefoot! And all of us barefoot!	Bianki 2013:4
		Poult: *Где сапог наберу?* ×2 [Gde sapog naberu? ×2] (Russian) Where could I pick up lots of boots? ×2	
		Tom: *Пообедать бы!* ×2 [Poobedat' by! ×2] (Russian) We want lunch! We want lunch!	
		Tom: *Куплю, куплю, куплю!* [Kuplyu, kuplyu, kuplyu!] (Russian) I will buy, I will buy, I will buy	
		Tom: *Балда, балда, балда!* [Balda, balda, balda!] (Russian) Fool, fool, fool (or stupid, stupid, stupid)	Bianki 2013:6
Twenty-eight Parrot, Australian Ringneck, *Barnardius zonarius*	Australia	Twenty eight, twenty eight, twenty eight	Hannah Tysoe (Personal communication)
Ugqotshane (Zulu) *Binomial?*	South Africa	Cock: *Ngizothi, nti, nti, nti, mawedelele.* ×3 (Zulu) Cock: I will say nti, nti, nti, to you (with a switch or slender stick such as a cane) if you continue being disobedient and insubordinate. ×3 (*Nti* is an adverbial expletive *... continued ...*	Dunning 1946:38

English Name, Other Name (language) Binominal name	Location	Warblish (Language); Translation (Explanation)	Source Author YEAR: page #
... Ugqotshane ... *continued ...?*	...	... *continued* ... denoting the sound caused by the contact of a switch with the body of the person being whipped.)	...
Ujenga (Zulu), *Binomial?*	South Africa	Cock: *Sekuyikho, sekuyikhoo, sekuyikho.* (Zulu) Cock: That's the very thing, that's the very thing, that's the very thing (i.e., That's the very thing the boys are talking about (discussing) now, that they are just about to pelt us with their throw-sticks.)	Dunning 1946:56
Undulated Tinamou, *Crypturellus undulatus*	Brazil	*Vamos-fazer-as-pazes* (Portuguese) Shall we make peace? Call and response. The two birds had been best friends but after an argument the red-winged went to the "open sunlit grasslands" and the undulated tinamou went to the dark forest. The undulated tinamou later regretted their falling out and said mournfully, *vamos-fazer-as-pazes* (shall we make peace?) (4 notes) The red-winged tinamou responded with *Eu, nunca mais* (me, never again).	Cocker 2013:13 citing Sick 1993:100
Upland Sandpiper, *Bartramia longicauda*	N. America	Whip-whee-ee you Respell: whip-will-you Quip-ip-ip	Burrows 202:124 Burrows 202:125
Ural Owl, *Strix uralensis*	Estonia	*Uhu, kas tüdrukud kodu* (Estonian), Uhu (chirpish) Are the girls at home? OR Uhu. Are the girls going home?	Bhattacharya 2019:43 citing Jüssi 2007:63

English Name, Other Name (language) *Binominal name*	Location	Warblish (Language); Translation (Explanation)	Source Author YEAR: page #
Varied Honeyeater, *Lichenostromus versicolor*	Australia	Be quick, be quick	Higgins et al. 2001:756
		Go-bidger-roo	Pizzey 1980:330
		Which-way, which-way-you-go	
		Get-your-whip	
		Hear-hear	
Variegated Fairy-Wren, *Malurus lamberti*	Australia	Seeeee Respell: see	Higgins et al. 2001:317 citing Schodde
		Tiin Respell: tin	
Vesper Sparrow, *Pooecetes gramineus*	N. America	Here-here there-there, everybody-down-the-hill	Burrows 2002:281
		Here, here, where, where? All together now	Feith 2003a Feith n.d.
		Here-here-where-where	Feith 2003b
		Here-here; where-where; all-together-down-the-hill	South Bay Birders n.d.
		Listen to my evening sing-ing-ing-ing	Mosco 2017b
Warbling Vireo, *Vireo gilvus*	N. America	When I see you I will squeeze you, and I'll squeeze you till you squirt	Feith n.d.; Feith 2003b
		When I see you /you will squirt	Feith 2003a
		If I could see one, I would seize one, and would squeeze one, till it squirts	Kawasaki 2018:12 citing Allen
		If I SEE you, I will SEIZE you, and I'll SQUEEZE you, till you SQUIRT	Kawasaki 2018:12 citing Proctor 2016
		First you seize it, then you squeeze it, then you please it, 'til it squirts.	Hannah Sarvasy (personal communication)
		Brigadier; brigadier; briga-tee	South Bay Birders n.d.

English Name, Other Name (language) Binominal name	Location	Warblish (Language); Translation (Explanation)	Source Author YEAR: page #
Wedge-Tailed Eagle, Bunjil, *Aquila audax*	Australia	Pseet-you pseet you Respell: beseech you?	Pizzey 2000:60
Wedge-Tailed Pigeon, *Treron sphenura*	Asia	Why, we want cheer, what are we waiting for?	King & Dickinson 1975 :168 citing Smythies
Weebill, *Smicrornis brevirostris*	Australia	I'm a weebill	Wheatbelt
Weka, *Gallirallus australis*	NZ	Wheat	L. Moon 2011:17
Western Bristlebird, Brown/Long-Billed Bristlebird, *Dasyornis longirostris*	Australia	Chip-pee-tee-peetle-pet: Respell: "chippie, tea, kettle, pet" or "chippie, tea, petal, pet" (in northern England 'pet' and 'petal' are terms of endearment)	Pizzey 1980:290
Western Meadowlark, X̱wix̱wił (Sahaptin), *Sturnella neglecta*	N. America	(missing in source) (Sahaptin) (sings taunting phrases)	Hunn 1991:143 Sarvasy 2016:775
		(missing in source) (Secwepemc) (advises on planting biscuit root)	Sarvasy 2016:775 citing Ignace & Ignace
		Chup; tree; took	Saunders 1951:296
Western Wattlebird, *Anthochaera lunulata*	Australian	I've got the hiccups	Higgins et al. 2001:506 citing Davies (n.d.)
		Cook-cook-cup-hook, cook-cook-cup-hook	Wheatbelt 2018:175
		Cook-cackle, cook-cackle, cook-cackle	

English Name, Other Name (language) *Binominal name*	Location	Warblish (Language); Translation (Explanation)	Source Author YEAR: page #
White Crowned Cuckoo/Koel, Bidɛli-ano (Kululi), *Cacomantis leucolophus*	PNG	Nɛ fɛs ɔn (Kaluli) My back hurts	Feld 2012:79
White-Bellied Cuckooshrike, *Coracina papuensis*	Australia	Kissik, kissik'or 'quzeek Respell: kiss it	Pizzey 1980:231
White-Breasted Nuthatch, *Sitta carolinensis*	N. America	Yank, yank, to what, what, what? Yank yank What, what, too, too	Jonas 1999:12 Schmalz n.d. Bent 1948:9
White-Browed Babbler, *Pomatostomus superciliosus*	Australia	Sweet-sweet-sweet-miaow	Pizzey 1980:271
White-Browed Robin-Chat, *Cossypha heuglini*	Africa	It's-up-to-you, it's-up-to-you, IT'S-UP-TO-YOU Think-of-it, think-of-it, THINK-OF-IT Don't-you-DO-it	Koopman 2018a:16 (Maclean 1985:524)
White-Browed Scrub Robin, *Cercotrichas leucophrys*	South Africa	Twee-too-too Respell: 3-2-2	Barnes & Behrens 2017:124
White-Browed Treecreeper, *Climacteris affinis*	Australia	Tinker-tinker-tinker Peter-peter	Higgins et al.2001:216 Pizzey 1980:312
White-Browed Woodswallow, *Artamus superciliosus*	Australia	Chap chap	Pizzey 1980:394
White-Cheeked Honeyeater, *Phylidonyris nigra*	Australia	Chip Hiccup Chip-chew, chippy-chew	Pizzey 1980:346

English Name, Other Name (language) *Binominal name*	Location	Warblish (Language); Translation (Explanation)	Source Author YEAR: page #
White-Crowned Sparrow, *Zonotrichia leucophrys*	N. America	More cheese cheese please please	Feith 2005
		My song is ever of thee (REPLY) sweet-heart, come live with me (OR) Now hill and pasture gay (OR) Smile with the flowers of May 'Sings a song approaching the first lines of the hymn: My faith looks up to Thee, but changes to "My song is ever of thee"...'	S. Mathews 1921:93
		I gotta go wee-wee now	Burrows 2002:289
White-Eared Brown Dove, *Phapitreron leucotis*	Philippines	Who-oo, who-oo, who-oo Also hoot-ho hoot-ho hoot hoot hoot-hoot-hoot	Kennedy et al. 2000:136
White-Eared Honeyeater, *Lichenostomus leucotis*	Australia	Be quick, be quick	Higgins et al. 2001:756
		Beer-brick, beer-brick	Pizzey 1980:331,
		Chock up, chock up	Wheatbelt 2018:155
		Chock-chock-chock	
		Cherrywheat, cherrywheat	Wheatbelt 2018:155
		Cheery-bob	
White-Eared Tailorbird, *Orthotomus cinereiceps*	Philippines	Chat-chat-chat-chat	Kennedy et al. 2000:282
White-Eyed Vireo, *Vireo griseus*	N. America	Pick up a real chick	Feith 2005
		Who are you there?... Go 'way... Get out!	S. Mathews 1921:163
		Quick give me a rain check	Roth 2012:79; Schmalz n.d.

English Name, Other Name (language) Binominal name	Location	Warblish (Language); Translation (Explanation)	Source Author YEAR: page #
... White-Eyed Vireo, ... continued ...	N. America	Tick wick whee! Tutututututu tip! Respell: dig quick weed! Tututututu-tulip!	Saunders 1951:162
		Spit and see if I care, spit!	Feith 2005
White-Faced Owl, *Ptilopsis leucotis?*	Sudan / Baggara	*Ghatt-o, ghatt-o* (Chadian Arabic?) Cover it up (referring to a corpse "if you hear that when you're sick all the fikis [sic] in Kordofan can't help you".)	Owen 1947:194
White-Fronted Honeyeater, *Phylidonyris albifrons*, *Purnella albifrons*	Australia	Quack-peter-peter-peter Peter-peter-pete Dick, dick	Pizzey 1980:346
White-Plumed Honeyeater, *Lichenostomus penicillatus?* *Ptilotula penicillata?*	Australia	Shit-a-brick! Due-wheat	Lobb 2019:81, Sarvasy 2016:779 Wheatbelt 2018:158
White-Throated Grasswren, *Amytornis woodwardi*	Australia	Treeee, chirp, trip-trip, treeee Respell: tree, chirp, trip-trip-tree	Higgins et al. 2001:317 citing Schodde
White-Throated Sparrow, *Zonotrichia albicollis*	N. America	Dear sweet Canada Canada Canada Oh sweet Canada Canada Canada	Burrows 2002:288 Young 2003:2, Sarvasy 2016:774, Mosco 2017a
		Poor Sam Peabody	Feith n.d.
		Poor Sam Peabody, Peabody, Peabody	Sarvasy 2016:774

English Name, Other Name (language) Binominal name	Location	Warblish (Language); Translation (Explanation)	Source Author YEAR: page #
... White-Throated Sparrow ... continued ...	N. America	Poor Sam Pea'body, Pea'body, Pea'body	Feith 2003b, Schmalz n.d.
		Oooh, poor Sam Peabody, Peabody, Peabody	Jonas 1999:11
		Old Sam Peabody, Peabody, Peabody	S. Mathews 1921:96, Young 2003:2
		Old Sam Peabiddy Peabiddy Peabiddy	Roth 2012:78
		Sow wheat Pe-ver-ley, Pe-ver-ley, Pe-ver-ly	S. Mathews 1921:96
		All day whit-tl-lin', whit-tl-lin', whit-tl-lin'	
		Oh hear me Ther-esa, Ther-esa- Ther-esa	
		All day fid-dle-in', fi-dle-in' fid-dle-in	
		Di Pro-sen-za-a-a (Italian?) (reminiscent of the Di Provenza from Verdi's Traviata)	S. Mathews 1921:98
	Philippines	Sweet sweet sweet sweet	Kennedy et al. 2000:283
White-Winged Crossbill, Loxia leucoptera	N. America	Kip kip	Feith 2003a
Wild Turkey, Meleagris gallopavo	NZ & N. America	Gobble gobble gobble	Chambers 2007:26, Jonas 1999:9
	Hungary	Csak úgy élünk csak-csak-csak! (Hungarian) We just live like this, just-just-just OR We only live like this, only-only-only!	Balint Koller (Personal communication)

English Name, Other Name (language) Binominal name	Location	Warblish (Language); Translation (Explanation)	Source Author YEAR: page #
... Wild Turkey ... continued	Hungary	Male: *Csak úgy élünk csak-csak-csak!* (Hungarian) We only live like this, only-only-only! (translator: Daisy Coles)	Ottó 1901:7
		Poult: *Még egy kicsit-csitt-csitt-csitt!* (Hungarian) For a little-ittle-ittle big longer! (translator: Coles)	
		Male: *Kúdúlással is eltartalak!* (Hungarian) Even in the struggle, I'll look after you (translator Daisy Coles: she notes this is hard to translate)	
Willet, *Catoptrophorus semipalmatus*	N. America	Will-will willet, will-will-willet Respell: will-will-will it? Will -will-will it?	Burrows 2002:123
		Pill-will-will-it	Feith 2005
Willie Wagtail, Black-and-White Fantail/ Flycatcher, Frogbird, Djidi Djidi (Noongar), *Rhipidura leucophrys*	Australia	Sweet pretty creature	Pizzey 1980:264
		Which are you, Willie, which are you? (In Noongar, this is a bird of ill omen, tries to lure children away from camp into the bush' p. 198)	Wheatbelt 2018:197
		I'm trying to an-NOY you	Young 2003:3
Willow Ptarmigan, *Lagopus lagopus*	N. America	Go-back go-back go-back Go-out, go-out, go-back, go-back	Burrows 2002:107 Jonas 1999:6
Willow Warbler, Lövsångare (Swedish), *Phylloscopus trochilus*	Sweden	*Och vi som hade det så bra och så blev det så här* (Swedish) We who had it so good and yet it became like this (falling, complaining tone)	Abelin 2011:14

English Name, Other Name (language) *Binominal name*	Location	Warblish (Language); Translation (Explanation)	Source Author YEAR: page #
... Willow Warbler, ... *continued* ...	Sweden	*Snälla lilla mamma, kan jag få gå ut ikväll?* (Swedish) Call: "Please, little mum, can I get out tonight?" (See response by Chaffinch)	Norudde 2009
		Snälla mamma, kan jag inte få gå på bio ikväll? (Swedish) Please mum, can't I go to the cinema tonight?"	
		Och vi som hade det så bra och så blev det så här (Swedish) And we who had it so good and then it ended up like this.	
		Snälla snälla mamma får jag gå på bio ikväll kl 10 (Swedish) Please please mum, can I go to the cinema tonight at 10 am (Chaffinch repeats the time)	
		Snälla lilla mamma kan jag få gå på bio ikväll? (Swedish) Please, little mum, can I go to the cinema tonight? (same as Chaffinch)	
Wilson's Phalarope, *Phalaropus tricolor*	N. America	Work work	Burrows 2002:143
		Wu wu wu, Respell: woo woo woo (It's the call on breeding grounds so I think the bird is wooing)	

English Name, Other Name (language) *Binominal name*	Location	Warblish (Language); Translation (Explanation)	Source Author YEAR: page #
Wilson's Warbler, *Cardellina pusilla*	N. America	Chchchchchew	Feith 2003a
Winter Wren, *Trolodytes troglodytes*	N. America	Chip-chip	Burrows 2002:228
Wonga Pigeon, *Leucosarcia melanoleuca*	Australia	Walk walk walk walk walk	Young 2003:2 citing Glen Threlfo
Wood Duck, *Aix sponsa*	N. America	What? What? What?	Feith 2003a
Wood Owl, *Strix genus*; *Strix woodfordii?*	Southern Africa?	Weh mame (Zulu) Oh my mother Who are you	Koopman 2018a:16 citing McLachlan & Liversidge 1978:259
Wood Pewee (now 2 species: Eastern W.P. *Contopus virens* & Western Wood Pewee, *Contopus sordidulus* *Muscicapa virens*	N. America	Plea-e-ease Ple-e-ease (pleading tone) Are they gone? I don't know. Are they gone? No.	Dormon 1969:103 Dormon 1969:24 Rothenberg 2005:125 citing Wallace Craig
Wood Thrush, *Hylocichla mustelina*	N. America	Will you live with me? Way up high in a tree, I'll come right down and . . . Seeee! Ravioli	Burrows 2002:241 Roth 2012:79; South Bay Birders n.d.
Woodcock, *Scolopax (genus)*	N. America	Fart fart fart peep! Fart fart fart peep! Fart fart peep! Warp!	Sewell 2013:29 Thomas 2019:

English Name, Other Name (language) Binominal name	Location	Warblish (Language); Translation (Explanation)	Source Author YEAR: page #
Woodford's Owl,	Southern Africa	*Wa gxebe! Wa gxebe! / Wa ndlebe zenja!* (Xhosa) *Wa gxebe! Wa gxebe! / Wa!* Dog's ears!	Wainwright 1983:300
Woodpecker, uSibawebe (Zulu), Ciocănitoare (Romanian), *Picidae* (family)	South Africa	*Sibagwebe, sibagwebe, sibagwege* (Zulu) Let us prod them, let us prod them, let us prod them	Bulpin 1966:27
	Romania	*Cioc, cioc, cioc* (Romanian) Beak, beak, beak	Cris Cucerzan (Personal communication)
Wood-Quail, *Odontophorus* (family)	Central America	Burst the bubble, burst the bubble	Young 2003:3
Yellow Honeyeater, *Lichenostomus flavus*	Australia	Tut tut tut	Higgins et al. 2001:775 citing Thompson 1935
Yellow Rail, *Coturnicops noveboracensis*	N. America	Tik, tik, tik-tik-tik Respell: tick, tick, tick-tick-tick Tic-tic-tic, tic-tic (like a typewriter)	Burrows 2002:109 Feith 2003a
Yellow Warbler, Wild Canaries, Yellowhammers, *Dendroica petechia*	N. America	Sweet-sweet-sweet summer sweet Sweet sweet sweet, little more sweet Sweet sweet sweet, I'm so sweet Sweet, sweet, I'm so very sweet	Burrows 2002:254 Feith 2003a Schmalz n.d. Mosco 2017a
Yellow White-Eye, *Zosterops nigrorum*	Philippines	Sip-it sip-it Sit-it sit-it	Kennedy et al. 2000:337
Yellow-Bellied Flycatcher, *Empidonax flaviventris*	N. America	Killit Respell: kill it	Feith 2003a; Feith 2005

English Name, Other Name (language) *Binominal name*	Location	Warblish (Language); Translation (Explanation)	Source Author YEAR: page #
Yellow-Billed Kite, Nhloile, kaMguphane, (Zulu), *Milvus aegyptius*	South Africa	Cock: *Aiwe, aiwe, aiwe.* ×3 (Zulu) Cock: Let it (the meat) fall (to me), let it (the meat) fall (to me), let it (the meat) fall (to me). ×3 (N.B.—meat in this case means the chicken (or any other bird, as the case may be).	Dunning 1946:53
Yellow-Breasted Barbet, *Lybiidae family*	Sudan / Baggara	Call: *Sherrat-o, sherrato* (Chadian Arabic?) Tear it up, tear it up (translator: Google) Response: *Khaiyat-o, khaiyat-o* (Chadian Arabic) Sew it up, sew it up (translator: Google) Call/response: The two birds always cry out together, and the Arabs along the river say that they are quarrelling about a piece of cloth; the cock wants to tear it up and keeps calling "*Sherrat-o, sherrato,*" and the hen is determined to sew it up and repeats after him "*Khaiyat-o, khaiyat-o.*" I think they sing more during the rains.	Owen 1947:195
Yellow-Breasted Chat, *Icteria virens*	N. America	Wha ha ha . . . . . . Whoo he he he . . . Pray wor whee tsuck hoo hoo hoo Respell: What? Ha ha . . . Who's he he he? . . . Pray were we stuck, who who who?	Saunders 1951:213
Yellow-Crowned Parakeet, *Cyanoramphus auriceps*	Australia	28 Pretty dick	Williams 1976:12
Yellow-Eyed Penguin, Hoiho (Māori), *Megadyptes antipodes*	NZ	Help!	L. Moon 2011:8

English Name, Other Name (language) *Binominal name*	Location	Warblish (Language); Translation (Explanation)	Source Author YEAR: page #
Yellow-Faced Honeyeater, *Lichenostomus chrysops*	Australia	Chick-up	Higgins et al. 2001:733 citing Kindwood 1932 & Officer 1971
Yellow-Finch Golden-Rump Canary Yellow Eye Mbalabe (Zulu) *Binomial nomenclature?*	South Africa	Cock: *Amaɓele, ayintilintili, ngidle ngaze ngashiya-nje, Zonke izinyoni, ziwadlile anhlamvana, avuthiwe ayintilintili.* ×3 Cock: The Amaɓele-corn (there) are (just) heaps of it, I ate it and just left it; all the birds have eaten it in quantities, it (the corn) is just in heaps. ×3 Cock: *Bacikize, bacikize, ɓathi kucikize Mbalane! Aku maɓele, ayintilintili!* ×3 Cock: They scattered it (the corn) and they scattered it (and) what they scattered (i.e., the huge quantities they scattered to the ground while eating it) Yellow Finch! It wasn't corn; it was real heaps! ×3	Dunning 1946:40
Yellow-Finch Golden-Rump Canary Yellow Eye Mbalabe (Zulu) *Binomial nomenclature?*	South Africa	Cock: *Mlindikazana, mlindikazana, Akuse 'Maɓele, ayintilintili Siwadlile anhlamvana anhlamvana.* ×3 Cock: Little girl! Little girl! (i.e., the girl who keep watch in the corn-fields and scares the birds away) this isn't corn, it's real heaps! We have eaten quantities upon quantities of it. ×3	Dunning 1946:41

English Name, Other Name (language) *Binominal name*	Location	Warblish (Language); Translation (Explanation)	Source Author YEAR: page #
... Yellow-Finch ... continued ...	South Africa	Cock: *Akumabele, intilintili! Yonke lentilintili ngizakuyenze njani?* ×3 Cock: This isn't corn, it's real heaps! What shall I do with all this abundance?	Dunning 1946:41–42
Yellowhammer, Gulsparv (Swedish), *Emberiza citrinella*	Czech Republic	*Kéž by si sedláčku chcip!* (Czech) Wish you were dead, farmer!	Pavel Pipek (Personal communication)
	UK	No, no, no, no, PLEASE	Mynott 2009:165
		A little bit of bread and no cheese	Thomas 2019:115, Gunson 2011:143
		A little bit of bread and no cheese, please	Thomas 2019:115
		Give me bread and some more cheese	Abelin 2011:15
		Give me bread and some more cheeeeeese	Norudde 2009
	Sweden	Bread and butter but no cheese	Abelin 2011:16 citing Norudde 2009
		Siit, sitt, sitt, sitt, sitt åskiiit (Swedish) Sit, sit, sit, sit, sit & shit (translator: Mikaela Nyman)	Norudde 2009, Abelin 2011:15
		Se se se se se shiiit (Swedish) See see see see see shit	
		Se-se-shiten (Swedish) See see shit	Norudde 2009
		Nu är sommaren snart slut (Swedish) Now the summer is over soon	Abelin 2011:15

English Name, Other Name (language) *Binominal name*	Location	Warblish (Language); Translation (Explanation)	Source Author YEAR: page #
... Yellowhammer ... *continued* ...	Sweden	*Nu är sommaren snart sluuuuut* (Swedish) Now the summer is soon over	Norudde 2009
		Vi-vi-vi-vi-visingsööö (Swedish) (name of an island)	Abelin 2011:15
		Vi-vi-vi-vi-visingsööö (Swedish) We-we-we-Visingsööö	Norudde 2009
		1, 2, 3, 4, 5, 6, sjuuuu (Swedish) 1, 2, 3, 4, 5, 6, seven	Norudde 2009; Abelin 2011:15
		Ett två tre fyra fem sex sjuuu, jag är liten jag är guuul (Swedish) One, two, three, four, five, six, seven, I am little, I am yellow	Abelin 2011:15
		Fy på dig Nisse lille fyyyy (Swedish) Shame on you little Nisse, shame on you	Norudde 2009; Abelin 2011:15
		Ett två tre fyra fem sex sjuuu ... jag är liten, jag är guuuuul (Swedish) 1,2,3,4,5,6,7...I'm small, I'm yellow (translator: Mikaela Nyman; seven [sju] rhymes with yellow [gul])	Norudde 2009
		Allt kommer tillbaks igen (Swedish) Everything returns/reappears (translator: Mikaela Nyman); Everything comes back again (translator: Google)	

English Name, Other Name (language) *Binominal name*	Location	Warblish (Language); Translation (Explanation)	Source Author YEAR: page #
...Doves ... continued	Sweden	*Skogsturken ringer* (Swedish) The forest pigeon rings / the woods call / the forest turkey is calling (Google translate)	Norudde 2009
Downy Woodpecker, *Dryobates pubescens*	N. America	Pick	Feith 2003a
		Keep, keep, keep	Saunders 1951:77
Drongo Cuckoo, *Surniculus lugubris*	Asia	One, two, three, four, five, six	King & Dickinson 1975:186
Duck, Утка (Russian), *Anas* (genus)	Russia	*Bpa-aa! Bpa-aa! Bpa-aa!* [Vra-ag! Vra-ag! Vra-ag!] (Russian); Enemy! Enemy! Enemy!	Bianki 2013:5
	Hungary	*Csak csapra! Csak csapra!* (Hungarian) Only on tap! Only on tap! (translator: Daisy Coles); (response to Rock Pigeon saying "we have wine")	Ottó 1901:7
	Southern Africa	Duck call: *Isifuba sam sithe. Gaa gaa gaa! Drake response: Uzithi, tshwe tshwe tshwe!* (Xhosa) (Duck) My chest goes: gaa gaa gaa! (Drake reply) You should say, tshwe, tshwe, tshwe!	Wainwright 1983:298
Dusky Myzomela, *Myzomela obscura*	Australia	See see see	Pizzey 1980:353
Eagle-owl? *Bubo* (genus)	Africa, Sudan / Baggara	*Kozi, -mmmm, Kosi, - mmmm* (Chadian Arabic?) (Brooding over daughter's (named Kozi) death	Owen 1947:194
Eastern Barn Owl, *Tyto alba delicatula*	Australia	Sk-air OR skee-air OR skee-aarr Respell: scare	Wheatbelt 2018:91

English Name, Other Name (language) Binominal name	Location	Warblish (Language); Translation (Explanation)	Source Author YEAR: page #
Yellow-Tufted Honeyeater, *Lichenostomus melanops*	Australia	Twee-twee-twee-twee-coffee-coffee-coffee-coffee Respell: twee as tea	Higgins et al. 2001:816 citing Wakefield 1958
'A bird'	Libya	Audrey! Audrey!	Fielding 1942:40
'Other birds'	France?	*Oci* (French) Could be '*occi*' which is 'kill' (translator: Luc Arnault)	Leach 2007:140
'Other birds'	France?	*Tue* (French) Kill (translator: Luc Arnault)	
'Other birds'	France?	*Il est temps* (French) It is time (translator: Luc Arnault)	

Appendix D: Animalopoeia Database

Common English Name (*Binominal name*)	Location	Animalopoeia (Language); Translation (Explanation)	Source Author YEAR: page #
Bull *Bos taurus*	Russia	Убью-у! [Ub'yu-u!] (Russian) I'll kill you	Bianki 2013:5
Cat *Felis catus*	NZ	Me? Ow!	Frank Lamb (Personal communication)
Chorus Cicada, *Amphipsalta zelandica*	NZ	What are you gonna do?	Helen Mae Innes
Dog *Canis familiaris*	Russia	Хам! Хам! Тррусы! [Xam! Xam! Trrusy!] (Russian) Woof! Woof! Coward!	Bianki 2013:5
Frog	NZ	Rip-it, rip-it	David Safonov-Innes (Personal communication)
Frog, Yellow-bellied frog? *Anura order*	Russia	Был кум [Byl kum] (Russian) There was a godfather На Дону [Na Donu] (Russian) On the Don (River) Где кум? [Gde kum?] (Russian) Where's the godfather? Утонул [Utonul] (Russian) Drowned!	Bianki 2013:14

Common English Name (*Binominal name*)	Location	Animalopoeia (Language); Translation (Explanation)	Source Author YEAR: page #
... Frog ... *continued* ...	Russia	Ну плакать? [Nu plakat'?] (Russian) Well, cry?	Bianki 2013:14
		Ну-нуу! [Nu-nu!] (Russian) No! Noooo! Дурра! Дурppa! [Durra! Durrra!] (Russian) Fool! Fool! OR Dope! Dope! Са-ма ка-ко-ва! Сама какова [Sa-ma ka-ko-va! Sama kakova] (Russian) You're the fool! What about you?	Bianki 2013:15
Goat *Capra aegagrus hircus*	Russia	Меня-я! Меня-я! [Menya-ya! Menya-ya!] (Russian) Me! Me!	Bianki 2013:5
Katydid, *Tettigoniidae* family	NZ	Katy did, Katy didn't Zip zip	Gunson 2011:89
Pig *Sus domesticus*	Russia	Рюхой! Рюхой! [Ryukhoy! Ryukhoy!] (Russian) With knucklebones! With knucklebones!	Bianki 2013:5

Appendix E: Ticktocklish Database

Common English Name	Location	Ticktocklish (Language); Translation (Explanation)	Source Author YEAR: page #
Clock	Mexico	*Tequiti* (Nahuatl) Work ("Listen to what the clock is telling you. Always, work this, and work that. That is what it was saying. Work. You have to work.")	Tammet 2017:81
Siren (old-style police or ambulance siren)	South Africa	*Ry daar, ry daar* (Afrikaans) Drive there, drive there	Michael Webber (Personal communication)
Train	NZ	Go-it go-it go-it de-light-ed-ly de-light-ed-ly the Lim-it-ed (Refers to the express train)	Frame 1957:146
	Romania	*Te duc, te a-duc* (Romanian) I take you, I take you back (or) I'll take you (there), I'll bring you (back)	Cris Cucerzan (Personal communication)
	N. America	I think I can	Piper 1930:5
		I thought I could	Piper 1930:24–25

Works Cited

Abelin, Åsa. (2011). Imitation of bird song in folklore – Onomatopoeia or not? *TMH - QPSR, 51*,13–16.

Adjaye, Joseph K. (1994). *Time in the black experience*. Greenwood Publishing Group.

Agnihotri, Samira & Si, Aung. (2012). Solega ethno-ornithology. *Journal of Ethnobiology, 32(*2), 185-211. https://doi.org/10.2993/0278-0771-32.2.185

Aikhenvald, Alexandra Y. (2003). *Tariana texts and cultural context*. Languages of the World/Texts 07 Lincom Europa.

Ali, S. & Ripley, S.D. (1986). *Handbook of the birds of India and Pakistan: Volume 5* (2nd ed.). Oxford University Press.

Allen, Nick. (2012). *Where to watch birds in Canterbury*. Canterbury Region of the Ornithological Society of New Zealand, Inc.

Allen, Pamela. (1996). *Waddle giggle gargle*. Puffin.

Andersen, Johannes Carl. (n.d.). *Johannes Carl Andersen. My Poetic Side*. https://mypoeticside.com/poets/johannes-carl-andersen-poems

Andersen, Johannes, Carl. (1926). *New Zealand song birds*. Whitcombe & Tombs Ltd.

Archer, John. (2020, October). *Ki kō, ki kō. New Zealand waiata poi*. http://folksong.org.nz/ki_ko_ki_ko/index.html

Artuso, Christain. (2017, Oct 21). *Bob-o-lincoln, Goglu, Charlatán, Rice Bird, Reed Bird, Long-toed Rice-eater... A Bobolink is still as sweet!* Birds, wildlife: Birding, conservation, ecology, and animal behaviour. http://artusobirds.blogspot.com/2017/10/bob-o-lincoln-goglu-charlatan-rice-bird.html

Barnes, Keith & Behrens, Ken. (2017). *Birds of Kruger National Park*. Princeton University Press.

Barnes, Simon. (2011). *Birdwatching with your eyes closed: an introduction to birdsong*. Short Books.

Barnes, Simon. (2016). *The meaning of birds*. Head of Zeus Ltd.

Bent, Arthur Cleveland. (1945). *Life histories of North American jays, crows, and titmice*. United States Governement Printing Office.

Bent, Arthur Cleveland. (1948). Life histories of North American nuthatches, wrens, thrashers, and their allies: Order Passeriformes. *Bulletin of the United States National Museum 195*, 205–16. https://doi.org/10.5479/si.03629236.195.1

Best, Elsdon. (1982). *Maori religion and mythology, part 2*. Government Printer.

Bhattacharya, Sugata. (2019). *The use of bird sound imitations and recordings among Estonian birders* [Master's thesis, University of Tartu]. *Eesti Ornitoloogiaühing* (Birdlife Estonia). https://www.eoy.ee/uurimistood/files/2019_Bhattacharya_Msc.pdf

Bianki, Vitaly Valentinovich [Бианки, Виталий Валентинович]. (2013). *Птичьи разговоры* [*Bird talk*]. Акварель, Команда А. [Watercolour, Team A].

Bird Academy. (2010). *I'm here, where are you?: Wails of the Common Loon*. https://academy.allaboutbirds.org/im-here-where-are-you-the-wails-of-the-common-loon/

Birdlife Australia. (2020). *Birds in backyards: Australian painted snipe*. https://www.birdsinbackyards.net/species/Rostratula-australis

Brown Creeper. (2020, October 14). In Wikipedia. https://en.wikipedia.org/wiki/Brown_creeper

Brown-Crested Flycatcher. (2020, April 15). In Wikipedia. https://en.wikipedia.org/wiki/Brown-crested_flycatcher

Browning, Robert. (1845). *Home thoughts from abroad*. https://www.poetryfoundation.org/poems/43758/home-thoughts-from-abroad

Budhwar, Kartika. (2019) To the redwing blackbird. In *Blue Mesa Review, 40*, p. 50. University of New Mexico. https://issuu.com/bluemesareview/docs/bmr_issue_40_issuu/50

Buff-Breasted Paradise Kingfisher (2025. March 3). In Wikipedia. https://en.wikipedia.org/wiki/Buff-breasted_paradise_kingfisher

Bulpin, Thomas Victor. (1966). *Natal and the Zulu country*. Protea Book House.

Burrows, Roger. (2002). *Birds of Atlantic N. America*. Lone Pine

Publishing.

Burroughs, John. (1901, December 1). The vesper sparrow. *Harper's Monthly Magazine, 104*, p. 127.

Callaway, Henry. (1868). *Nursery tales, traditions, and histories of the Zulus, in their own words, with a translation into English and notes, Volume l*. John A. Blair.
https://archive.org/details/cu31924026950968/page/n163

Cambridge Dictionary. (2021). Bang. In *Cambridge Dictionary*.
https://dictionary.cambridge.org/dictionary/english/bang

Cambridge Dictionary. (2021). Nonce. In *Cambridge Dictionary*.
https://dictionary.cambridge.org/dictionary/english/nonce

Cambridge Dictionary. (2021). Onomatopoeia. In *Cambridge Dictionary*.
https://dictionary.cambridge.org/dictionary/english/onomatopoeia

Castlemaine Bird List. (n.d). [Google Docs Spreadsheet].
https://docs.google.com/spreadsheets/d/1eLqGthUKnKKCiTlDQZsCoAleiZQ7nzI0QcpgQIjHlcc/edit?gid=0#gid=0

Chadd, Rachel W., & Taylor, Marianne. (2016). *Birds: Myth, lore and legend*. Bloomsbury Natural History.

Chambers, Stuart. (2007). *New Zealand Birds: An identification guide*. Reed.

Clark, Gary. (2017, Sept 02). *Why blue jays are such noisy birds: Bird vocalizations range from shrill jeers to whistles and bell tones*. Houston Chronicle.
https://www.houstonchronicle.com/life/clark/article/Why-blue-jays-are-such-noisy-birds-12220444.php

Cleere, Nigel. (2010). *Nightjars, potoos, frogmouths, oilbird, and owlet-nightjars of the world*. Princeton University Press.
https://doi.org/10.1515/9781400836161

Cocker, Mark. (2013) *Birds and people*. Random House.

CoEDLang. (2017, October 23). *A new term for birdwatchers: Warblish*. ARC Centre of Excellence for the Dynamics of Language.
http://www.dynamicsoflanguage.edu.au/news-and-media/latest-headlines/article/?id=a-new-term-for-birdwatchers-warblish

Common Bulbul (2025, March 1). In *Wikipedia*.
https://en.wikipedia.org/wiki/Common_bulbul

Common Quail. (2020, October 12). In *Wikipedia*.
https://en.wikipedia.org/wiki/Common_quail

Compare the Marsh Tit. (2012, April 28). *Trade Secrets* [Blog Post].

https://comparethemarshtit.blogspot.com/2012/04/
Cook, Guy. (2000). *Language play, language learning.* Oxford University Press.
Cooke, W. W. (1884, July 3). Bird nomenclature of the Chippewa Indians. *The Auk, 1*(3), 242–250. American Ornithological Society.
Cowser, Robert. (1969). Bird talk [Letter to the Editor]. *Western Folklore, 28*(1), 42–43.
https://doi.org/10.2307/1499107
Crowe, Andrew. (2001). *Which New Zealand bird?* Penguin.
Darwin, Charles. (1839). *Narrative of the surveying voyages of His Majesty's Ships Adventure and Beagle between the years 1826 and 1836, describing their examination of the southern shores of South America, and the Beagle's circumnavigation of the globe. Volume 3.* Henry Colburn.
https://www.biodiversitylibrary.org/page/45333283#page/82/mode/1up
Dingemanse, Mark. (2019). 'Ideophone' as a comparative concept. In Kimi Akita & Prashant Pardeshi (Eds.), *Ideophones, mimetics and expressives* (pp. 13–34). John Benjamins Publishing Company.
https://pure.mpg.de/rest/items/item_3006532_3/component/file_3053674/content
Donaldson, Julia. (2019). *The go-away bird.* MacMillian.
Dormon, Caroline. (1969). *Bird talk.* Claitor's Pub. Division.
Duggan, Eileen. (1929). *New Zealand bird songs.* Whitcombe & Tombs Ltd.
Dunning, R. G. (1946). *Two hundred and sixty-four Zulu proverbs, idioms, etc. and the cries of thirty seven birds.* Knox Print and Publishers.
Feith, John. (2003a) [Liner notes]. In *Bird song ear training guide: Who cooks for poor Sam Peabody* [CD]. Independent Records.
Feith, John. (2003b). *Bird song ear training guide: Who cooks for poor Sam Peabody* [CD]. Independent Records.
Feld, Steven. (2012). *Sound and sentiment: Birds, weeping, poetics, and song in Kaluli expression* (3rd ed.). Duke University Press.
Fielding, Sean. (1942). *They sought out Rommel.* Whitefriars Press Ltd.
Frame, Janet. (1957). *Owls do cry.* Pegasus Press.
Frances, Peter, & Burnie, David. (2007). *Bird: The definitive visual guide.* Dorling Kindersley.

Fugl (username). (2014, September 5; Post#6). *3 regulars from my backyard in Reno--"Where are you, where are you"* [online forum post]. Bird Forum. https://www.birdforum.net/showthread.php?t=290445

Giacon, John. (2013). Etymology of Yuwaalaraay Gamilaraay bird names. In Robert Mailhammer (Ed.), *Lexical and structural etymology beyond word histories* (pp. 251–291).

Glover, Denis. (1964). The Magpies. In *Enter without knocking*. https://allpoetry.com/The-Magpies

Goodrich, S.G. (1849). *Merry's Museum Volume 17*. D. MacDonald & Co.

Gorst, Emma. (2010). Interspecies mimicry: Birdsong in Chaucer's 'Maniciple's Tale' and the Parlement of Fowles. *New Medieval Literatures, 12*, 147–154. https://doi.org/10.1484/J.NML.1.102183

Greene, R., Cushman, S., Cavanagh, C., Ramazani, J., Rouzer, J., Feinsod, H., Marno., D. & Slessarev, A. (Eds.). (2012). *Princeton encyclopedia of poetry and poetics* (4th ed.). Princeton University Press.

Gunson, David. (2011). *The big book of New Zealand wildlife*. New Holland Publications.

He, Li., Frodsham, J., & Rouzer, P. (2016). *The collected poems of Li He*. New York Review Books.

Higgins, P. J., Peter, J. M., & Steele, W. K. (Eds.). (2001). *Handbook of Australian, New Zealand and Antarctic Birds. Volume 5: Tyrant-flycatchers to Chats*. Melbourne: Oxford University Press.

Holmer, Nils M., & Holmer, Vanja E., (1969). *Stories from two native tribes of Eastern Australia*. A.-B. Lundequistska Bokhandeln.

Hunn, Eugene S. (1991). Sahaptin bird classification. In A. Pawley (Ed.), *Man and a half: Essays in Pacific anthropology and ethnobiology in honour of Ralph Bulmer* (pp. 137–147). The Polynesian Society.

Indian Cuckoo (2025, January 6). In *Wikipedia*. https://en.wikipedia.org/wiki/Indian_cuckoo

Jan (username). (2009, July, 3). *Yellowhammers have other calls too* [online forum post]. General Birding Discussion. http://www.birdingnz.net/forum/

Jonas, Ann. (1999). *Bird talk*. Greenwillow Books.

Kawasaki, Akiko. (2018). アメリカ英語の鳥声記述：聞きなしとオ

ノマトペ [Birdsongs in American English: Mnemonics]. ことば・文化・コミュニケーション [*Language, Culture, and Communication*], *10*, 1–17. https://rikkyo.repo.nii.ac.jp/?action=pages_view_main&active_action=repository_view_main_item_detail&item_id=15859&item_no=1&page_id=13&block_id=49

Keane-Tuala, Kelly. (2015). *Story: Ngā manu – birds: Birds' names*. Te Ara - The Encyclopedia of New Zealand. http://www.TeAra.govt.nz/en/nga-manu-birds/page-6

King, Ben F., & Dickinson, Edward C. (1975) *Field guide to the birds of Southeast Asia*. Collins.

Koopman, Adrian. (1990). Ornimatopoeia: Song reference in English, Afrikaans, and Zulu bird names. *Nomina Africana: Journal of the Names Society of Southern Africa, 4*(1), 67–87.

Koopman, Adrian. (2018a). From vocalisation to verbalisation: Strategies for turning bird calls into language. *Language Matters, 49*(2), 3–22.

Koopman, Adrian. (2018b). Zulu bird names: A progression over the decades. *South African Journal of African Languages, 38*(3), 261–267. http://doi.org/10.1080/02572117.2018.1518029

Leach, Elizabeth. (2007). *Sung birds: Music, nature, and poetry in the later middle ages*. Cornell University Press.

Leary, S. (2016). *California quail*. New Zealand Birds Online. https://www.nzbirdsonline.org.nz

Legris, André. (n.d.). *Using bird song mnemonics*. Birding World. http://birding-world.com/using-bird-song-mnemonics/

LesleytheBirdNerd. (2013, Oct 25). Black-Capped Chickadee calls and sounds - fee-bee call, chickadee-dee-dee call, seet call etc [Video]. YouTube. https://www.youtube.com/watch?v=rYoZgpAEkFs

Lobb, Joshua. (2019). *The flight of birds: a novel in 12 stories*. Sydney University Press.

Lorenzin, Tomm. (2011). *Bird Song Mnemonics*. 1000 Plus. www.1000plus.com/BirdSong/birdsngb.html

Louv, Richard. (2013). *Last child in the woods: Saving our children from nature-deficit disorder*. Algonquin Books.

Majnep, Ian Saem & Bulmer, Ralph. (1977). *Birds of my Kalam country*. Auckland University Press.

Manhire, Bill [@pacificraft]. (2020, October 2nd). *The Dotterel*. X (formally Twitter). https://twitter.com/pacificraft/status/1311776714205224961/photo/

Marler, Peter. (1956). *Behaviour of the chaffinch (Fringilla coelebs)*. E.J. Brill.

Mathews, P. H. (2007). Nonce-word. In *The Concise Oxford Dictionary of Linguistics* (2nd ed.). Oxford University Press. https://www.oxfordreference.com/view/10.1093/acref/9780199202720.001.0001/acref-9780199202720-e-2239?rskey=0icJkR&result=2221

Mathews, Schuyler. (1921). *Field book of wild birds and their music*. Putnam.

McEwen, John. (2017, December). *Bird of the month: Sparrow*. The Oldie. https://www.theoldie.co.uk/article/bird-of-the-month-sparrow

McGehee, Judson D. (1958). *The nature essay as a literary genre: An intrinsic study of the works of six English and American nature writers* [Doctoral dissertation, University of Michigan]. ProQuest Dissertations and Theses.

McKay, Don. (2005). *Deactivated west 100*. Gaspereau Press

Mincing Mockingbird. (2014). *Guide to troubled birds*. Blue Rider Press.

Moon, Geoff. (1967). *Refocus on New Zealand birds*. A.H & A.W. Reed.

Moon, Geoff. (2018). *New Zealand forest birds and their world*. New Holland Publishers Ltd.

Moon, Lynnette, Moon, Geoff, Kendrick, J., Baird, K. (2011). *New Zealand bird calls*. New Holland Publishers Ltd.

Moreau, A. J. (1940, Dec). Bird names used in coastal North-Eastern Tanganyika. *Tanganyika Notes and Records*, *10*, 47–72.

Moreau, Reginald Ernest. (1942). Bird-nomenclature in an East African area. *Bulletin of the School of Oriental and African Studies, 10*(4), 998–1006. https://www.jstor.org/stable/609139?seq=1

Moreno Cabrera, Juan C. (2016). Onomatopoeia and the meaningful interpretation of bird calls. In M. A. Flaksman & O. I. Brodovich (Eds.) *Phonosemantics. In commemoration of Professor Dr. Stanislav Voronin's 80th anniversary, St. Petersburg, ANCO 'University of Education Districts'* (pp.73–78). ANCO University of Education Districts. Retrieved from ResearchGate https://tinyurl.com/ycyk3hbc

Mosco, Rosemary. (2017a). Bird song mnemonics: Songs and calls of Eastern North American birds. *Bird and Moon Comics.*
https://www.birdandmoon.com/comic/eastern-bird-sounds/

Mosco, Rosemary. (2017b). Bird song mnemonics: Songs and calls of Western North American birds. *Bird and Moon Comics.*
https://www.birdandmoon.com/comic/western-bird-sounds/

Mrpjdavis (username). (2006, Aug, 6: Post#16). *Collins Bird Guide describes the song as* [online forum post]. BirdForum.
https://www.birdforum.net/showthread.php?t=58484

Muiruri, Mercy Njeri & Maundu, Patrick. (2010). Birds, people and conservation in Kenya. In Sonia Tidemann & Andrew Gosler (Eds.). *Ethno-ornithology birds, indigenous peoples, culture and society* (pp. 279–290). Earthscan.

Müller, Wolfgang. (2009, February). *Séance vocibus avium* (*audio project*) Great Auk [*Pinguinus impennis*] (track)
https://www.thewire.co.uk/audio/tracks/p=14851

Mynott, Jeremy. (2009). *Birdscapes: Birds in our imagination and experience.* Princeton University Press.

Ngā Taonga Sound and Vision. (2021). *The Huia.*
https://www.ngataonga.org.nz/collections/catalogue/catalogue-item?record_id=217473

Norudde, Ingrid. (2009). *Svenska folkets fågelramsor* (The Swedish people's bird rhymes). [Unpublished manuscript].

Ottó, Herman. (1901). *A madarak hasznáról és káráról* [*On the benefits and harm of birds*]. A. M. Kir. Földmivelésügyi Minister Kiadványai [A. M. Kir. Publications of the Minister of Agriculture].
https://tinyurl.com/3pxbz5kz

Ovenbird43 (username) (2014, Sept 14). *Perhaps I'm just weird but I never found mnemonics helpful* [online forum post]. Bird Forum.
https://www.birdforum.net/showthread.php?t=290445

Owen, T. (1947). Bird talk. *Sudan Notes and Records, 28,* 193–196.
http://www.jstor.org/stable/41716525

Paine, Robert P. (2020, March 4). *African Emerald Cuckoo: Sounds and vocal behaviour.* The Cornell Lab of Ornithology Birds of the World.
https://birdsoftheworld.org/bow/species/afecuc1/cur/introduction

Pied-Billed Grebe. (2025, March 3). In Wikipedia.

https://en.wikipedia.org/wiki/Pied-billed_grebe#cite_note-F19-17

Piper, Watty. (1930). *The little engine that could.* The Platt & Munk Co Inc Publishers. https://www.printmag.com/post/watty-pipers-1930-the-little-engine-that-could

Pizzey, Graham. (1958). *A time to look.* William Heinemann Ltd.

Pizzey, Graham. (1980). *A field guide to the birds of Australia.* Collins

Pizzey, Graham. (Ed). (1985). *A separate creation. discovery of wild Australia by explorers and naturalists.* Currey O'Neil Ross.

Pizzey, Graham. (1997). *The Graham Pizzey & Frank Knight field guide to the birds of Australia.* Angus & Robertson.

Pizzey, Graham. (2000). *Journey of a lifetime: Selected pieces by Australia's foremost birdwatcher and nature writer.* Angus & Robertson.

Poe, Edgar Allen. (1898). *The raven.* R. G. Badger & Company

Preston, Alex & Gower, Neil. (2018). *As Kingfishers Catch Fire: Birds & Books.* Corsair.

Pușcariu, Sextil. (1920-1921). Din perspectiva Dicționarului. I. [From the perspective of the Dictionary. I.] Despre onomatopee în limba română [About onomatopoeias in Romanian]. *Dacoromania Buletinul „Muzeului Limbei Române", I*, p. 73 [The '*Museum of the Romanian Language*' Bulletin, I, p. 73].

Quinion, Michael. (2016, Mar 16). *Oryzivorous.* World Wide Words: Investigating the English language across the globe. http://www.worldwidewords.org/weirdwords/ww-ory1.htm

Reynolds, Aaron. (2019). *Effin' birds: A guide to field identification.* Ten Speed Press.

Roth, Sally. (1998). *Attracting birds to your backyard: 536 ways to turn your yard and garden into a haven for your favorite birds.* Rodale.

Roth, Sally. (2012). *Attracting songbirds to your backyard: Hundreds of easy ways to bring the music and beauty of songbirds to your yard.* Rodale.

Rothenberg, David. (2005). *Why birds sing: A journey into the mystery of bird song.* Basic Books.

RSPB. (n.d.). *Woodpigeon.* https://www.rspb.org.uk/birds-and-wildlife/wildlife-guides/bird-a-z/woodpigeon/?utm_source=subsectionlandingpage&campaign_medium=standalone_cta&utm_content=woodpigeon_standardcontentblock

Sarvasy, Hannah. (2016). Warblish: Verbal mimicry of birdsong. *Journal of Ethnobiology, 36*(4), 765–782. https://doi.org/10.2993/0278-0771-36.4.765

Saunders, Aretas A. (1951). *A guide to bird songs* (2nd ed.). Doubleday.

Schlitz Audubon Nature Center. (2017, June 22). Schlitz Audubon presents: Spring 2017 bird call mnemonics [Video]. YouTube. https://www.youtube.com/watch?v=qWLDkGLSvR8

Schmalz, Georgann. (n.d.). *Birdsong mnemonics*. Fernbank Science Centre. http://www.fernbank.edu/Birding/mnemonics.htm

Sewell, Matt. (2013). *Our songbirds: a songbird for every week of the year*. Ebury Press.

Singh, Simon. (2013). *The Simpsons and their mathematical secrets*. Bloomsbury.

Skatebirder (username). (2008, April, 28: Post#12). *It's interesting to me to see how one person's rendering of a Cetti's Warbler song can be confused* [online forum post]. BirdForum. https://www.birdforum.net/showthread.php?t=112534&highlight=mnemonics

Smythies, Bertram. (1953). *The birds of Burma*. Oliver and Boyd.

Smythies, Bertram. (1960). *The birds of Borneo*. Oliver and Boyd.

Smythies, B. G., Davidson, W.H., Harrison, Tom, & Hughes, A.M. (Eds.). (1999). *The birds of Borneo*. (4th ed.). Natural History Publishing.

Soper, Gary R. (2019, June 20). *A Grassland Migrant*. Wildlife In Nature: Gary R. Soper Wildlife Photography. https://wildlifeinnature.com/wp/2019/06/20/a-grassland-migrant/

Souter, Gavin. (2004). *Time and Tides*. Simon & Schuster.

South Bay Birders (n.d.). *Mnemonic bird songs*. https://web.archive.org/web/20160319131746/http://web.stanford.edu/~kendric/birds/

Southey, Ian (username). (2009, Sept, 8). *Actually, the version of the Yellowhammer call given is onomatopoeia too* [online forum post]. General Birding Discussion. http://www.birdingnz.net/forum/

Standing Bear, Luther. (1928). *My people the Sioux*. The Riverside Press.

Stevens, E. S. (1931). *Folk-tales of Iraq: Set down and translated from the vernacular*. Oxford University Press.

Strandman (username) (2006, July 31: Post#15). *Or as Simon Barnes puts it: "Me? Cetti's? If you don't like it - f*ck off!"* [Online forum post]. Bird Forum. https://www.birdforum.net/threads/cettis-warbler-song.58484/

Strong, Charles. (2017). The third paeon. In *Ad Lapidem*. https://web.archive.org/web/20211019015903/https://adlapidemessays.com/the-third-paeon/

Svensson, Lars. (2009). *Collins bird guide* (2nd ed.). Harper Collins.

Tammet, Daniel. (2017). *Every word is a bird we teach to sing.* Hodder & Stoughton.

The Octagon (username). (2008, April, 25: Post#1). *Heard many times first from a bird hide tonight* [online forum post]. BirdForum. https://www.birdforum.net/showthread.php?t=112534&highlight=mnemonics

The Octagon (username). (2008, April, 25: Post#10). *I went back to Brandon this evening with my minidisc recorder* [online forum post]. BirdForum. https://www.birdforum.net/showthread.php?t=112534&highlight=mnemonics

Thomas, Adrian. (2019). *RSPB Guide to birdsong.* Bloomsbury Publishing Plc.

Thorpe, William Homan. (1961). *Bird-song: The biology of vocal communication and expression in birds.* Cambridge University Press.

Tidemann, Sonia and Whiteside, Tim. (2010). Aboriginal stories: The riches and colour of Australian birds. In S. Tidemann and A. Gosler (Eds.), *Ethno-Ornithology* (pp. 153–179). Earthscan.

Torrey, Bradford. (1893). *Birds in the Bush* (6th ed.). The Riverside Press. https://www.gutenberg.org/ebooks/28019

Tracey, John, Bomford, M., Hart, Q., Saunders, G., & Sinclair, R. (2007) *Managing bird damage to fruit and other horticultural crops.* Bureau of Rural Sciences.

Turpin, Myfany, Ross, A., Dobson, V., & Turner, M. (2013). The spotted nightjar calls when dingo pups are born: ecological and social indicators in Central Australia. *Journal of Ethnobiology, 33*(1), 7–32. https://doi.org/10.2993/0278-0771-33.1.7

Vadim_mikhaylin (username) (2019, June 18). Витю видел? [Have you seen the wind?] [Online forum post]. Ru-Birds. https://ru-birds.livejournal.com/868632.html

Van der Post, Laurens. (1961). *The heart of the hunter.* Morrow.

Van Dyke, Henry. (1925). 'The Song Sparrow'. In *The Songs out of* doors: Later poems. (p. 31). The Scribner Press. http://www.gutenberg.org/files/16229/16229-h/16229-h.htm

Wainwright, A.T. (1983). Bird names and Xhosa oral poetry. *Names 1983*. Paper presented at the Second South African Names Congress for the Institute for Research into Language and the Arts, Onomastic Research Centre. Human Sciences Research Council.

Wells, Diane. (2002). *100 Birds and how they got their names*. Algonquin Books.

Wheatbelt NRM (2018). *Birds of the Avon River basin*. https://web.archive.org/web/20241015194850/https://www.wheatbeltnrm.org.au/sites/default/files/knowledge_hub/documents/Birds%20of%20the%20Avon%20River%20Basin%20-%20Web%20-%20Version.pdf

Wilde, Oscar. (1909). *The happy prince and other tales*. D. Nutt. https://archive.org/details/happyprinceother00wild1/page/12/mode/2up

Williams, Gorden. (1976). *Birds and birdsongs of New Zealand*. Reed.

Winter, Matt. (2020). *A guide to New Zealand's backyard birds*. This NZ Life. https://thisnzlife.co.nz/guide-new-zealands-backyard-birds/

Wright, Frederick, A. (2014). The short story just got shorter: Hemingway, narrative, and the six-word urban legend. *The Journal of Popular Culture, 47*(2), 327–340.

Xenospiza (username). (2014, September 5: Post#9). *The call of the Red-browed parrot* [online forum post]. Bird Forum. https://www.birdforum.net/showthread.php?t=290445

Yellow Warbler (2025, March 3). In *Wikipedia*. https://en.wikipedia.org/wiki/Yellow_warbler

Young, William. (2003, Winter). Translating the language of birds. *Verbatim, 28*(1), 2–5.

Yuhas, Daisy. (2024). *Kids' field guide to birds*. Cool Springs Press.

Zheljko (username). (2014, September 6: Post#21). *My friend shared that in one area they heard Golden Oriole's song* [Online forum post]. Bird Forum. https://www.birdforum.net/showthread.php?t=290445

Endnotes

Foreword

[1] Abelin, 2011, p. 13.
[2] Young, 2003, p. 2.

1. Introduction

[1] Torrey, 1893, p. 83.
[2] Andersen, 1926, p. 23.
[3] Why the Nightingale Sings, 1887
[4] Burrows 2002, p. 288
[5] Mosco, 2017a; Sarvasy, 2016, p. 774; Young, 2003, p. 2.
[6] Sarvasy, 2016, p. 774.
[7] Roth, 2012, p. 78.
[8] Mathews, 1921, p. 96.
[9] Mathews, 1921, p. 96.
[10] Mathews, 1921, p. 96.
[11] E.g., www.fernbank.edu/Birding/mnemonics.htm
[12] E.g., www.birdforum.net or www.birdingnz.net/forum/
[13] Burrows, 2002, p. 198.
[14] Koopman, 1990.
[15] Dunning, 1946, p. i
[16] Sarvasy, 2016, p. 780.
[17] Sarvasy, 2016, p. 765.
[18] R. E. Moreau, 1942, p. 1005.
[19] https://dictionary.cambridge.org

2. Defining the Phenomenon

[1] Proctor, 2016, as cited in Kawasaki, 2018, p. 1216.
[2] Rachel Kirkwood (personification communication).
[3] Burrows, 2002, p. 300.
[4] Pizzey, 1980, p. 266.
[5] "Indian Cuckoo", 2025.
[6] "Indian Cuckoo", 2025.
[7] Majnep and Bulmer, 1977, p. 102.
[8] Xenospiza 2014
[9] Andersen 1926:58-59
[10] Stevens, 1931, p. 294.
[11] Holmer and Holmer, 1969, p. 38.
[12] Standing Bear, 1928, p. 39.
[13] McGehee, 1958, p. 94.
[14] Cowser, 1969, p. 43.
[15] Torrey, 1893, p. 83; Most other sources (Feith 2003b; Jonas 1999, p. 11; Mathews, 1921, p. 96; Sarvasy, 2016, p. 774; Schmalz, n.d., Young, 2003, p. 2) have it saying 'Poor/Old Sam Peabody, Peabody, Peabody' hence it is often called the Peabody bird, but it is also known to say, 'Old Sam Peabiddy, Peabiddy, Peabiddy' (Roth, 2012, p. 78).
[16] Owen, 1947, p. 193.
[17] Stevens, 1931, p. 294.
[18] Dunning, 1946, p. i.
[19] Tidemann and Whiteside, 2010, p. 170.
[20] Callaway, 1868, p. 140.
[21] Cowser, 1969, p. 43.
[22] Norudde, 2009.
[23] Abelin, 2011, p. 13.
[24] Abelin, 2011, p.14.
[25] Abelin, 2011, p. 14.
[26] Abelin, 2011, p. 15; note: she spells this 'herrarna' but Norudde, 2009, p. 5, spells it 'herarna'.
[27] Norudde, 2009.
[28] Sarvasy, 2016.
[29] Mynott, 2009, p. 167.
[30] Sarvasy, 2016, p. 772.
[31] Sarvasy, 2016, p. 775.
[32] Sarvasy, 2016, p. 775.

33 Moreno Cabrera, 2016, p. 73–74.
34 Moreno Cabrera, 2016, p. 75.
35 Moreno Cabrera, 2016, p. 75.
36 Abelin, 2011, p.13.
37 Moreno Cabrera, 2016, p. 75.
38 Mosco, 2017.
39 Burrows, 2002, p. 258.
40 Schmalz, n.d.
41 Koopman, 2018a, p. 14.
42 Mynott, 2009, p. 163.
43 Svensson 2009, p. 314.
44 Koopman, 2018a, p. 14.
45 Svensson, 2009, p. 298.
46 Svensson, 2009, p. 11.
47 Abelin, 2011, p. 13.
48 Abelin, 2011, p. 16.
49 Although, I think it should be noted, this is not the bird's natural food; Abelin, 2011, p. 15.
50 Abelin, 2001, p. 15.
51 Abelin, 2011, p. 14.
52 Sarvasy, 2016, p. 777.
53 Muiruri and Maundu, 2010, p. 287.
54 Majnep and Bulmer, 1977, p. 85.
55 Sarvasy, 2016, p. 775.
56 Feld, 2012, p. 79.
57 Dunning, 1946, p. 32–58.
58 Abelin, 2011, p. 16.
59 Now known as White-Browed Robin-Chat (*Cossypha heuglini*)
60 Koopman, 2018, p. 16.
61 Ottó, 1901, p. 7.
62 Thorpe, 1961, p. 12.
63 Why the Nightingale sings, 1887.
64 Holmer and Holmer, 1969, p. 38.
65 Majnep and Bulmer, 1977, p. 95.
66 Thomas, 2019, p. 83.
67 Akiko Kawasaki, personal communication, 20/03/2020.
68 Includes languages from tribes in Wadigo, Wabondei, Wasambaa, Wazigue, Wakami, Wambwera, R. E. Moreau, 1942, p. 998.

[69] R. E. Moreau, 1942, p. 1005.
[70] R. E. Moreau, 1942, p. 1002.
[71] Moreau refers to it by the older name, Bronze Cuckoo (*Lampromorpha klaasi*). Koopman (2018a) and I use the modern name.
[72] R. E. Moreau, 1942, p. 1002.
[73] Feld, 2012, p. 76.
[74] Feld, 2012, p. 76.
[75] Feld, 2012, p. 77.
[76] Koopman, 1990, p. 67.
[77] Hadada Ibis.
[78] Koopman, 1990, p. 74.
[79] Koopman, 1990, p. 73.
[80] Koopman, 1990, p. 81 citing Maclearn, 1985, p. 355.
[81] Koopman, 2018a.
[82] It is interesting to note that R. E. Moreau's (1942) 'meaningless' category corresponds with 'partial-verbalisation'; his 'interpretable words' category corresponds with 'full-verbalisation'; and his 'descriptive' category is a combination of Koopman's (2018a) first two categories. However, R. E. Moreau's categories are all for bird names and Koopman has moved bird names into its own category that can include the other features.
[83] Koopman, 2018a, p. 14.
[84] Koopman, 2018a, p. 16.
[85] I also consider bird names to be meaningless (i.e., Type I) unless they have another independent meaning.
[86] Moreno Cabrera, 2016, p. 73.
[87] Moreno Cabrera, 2016, p. 73.
[88] Moreno Cabrera, 2016, p. 76.
[89] Sarvasy, 2016, p. 766.
[90] Sarvasy, 2016, p. 766.
[91] Koopman, 1990.
[92] Koopman, 2018a.
[93] Gorst, 2010.
[94] Gorst, 2010, p. 149.
[95] Gorst, 2010, p. 150.
[96] To copulate/to fuck
[97] Gorst, 2010, p. 151; Note: Gorst uses more than one spelling for *Parlement of Fowles*.

[98] Kawasaki, 2018.

3. Revised Terminology

[1] Sarvasy, 2016, p. 773.
[2] Young, 2003.
[3] Feith, 2003a, 2003b.
[4] Gorst, 2010; Koopman, 2018a; R. E. Moreau, 1942; Moreno Cabrera, 2016; Sarvasy, 2016; Wainwright, 1986.
[5] Koopman, 2018a.
[6] Moreno Cabrera, 2016, p. 73.
[7] Sarvasy, 2016, p. 770.
[8] Koopman, 1990.
[9] Sarvasy, 2016, p. 771.
[10] Cambridge Dictionary, 2021.
[11] P. H. Mathews, 2007.
[12] Cambridge Dictionary, 2021.

4. What is the Function of Warblish?

[1] Sarvasy refers to the 2002 version; I used the 2003 version.
[2] Sarvasy has just one other English example which is part of a story, from Goodrich (1849).
[3] Thomas, 2019, p. 33; This last comment is reminiscent of Sarvasy's (2016) and Moreno Cabrera's (2016) comments earlier about approximations in sound, rather than imitation.
[4] Crowe, 2001, p. 5.
[5] Koopman, 2018a.
[6] Svensson, 2009, p. 11.
[7] Young, 2003, p. 2.
[8] Norudde, 2009, p. 12–13.
[9] Thomas, 2019, p. 115.
[10] Thomas, 2019, p. 115; Gunson, 2011, p. 143.
[11] Abelin, 2011, p. 15.
[12] Abelin, 2011, p. 16; Norudde, 2009.
[13] Burrows, 2002, p. 284.
[14] Lobb, 2019, p. 80.
[15] Mathews, 1921, p. 112.

[16] Mathews, 1921, p. 113.
[17] Mathews, 1921, p. 114.
[18] Mathews, 1921, p. 117.
[19] Mathews, 1921, p. 117.
[20] Mathews, 1921, p. 118.
[21] Feith, 2003b.
[22] Walton, as cited in Young, 2003, p. 2.
[23] Bianki, 1939/2013.
[24] Allen, 1999.
[25] Jonas, 1999.
[26] Donaldson, 2019.
[27] Mosco, 2017a, 2017b.
[28] Mosco, 2017a.
[29] Donaldson, 2019.
[30] See *Sparrows say 'Cheer up! Cheer up!* by Helen Mae Innes for a reinterpretation in English. To be published in 2025.
[31] Glover, 1964.
[32] Allen, 1999, p. 5.
[33] Jonas, 1999, p. 21.
[34] Bush, 1999, p. 317.
[35] Bhattacharya, 2019, p. 43.
[36] Jüssi, 2007, p. 63, as cited in Bhattacharya, 2019, p. 43.
[37] Bulpin, 1966, p. 26.
[38] Bulpin, 1966, p 26–27. Note: Callaway's (1868, p. 140) example for the same bird was similar: '*Nga ngi ba ngi muhle; ng'oniwa I loku na loku*' (I should be beautiful, but I am spoiled by this and by this).
[39] Sarvasy, 2016, p. 775.
[40] Sarvasy, 2016, p. 779.
[41] A. J. Moreau, 1940, p. 49.
[42] Barnes, 2011, p. 67.
[43] Norudde, 2009, p. 7.
[44] Abelin, 2011, p. 14.
[45] Sarvasy, 2016, p. 779
[46] Feith, 2003a.
[47] Burrows, 2002, p. 201.
[48] Feld, 2012, p. 78–79.
[49] I am not sure of the English common name nor the species, but I believe this bird is from the Berrypicker and Longbill family (*Melanocharitidae* family)

[50] "Indian Cuckoo", 2021; It says, *kafal pako* (bayberry ripe)
[51] Proctor, as cited in Kawasaki, 2018, p. 12.
[52] Pizzey, 1980, p. 251.
[53] Mason, as cited in King and Dickinson, 1975, p. 342.
[54] Burrows, 2002, p. 141.
[55] Torrey, 1893, p. 83.
[56] "Indian Cuckoo", 2020.
[57] Koopman, 2018a.
[58] A. J. Moreau, 1940.
[59] Mincing Mockingbird, 2014.
[60] Sarvasy, 2016.
[61] Hannah Sarvasy, personal communication, 29/11/2019.
[62] Feld, 2012, p. 77–78.
[63] Feld, 2012, p. 78.
[64] Smythies, 1953, p. 19.
[65] Pizzey, 1980, p. 354.
[66] R. E. Moreau, 1942, p. 1001.
[67] Schmalz, n.d.
[68] Giacon, 2013, p. 258
[69] Giacon, 2013, p. 270.
[70] Majnep and Bulmer use the English name: Cinnamon-Breasted Wattle-Bird.
[71] Majnep and Bulmer, 1977, p. 62.
[72] R. E. Moreau, 1942, p. 1005.
[73] Majnep and Bulmer 1977, p. 62.
[74] Burrows, 2002, p. 289.
[75] King and Dickinson 1975, p. 298.
[76] King and Dickinson 1975, p. 307.
[77] Both *shit* and *skit* translate as 'shit'; Abelin, 2010, p. 15.
[78] Lobb, 2019, p. 81.
[79] Abelin 2011, p. 14.
[80] Abelin, 2011, p. 15.
[81] Pizzey, 1980, p. 380.
[82] Abelin, 2011, p. 15.
[83] Barnes, as cited in Moss, 2018, chapter 2.
[84] Koopman, 2018a.
[85] Feith, 2003b.
[86] Feith, n.d.; other versions: Feith, 2003; Feith 2003b; Kawasaki, 2018, p. 12.

[87] Legris, n.d.; other versions: see Mosco, 2017a. Similar phrases to the Black-Throated Blue Warbler.
[88] Burrows, 2002, p. 241.
[89] Cocker, 2013, p. 69.
[90] Wainwright, 1983, p. 300.
[91] Mathews, 1921, p. 184; other versions: Young, 20023, p. 2; South Bay Birders Unlimited, n.d.
[92] Norudde, 2009.
[93] Abelin, 2011, p. 13–14.
[94] Dormon, 1969, p. 33.
[95] Wainwright, 1986, p. 293.
[96] Wainwright, 1986, p. 295.
[97] Koopman, 2018a.
[98] Wainwright, 1986, p. 302.
[99] Wainwright, 1986, p. 303.
[100] Dunning, 1946.
[101] Dunning, 1946, p. 32.
[102] Wainwright, 1986, p. 294.
[103] Callaway, 1896.
[104] Dunning gives the English name as, Hornbill/Turkey-Buzzard.
[105] Dunning, 1946, p. 33.
[106] Callaway, 1868; Puşcariu, 1920–1921.
[107] Stevens, 1931.
[108] Thomas, 2019.
[109] Mynott, 2009; Ottó, 1901; Standing Bear, 1928; Torrey, 1893.
[110] I have been unable to find Lugg's paper from 1970.
[111] Bent, 1948, p. 212.
[112] Bent, 1948, p. 370.
[113] Koopman, 1990.
[114] Andersen, 1921, p. 51.
[115] Norudde, 2009.
[116] Bent, 1948, p. 370.
[117] Browning, 1845.
[118] Tennyson, 1896.
[119] Budhwar, 2019, p. 50.
[120] Van Dyke, 1925, p. 31.
[121] Burroughs, 1901, p. 127.
[122] Duggan, 1929, p. 37.

[123] Manhire, 2020.
[124] Bill Manhire, personal communication, 02/10/2020.
[125] Frame, 1957, p. 7.
[126] Wilde, 1909, p. 13.
[127] Young, 2003, compiled a list of warblish with some commentary in an article entitled 'Translating the language of bird'. I thought it was interesting that in his biography at the end of the article he lists anagrams and limericks as his interests but not birdwatching.
[128] Miller, 2005, wrote an interesting thesis on phonemic iconicity in haiku.
[129] Wright, 2014, p. 327
[130] Abelin, 2011, p. 14.
[131] Proctor, 2016, as cited in Kawasaki, 2018, p. 12.
[132] Greene et. al, 2012, p. 990.
[133] Strong, 2017.
[134] Singh, 2013, p. 42–43.
[135] Mosco, 2017b.

5. Does Warblish Exist for Other Creatures or Objects?

[1] Gunson, 2011, p. 89.
[2] Originally published in 1939. I used the 2013 version.
[3] The blocks of wood are short sticks somewhat like bowling pins used in a children's game. Instead of bowling a ball the child throws a longer stick at the 'pins'. They also happen to be the perfect size and shape to use as a weapon.
[4] Stevens, 1931, p. 294.
[5] Michael Weber, personal communication, 01/12/19.
[6] Tammet, 2017, p. 81.
[7] Cris Cucerzan, personal communication, 14/07/19.
[8] Frame, 1957, p. 146.
[9] Piper, 1930, p. 5.
[10] Piper, 1930, p. 16–17.
[11] Piper, 1930, p. 21.
[12] Piper, 1930, p. 22–23.
[13] Piper, 1930, p. 24–25.

6. Looking at the Wider Context: The Shared Features of Different Interpretations

[1] Gorst, 2010.
[2] Koopman, 2018a.
[3] Ngā Taonga Sound and Vision, 2021.
[4] Wainwright, 1986, p. 307.
[5] Koopman, 2018a
[6] Barnes, 2016, p. 56.
[7] Müller, 2009.

7. Is Warblish Endangered?

[1] MacFarlane, 2015, p. 4.
[2] Norrude's document was never published but it states it was updated in 2009.
[3] Bulpin, 1966, p. 27.
[4] Sarvasy, 2016, p. 777.
[5] Goodrich, 1849, p. 183.
[6] Kawasaki, 2018, p. 7.
[7] Feith, 2003b; South Bay Birders Unlimited n.d.
[8] Thoreau, as cited in Bent, 1948, p. 367.
[9] Mathews, 1921, p. 213.
[10] Mathews, 1921, p. 214.
[11] Mathews, 1921, p. 214.
[12] Feld, 2012, p. xiii.
[13] Feld, 2012, p. xiii.
[14] Mathews, 1921, p. 159.
[15] Mathews 1921, p. 54
[16] Nic Wynne, personal communication, 01/01/18.
[17] Owen is the only source I can find anywhere that calls this bird a Lesser Grey Hornbill
[18] Species and name are unclear, it maybe the Northern Red-Billed Hornbill
[19] Owen, 1947, p. 194
[20] Which I often appreciated as their language and approach was often more poetic and joyful.

8. Warblish as a Creative Process

[1] Dunning, 1946.
[2] Anne-Marie Thorby, personal communication, 01/06/2018.
[3] David Safonov-Innes, personal communication, 01/02/2021.
[4] Frank Lamb, personal communication, 01/02/2021.
[5] Louv, 2013, back cover.

9. Further Research

[1] Koopman, 2018b, p. 5.
[2] Cook, 2000, p. 1.
[3] Cook, 2000, p. 2.
[4] Feld, 2012.

Appendix C: Methodology for the Warblish, Animalopoeia, and Ticktocklish Database

[1] Hannah Sarvasy, personal communication, 4/5/2017.
[2] https://warblish.weebly.com/;
   https://warblish.wordpress.com/
[3] Both Koopman, 2018a and Koopman, 2018b
[4] Thomas, 2019, p. 30.
[5] Koopman, 2018a, p. 4.
[6] Feith, 2003a.

www.ingramcontent.com/pod-product-compliance
Lightning Source LLC
Chambersburg PA
CBHW081154020426
42333CB00020B/2503